MW00782173

SURPRISED BY JOY

———

THE FOUR LOVES

BOOKS BY C.S. LEWIS

The Pilgrim's Regress

The Problem of Pain

The Screwtape Letters and
   Screwtape Proposes a Toast

Broadcast Talks

The Abolition of Man

Christian Behavior

Beyond Personality

The Great Divorce

George MacDonald: An Anthology

Miracles

Transportation and Other Addresses

Mere Christianity

*Surprised by Joy: The Shape of My
   Early Life*

Reflections on Psalms

*The World's Last Night and Other
   Essays*

The Four Loves

*Letters to Malcolm: Chiefly on
   Prayer*

Poems

Of Other Worlds: Essays and Stories

Letters of C.S. Lewis

Narrative Poems

A Mind Awake

*On Stories: And Other Essays on
   Literature*

Spirits in Bondage: A Cycle of Lyrics

*The Business of Heaven: Daily
   Readings from C.S. Lewis*

Present Concerns

*All My Road Before Me: The Diary
   of C.S. Lewis, 1922–1927*

FOR CHILDREN

*The Chronicles of Narnia: The Lion,
   the Witch, and the Wardrobe*

Prince Caspian

The Voyage of the Dawn Treader

The Silver Chair

The Horse and His Boy

The Magician's Nephew

The Last Battle

FICTION

Out of the Silent Planet

Perelandra

That Hideous Strength

Till We Have Faces: A Myth Retold

The Dark Tower and Other Stories

*Boxen: The Imaginary World of
   Young C.S. Lewis*

Surprised by Joy

The Four Loves

C.S. LEWIS

Houghton Mifflin Harcourt

BOSTON • NEW YORK

Surprised by Joy, Copyright © 1955 by C. S. Lewis PTE Unlimited

The Four Loves, Copyright © 1960 by Helen Joy Lewis,
renewed 1988 by Arthur Owen Barfield

ALL RIGHTS RESERVED

For information about permission to reproduce selections
from this book, write to Permissions, Houghton Mifflin Harcourt
Publishing Company, 215 Park Avenue South, New York,
New York 10003.

www.hmhbooks.com

Library of Congress Cataloging-in-Publication Data
Lewis, C. S. (Clive Staples), 1898–1963.
Surprised by joy : the shape of my early life ; The four loves / C. S. Lewis.
p. cm.
ISBN 978-0-547-59939-7
1. Lewis, C. S. (Clive Staples), 1898–1963 — Childhood and youth.
2. Authors, English — 20th century — Biography. 3. Anglican converts —
England — Biography. 4. Christian biography — England.
5. Love — Religious aspects — Christianity. I. Lewis, C. S. (Clive Staples),
1898–1963. Four Loves. II. Title. III. Title: Four Loves.
BV4935.L43A3 2011
248.2'46092 — dc22   [B]

Book design by Melissa Lotfy

Printed in the United States of America
DOC 10 9 8 7 6 5 4 3 2

Surprised by Joy

The Shape of My Early Life

To
Dom Bede Griffiths, O.S.B.

Surprised by joy—impatient as the wind.

— WORDSWORTH

Contents

Preface

THIS book is written partly in answer to requests that I would tell how I passed from Atheism to Christianity and partly to correct one or two false notions that seem to have got about. How far the story matters to anyone but myself depends on the degree to which others have experienced what I call "joy." If it is at all common, a more detailed treatment of it than has (I believe) been attempted before may be of some use. I have been emboldened to write of it because I notice that a man seldom mentions what he had supposed to be his most idiosyncratic sensations without receiving from at least one (often more) of those present the reply, "What! Have *you* felt that too? I always thought I was the only one."

The book aims at telling the story of my conversion and is not a general autobiography, still less "Confessions" like those of St. Augustine or Rousseau. This means in practice that it gets less like a general autobiography as it goes on. In the earlier chapters the net has to be spread pretty wide in order that, when the explicitly spiritual crisis arrives, the reader may understand what sort of person my childhood and adolescence had made me. When the "build-up" is complete, I confine myself strictly to business and omit everything (however important by ordinary biographical standards) which seems, at that stage, irrelevant. I do not think there is much loss; I never read an autobiography in which the parts devoted to the earlier years were not far the most interesting.

The story is, I fear, suffocatingly subjective; the kind of thing I have never written before and shall probably never write again. I have tried so to write the first chapter that those who can't bear such a story will see at once what they are in for and close the book with the least waste of time.

C.S.L.

I

The First Years

Happy, but for so happy ill secured.

MILTON

I WAS born in the winter of 1898 at Belfast, the son of a solicitor and of a clergyman's daughter. My parents had only two children, both sons, and I was the younger by about three years. Two very different strains had gone to our making. My father belonged to the first generation of his family that reached professional station. His grandfather had been a Welsh farmer; his father, a self-made man, had begun life as a workman, emigrated to Ireland, and ended as a partner in the firm of Macilwaine and Lewis, "Boiler-makers, Engineers, and Iron Ship Builders." My mother was a Hamilton with many generations of clergymen, lawyers, sailors, and the like behind her; on her mother's side, through the Warrens, the blood went back to a Norman knight whose bones lie at Battle Abbey. The two families from which I spring were as different in temperament as in origin. My father's people were true Welshmen, sentimental, passionate, and rhetorical, easily moved both to anger and to tenderness; men who laughed and cried a great deal and who had not much of the talent for happiness. The Hamiltons were a cooler race. Their minds were critical and ironic and they had the talent for happiness in a high degree—went straight for it as experienced travelers go for the best seat in a train. From my earliest years I was aware of the vivid contrast between my mother's cheerful and tranquil affection and the ups and downs of my father's emotional life, and this bred in me long before I was old enough to give it a name a certain distrust or dislike of emotion as something uncomfortable and embarrassing and even dangerous.

Both my parents, by the standards of that time and place, were bookish or "clever" people. My mother had been a promising mathematician in her youth and a B.A. of Queen's College, Belfast, and before her death was able to start me both in French and Latin. She was a voracious reader of good novels, and I think the Merediths and Tolstoys which I have inherited were bought for her. My father's tastes were quite different. He was fond of oratory and had himself spoken on political platforms in England as a young man; if he had had independent means he would certainly have aimed at a political career. In this, unless his sense of honor, which was fine to the point of being Quixotic, had made him unmanageable, he might well have succeeded, for he had many of the gifts once needed by a Parliamentarian—a fine presence, a resonant voice, great quickness of mind, eloquence, and memory. Trollope's political novels were very dear to him; in following the career of Phineas Finn he was, as I now suppose, vicariously gratifying his own desires. He was fond of poetry provided it had elements of rhetoric or pathos, or both; I think *Othello* was his favorite Shakespearean play. He greatly enjoyed nearly all humorous authors, from Dickens to W. W. Jacobs, and was himself, almost without rival, the best *raconteur* I have ever heard; the best, that is, of his own type, the type that acts all the characters in turn with a free use of grimace, gesture, and pantomime. He was never happier than when closeted for an hour or so with one or two of my uncles exchanging "wheezes" (as anecdotes were oddly called in our family). What neither he nor my mother had the least taste for was that kind of literature to which my allegiance was given the moment I could choose books for myself. Neither had ever listened for the horns of elfland. There was no copy either of Keats or Shelley in the house, and the copy of Coleridge was never (to my knowledge) opened. If I am a romantic my parents bear no responsibility for it. Tennyson, indeed, my father liked, but it was the Tennyson of *In Memoriam* and *Locksley Hall*. I never heard from him of the *Lotus Eaters* or the *Morte d'Arthur*. My mother, I have been told, cared for no poetry at all.

In addition to good parents, good food, and a garden (which then seemed large) to play in, I began life with two other blessings. One was our nurse, Lizzie Endicott, in whom even the exacting memory of childhood can discover no flaw — nothing but kindness, gaiety, and good sense. There was no nonsense about "lady nurses" in those days. Through Lizzie we struck our roots into the peasantry of County Down. We were thus free of two very different social worlds. To this I owe my lifelong immunity from the false identification which some people make of refinement with virtue. From before I can remember I had understood that certain jokes could be shared with Lizzie which were impossible in the drawing room; and also that Lizzie was, as nearly as a human can be, simply good.

The other blessing was my brother. Though three years my senior, he never seemed to be an elder brother; we were allies, not to say confederates, from the first. Yet we were very different. Our earliest pictures (and I can remember no time when we were not incessantly drawing) reveal it. His were of ships and trains and battles; mine, when not imitated from his, were of what we both called "dressed animals" — the anthropomorphized beasts of nursery literature. His earliest story — as my elder he preceded me in the transition from drawing to writing — was called *The Young Rajah*. He had already made India "his country"; Animal-Land was mine. I do not think any of the surviving drawings date from the first six years of my life which

I am now describing, but I have plenty of them that cannot be much later. From them it appears to me that I had the better talent. From a very early age I could draw movement—figures that looked as if they were really running or fighting—and the perspective is good. But nowhere, either in my brother's work or my own, is there a single line drawn in obedience to an idea, however crude, of beauty. There is action, comedy, invention; but there is not even the germ of a feeling for design, and there is a shocking ignorance of natural form. Trees appear as balls of cotton wool stuck on posts, and there is nothing to show that either of us knew the shape of any leaf in the garden where we played almost daily. This absence of beauty, now that I come to think of it, is characteristic of our childhood. No picture on the walls of my father's house ever attracted—and indeed none deserved—our attention. We never saw a beautiful building nor imagined that a building could be beautiful. My earliest aesthetic experiences, if indeed they were aesthetic, were not of that kind; they were already incurably romantic, not formal. Once in those very early days my brother brought into the nursery the lid of a biscuit tin which he had covered with moss and garnished with twigs and flowers so as to make it a toy garden or a toy forest. That was the first beauty I ever knew. What the real garden had failed to do, the toy garden did. It made me aware of nature—not, indeed, as a storehouse of forms and colors but as something cool, dewy, fresh, exuberant. I do not think the impression was very important at the moment, but it soon became important in memory. As long as I live my imagination of Paradise will retain something of my brother's toy garden. And every day there were what we called "the Green Hills"; that is, the low line of the Castlereagh Hills which we saw from the nursery windows. They were not very far off but they were, to children, quite unattainable. They taught me longing—*Sehnsucht*; made me for good or ill, and before I was six years old, a votary of the Blue Flower.

If aesthetic experiences were rare, religious experiences did not occur at all. Some people have got the impression from my books that I was brought up in strict and vivid Puritanism, but this is quite untrue. I was taught the usual things and made to say my prayers and in due time taken to church. ı naturally accepted what I was told but I cannot remember feeling much interest in it. My father, far from being specially Puritanical, was, by nineteenth-century and Church of Ireland standards, rather "high," and his approach to religion, as to literature, was at the opposite pole from what later became my own. The charm of tradition and the verbal beauty of Bible and Prayer Book (all of them for me late and acquired tastes) were his natural delight, and it would have been hard to find an equally intelligent man who cared so little for metaphysics. Of my mother's religion I can say almost nothing from my own memory. My childhood, at all events, was not in the least other-worldly. Except for the toy garden and the Green Hills it was not even imaginative; it lives in my memory mainly as a period of humdrum, prosaic happiness and awakes none of the poignant nostalgia with which I look back on my much less happy boyhood. It is not settled happiness but momentary joy that glorifies the past.

To this general happiness there was one exception. I remember nothing earlier than the terror of certain dreams. It is a very common trouble at that age, yet it still seems to me odd that petted and guarded childhood should so often have in it a window opening on what is hardly less than Hell. My bad dreams were of two kinds, those about specters and those about insects. The second were, beyond comparison, the worse; to this day I would rather meet a ghost than a tarantula. And to this day I could almost find it in my heart to rationalize and justify my phobia. As Owen Barfield once said to me, "The trouble about insects is that they are like French locomotives—they have all the works on the outside." *The works*—that is the trouble. Their angular limbs, their jerky movements, their dry, metallic noises, all suggest either machines that have come to life or life degenerating into mechanism. You may add that in the hive and the anthill we see fully realized the two things that some of us most dread for our own species—the dominance of the female and the dominance of the collective. One fact about the history of this phobia is perhaps worth recording. Much later, in my teens, from reading Lubbock's *Ants, Bees and Wasps*, I developed for a short time a genuinely scientific interest in insects. Other studies soon crowded it out; but while my entomological period lasted my fear almost vanished, and I am inclined to think a real objective curiosity will usually have this cleansing effect.

I am afraid the psychologists will not be content to explain my insect fears by what a simpler generation would diagnose as their cause—a certain detestable picture in one of my nursery books. In it a midget child, a sort of Tom Thumb, stood on a toadstool and was threatened from below by a stag beetle very much larger than himself. This was bad enough; but there is worse to come. The horns of the beetle were strips of cardboard separate from the plate and working on a pivot. By moving a devilish contraption on the *verso* you could make them open and shut like pincers: snip-snap—snip-snap—I can see it while I write. How a woman ordinarily so wise as my mother could have allowed this abomination into the nursery is difficult to understand. Unless, indeed (for now a doubt assails me), unless that picture itself is a product of nightmare. But I think not.

In 1905, my seventh year, the first great change in my life took place. We moved house. My father, growing, I suppose, in prosperity, decided to leave the semidetached villa in which I had been born and build himself a much larger house, further out into what was then the country. The "New House," as we continued for years to call it, was a large one even by my present standards; to a child it seemed less like a house than a city. My father, who had more capacity for being cheated than any man I have ever known, was badly cheated by his builders; the drains were wrong, the chimneys were wrong, and there was a draft in every room. None of this, however, mattered to a child. To me, the important thing about the move was that the background of my life became larger. The New House is almost a major character in my story. I am a product of long corridors, empty sunlit rooms, upstairs indoor silences, attics explored in solitude, distant noises of gurgling cisterns and pipes, and the noise of wind under the tiles. Also, of endless books. My father bought all the books he read and never got rid of any of them. There were books in the study, books in the drawing room, books in the cloakroom, books (two deep) in the great bookcase on the landing, books in a bedroom, books piled as high as my shoulder in the cistern attic, books of all kinds reflecting every transient stage of my parents' interest, books readable and unreadable, books suitable for a child and books most emphatically not. Nothing was forbidden me. In the seemingly endless rainy afternoons I took volume after volume from the shelves. I had always the same certainty of finding a book that was new to me as a man who walks into a field has of finding a new blade of grass. Where all these books had been before we came to the New House is a problem that never occurred to me until I began writing this paragraph. I have no idea of the answer.

Out of doors was "the view" for which, no doubt, the site had principally been chosen. From our front door we looked down over wide fields to Belfast Lough and across it to the long mountain line of the Antrim shore—Divis, Colin, Cave Hill. This was in the far-off days when Britain was the world's carrier and the Lough was full of shipping; a delight to both us boys, but most to my brother. The sound of a steamer's horn at night still conjures up my whole boyhood. Behind the house, greener, lower, and nearer than the Antrim mountains, were the Holywood Hills, but it was not till much later that they won my attention. The northwestern prospect was what mat-

tered at first; the interminable summer sunsets behind the blue
ridges, and the rooks flying home. In these surroundings the
blows of change began to fall.

First of all, my brother was packed off to an English boarding school and thus removed from my life for the greater part
of every year. I remember well the rapture of his homecom-
ings for the holidays but have no recollection of any corresponding anguish at his departures. His new life made no difference to the relations between us. I, meanwhile, was going
on with my education at home; French and Latin from my
mother and everything else from an excellent governess, Annie Harper. I made rather a bugbear of this mild and modest
little lady at the time, but all that I can remember assures me
that I was unjust. She was a Presbyterian; and a longish lecture
which she once interpolated between sums and copies is the
first thing I can remember that brought the other world to my
mind with any sense of reality. But there were many things that
I thought about more. My real life—or what memory reports
as my real life—was increasingly one of solitude. I had indeed
plenty of people to talk to: my parents, my grandfather Lewis,
prematurely old and deaf, who lived with us; the maids; and
a somewhat bibulous old gardener. I was, I believe, an intolerable chatterbox. But solitude was nearly always at my command, somewhere in the garden or somewhere in the house. I
had now learned both to read and to write; I had a dozen things
to do.

What drove me to write was the extreme manual clumsiness
from which I have always suffered. I attribute it to a physical
defect which my brother and I both inherit from our father;
we have only one joint in the thumb. The upper joint (that furthest from the nail) is visible, but it is a mere sham; we cannot
bend it. But whatever the cause, nature laid on me from birth
an utter incapacity to make anything. With pencil and pen I
was handy enough, and I can still tie as good a bow as ever lay
on a man's collar; but with a tool or a bat or a gun, a sleeve link

or a corkscrew, I have always been unteachable. It was this that forced me to write. I longed to make things, ships, houses, engines. Many sheets of cardboard and pairs of scissors I spoiled, only to turn from my hopeless failures in tears. As a last resource, as a *pis aller*, I was driven to write stories instead; little dreaming to what a world of happiness I was being admitted. You can do more with a castle in a story than with the best cardboard castle that ever stood on a nursery table.

I soon staked out a claim to one of the attics and made it "my study." Pictures, of my own making or cut from the brightly colored Christmas numbers of magazines, were nailed on the walls. There I kept my pen and inkpot and writing books and paintbox; and there

> *What more felicity can fall to creature*
> *Than to enjoy delight with liberty?*

Here my first stories were written, and illustrated, with enormous satisfaction. They were an attempt to combine my two chief literary pleasures—"dressed animals" and "knights in armor." As a result, I wrote about chivalrous mice and rabbits who rode out in complete mail to kill not giants but cats. But already the mood of the systematizer was strong in me; the mood which led Trollope so endlessly to elaborate his Barsetshire. The Animal-Land which came into action in the holidays when my brother was at home was a modern Animal-Land; it had to have trains and steamships if it was to be a country shared with him. It followed, of course, that the medieval Animal-Land about which I wrote my stories must be the same country at an earlier period; and of course the two periods must be properly connected. This led me from romancing to historiography; I set about writing a full history of Animal-Land. Though more than one version of this instructive work is extant, I never succeeded in bringing it down to modern times; centuries take a deal of filling when all the events have to come out of the historian's head. But there is one touch in the

History that I still recall with some pride. The chivalric adventures which filled my stories were in it alluded to very lightly and the reader was warned that they might be "only legends." Somehow—but heaven knows how—I realized even then that a historian should adopt a critical attitude toward epic material. From history it was only a step to geography. There was soon a map of Animal-Land—several maps, all tolerably consistent. Then Animal-Land had to be geographically related to my brother's India, and India consequently lifted out of its place in the real world. We made it an island, with its north coast running along the back of the Himalayas; between it and Animal-Land my brother rapidly invented the principal steamship routes. Soon there was a whole world and a map of that world which used every color in my paintbox. And those parts of that world which we regarded as our own—Animal-Land and India—were increasingly peopled with consistent characters.

Of the books that I read at this time very few have quite faded from memory, but not all have retained my love. Conan Doyle's *Sir Nigel*, which first set my mind upon "knights in armor," I have never felt inclined to reread. Still less would I now read Mark Twain's *A Connecticut Yankee in King Arthur's Court*, which was then my only source for the Arthurian story, blissfully read for the sake of the romantic elements that came through and with total disregard of the vulgar ridicule directed against them. Much better than either of these was E. Nesbit's trilogy, *Five Children and It, The Phoenix and the Wishing Carpet*, and *The Amulet*. The last did most for me. It first opened my eyes to antiquity, the "dark backward and abysm of time." I can still reread it with delight. *Gulliver* in an unexpurgated and lavishly illustrated edition was one of my favorites, and I pored endlessly over an almost complete set of old *Punches* which stood in my father's study. Tenniel gratified my passion for "dressed animals" with his Russian Bear, British Lion, Egyptian Crocodile and the rest, while his slovenly and perfunctory treatment of vegetation confirmed my own deficiencies. Then came the Beatrix Potter books, and here at last beauty.

It will be clear that at this time — at the age of six, seven, and eight — I was living almost entirely in my imagination; or at least that the imaginative experience of those years now seems to me more important than anything else. Thus I pass over a holiday in Normandy (of which, nevertheless, I retain very clear memories) as a thing of no account; if it could be cut out of my past I should still be almost exactly the man I am. But imagination is a vague word and I must make some distinctions. It may mean the world of reverie, daydream, wish-fulfilling fantasy. Of that I knew more than enough. I often pictured myself cutting a fine figure. But I must insist that this was a totally different activity from the invention of Animal-Land. Animal-Land was not (in that sense) a fantasy at all. I was not one of the characters it contained. I was its creator, not a candidate for admission to it. Invention is essentially different from reverie; if some fail to recognize the difference that is because they have not themselves experienced both. Anyone who has will understand me. In my daydreams I was training myself to be a fool; in mapping and chronicling Animal-Land I was training myself to be a novelist. Note well, a novelist; not a poet. My invented world was full (for me) of interest, bustle, humor, and character; but there was no poetry, even no romance, in it. It was almost astonishingly prosaic.[1] Thus if we use the word imagination in a third sense, and the highest sense of all, this invented world was not imaginative. But certain other experiences were, and I will now try to record them. The thing has been much better done by Traherne and Wordsworth, but every man must tell his own tale.

1. For readers of my children's books, the best way of putting this would be to say that Animal-Land had nothing whatever in common with Narnia except the anthropomorphic beasts. Animal-Land, by its whole quality, excluded the least hint of wonder.

The first is itself the memory of a memory. As I stood beside a flowering currant bush on a summer day there suddenly arose in me without warning, and as if from a depth not of years but of centuries, the memory of that earlier morning at the Old House when my brother had brought his toy garden into the nursery. It is difficult to find words strong enough for the sensation which came over me; Milton's "enormous bliss" of Eden (giving the full, ancient meaning to "enormous") comes somewhere near it. It was a sensation, of course, of desire; but desire for what? not, certainly, for a biscuit tin filled with moss, nor even (though that came into it) for my own past. ᾽Ιούλίανποθῶ[2] — and before I knew what I desired, the desire itself was gone, the whole glimpse withdrawn, the world turned commonplace again, or only stirred by a longing for the longing that had just ceased. It had taken only a moment of time; and in a certain sense everything else that had ever happened to me was insignificant in comparison.

The second glimpse came through *Squirrel Nutkin;* through it only, though I loved all the Beatrix Potter books. But the rest of them were merely entertaining; it administered the shock, it was a trouble. It troubled me with what I can only describe as the Idea of Autumn. It sounds fantastic to say that one can be enamored of a season, but that is something like what happened; and, as before, the experience was one of intense desire. And one went back to the book, not to gratify the desire (that was impossible — how can one *possess* Autumn?) but to reawake it. And in this experience also there was the same surprise and the same sense of incalculable importance. It was something quite different from ordinary life and even from ordinary pleasure; something, as they would now say, "in another dimension."

The third glimpse came through poetry. I had become fond of Longfellow's *Saga of King Olaf:* fond of it in a casual, shallow

---

2. Oh, I desire too much.

way for its story and its vigorous rhythms. But then, and quite different from such pleasures, and like a voice from far more distant regions, there came a moment when I idly turned the pages of the book and found the unrhymed translation of *Tegner's Drapa* and read

> *I heard a voice that cried,*
> *Balder the beautiful*
> *Is dead, is dead*——

I knew nothing about Balder; but instantly I was uplifted into huge regions of northern sky, I desired with almost sickening intensity something never to be described (except that it is cold, spacious, severe, pale, and remote) and then, as in the other examples, found myself at the very same moment already falling out of that desire and wishing I were back in it.

The reader who finds these three episodes of no interest need read this book no further, for in a sense the central story of my life is about nothing else. For those who are still disposed to proceed I will only underline the quality common to the three experiences; it is that of an unsatisfied desire which is itself more desirable than any other satisfaction. I call it Joy, which is here a technical term and must be sharply distinguished both from Happiness and from Pleasure. Joy (in my sense) has indeed one characteristic, and one only, in common with them; the fact that anyone who has experienced it will want it again. Apart from that, and considered only in its quality, it might almost equally well be called a particular kind of unhappiness or grief. But then it is a kind we want. I doubt whether anyone who has tasted it would ever, if both were in his power, exchange it for all the pleasures in the world. But then Joy is never in our power and pleasure often is.

I cannot be absolutely sure whether the things I have just been speaking of happened before or after the great loss which befell our family and to which I must now turn. There came a night when I was ill and crying both with headache and toothache and distressed because my mother did not come to me. That was because she was ill too; and what was odd was that there were several doctors in her room, and voices and comings and goings all over the house and doors shutting and opening. It seemed to last for hours. And then my father, in tears, came into my room and began to try to convey to my terrified mind things it had never conceived before. It was in fact cancer and followed the usual course; an operation (they operated in the patient's house in those days), an apparent convalescence, a return of the disease, increasing pain, and death. My father never fully recovered from this loss.

Children suffer not (I think) less than their elders, but differently. For us boys the real bereavement had happened before our mother died. We lost her gradually as she was gradually withdrawn from our life into the hands of nurses and delirium and morphia, and as our whole existence changed into something alien and menacing, as the house became full of strange smells and midnight noises and sinister whispered conversations. This had two further results, one very evil and one very good. It divided us from our father as well as our mother. They say that a shared sorrow draws people closer together; I can hardly believe that it often has that effect when those who share it are of widely different ages. If I may trust my own experience, the sight of adult misery and adult terror has an effect on children which is merely paralyzing and alienating. Perhaps it was our fault. Perhaps if we had been better children we might have lightened our father's sufferings at this time. We certainly did not. His nerves had never been of the steadiest and his emotions had always been uncontrolled. Under the pressure of anxiety his temper became incalculable; he spoke wildly and acted unjustly. Thus by a peculiar cruelty of fate, during those months the unfortunate man, had he but known it, was really losing his sons as well as his wife. We were coming, my brother and I, to rely more and more exclusively on each other for all that made life bearable; to have confidence only in each other.

I expect that we (or at any rate I) were already learning to lie to him. Everything that had made the house a home had failed us; everything except one another. We drew daily closer together (that was the good result)—two frightened urchins huddled for warmth in a bleak world.

Grief in childhood is complicated with many other miseries. I was taken into the bedroom where my mother lay dead; as they said, "to see her," in reality, as I at once knew, "to see it." There was nothing that a grown-up would call disfigurement—except for that total disfigurement which is death itself. Grief was overwhelmed in terror. To this day I do not know what they mean when they call dead bodies beautiful. The ugliest man alive is an angel of beauty compared with the loveliest of the dead. Against all the subsequent paraphernalia of coffin, flowers, hearse, and funeral I reacted with horror. I even lectured one of my aunts on the absurdity of mourning clothes in a style which would have seemed to most adults both heartless and precocious; but this was our dear Aunt Annie, my maternal uncle's Canadian wife, a woman almost as sensible and sunny as my mother herself. To my hatred for what I already felt to be all the fuss and flummery of the funeral I may perhaps trace something in me which I now recognize as a defect but which I have never fully overcome—a distaste for all that is public, all that belongs to the collective; a boorish inaptitude for formality.

My mother's death was the occasion of what some (but not I) might regard as my first religious experience. When her case was pronounced hopeless I remembered what I had been taught; that prayers offered in faith would be granted. I accordingly set myself to produce by will power a firm belief that my prayers for her recovery would be successful; and, as I thought, I achieved it. When nevertheless she died I shifted my ground and worked myself into a belief that there was to be a miracle. The interesting thing is that my disappointment produced no results beyond itself. The thing hadn't worked, but I was used to things not working, and I thought no more about it. I think the truth is that the belief into which I had hypnotized myself was itself too irreligious for its failure to cause any religious revolution. I had approached God, or my idea of God, without love, without awe, even without fear. He was, in my mental picture of this miracle, to appear neither as Savior nor as Judge, but merely as a magician; and when He had done what was required of Him I supposed He would simply—well, go away. It never crossed my mind that the tremendous contact which I solicited should have any consequences beyond restoring the *status quo*. I imagine that a "faith" of this kind is often generated in children and that its disappointment is of no religious importance; just as the things believed in, if they could happen and be only as the child pictures them, would be of no religious importance either.

With my mother's death all settled happiness, all that was tranquil and reliable, disappeared from my life. There was to be much fun, many pleasures, many stabs of Joy; but no more of the old security. It was sea and islands now; the great continent had sunk like Atlantis.

II

Concentration Camp

Arithmetic with Coloured Rods.

TIMES EDUCATIONAL SUPPLEMENT,
NOV. 19, 1954

C LOP-clop-clop-clop . . . we are in a four-wheeler rattling over the uneven squaresets of the Belfast streets
through the damp twilight of a September evening, 1908; my
father, my brother, and I. I am going to school for the first time.
We are in low spirits. My brother, who has most reason to be
so, for he alone knows what we are going to, shows his feelings least. He is already a veteran. I perhaps am buoyed up by
a little excitement, but very little. The most important fact at
the moment is the horrible clothes I have been made to put on.
Only this morning — only two hours ago — I was running wild
in shorts and blazer and sand shoes. Now I am choking and
sweating, itching too, in thick dark stuff, throttled by an Eton
collar, my feet already aching with unaccustomed boots. I am
wearing knickerbockers that button at the knee. Every night
for some forty weeks of every year and for many a year I am
to see the red, smarting imprint of those buttons in my flesh
when I undress. Worst of all is the bowler hat, apparently made

of iron, which grasps my head. I have read of boys in the same predicament who welcomed such things as signs of growing up; I had no such feeling. Nothing in my experience had ever suggested to me that it was nicer to be a schoolboy than a child or nicer to be a man than a schoolboy. My brother never talked much about school in the holidays. My father, whom I implicitly believed, represented adult life as one of incessant drudgery under the continual threat of financial ruin. In this he did not mean to deceive us. Such was his temperament that when he exclaimed, as he frequently did, "There'll soon be nothing for it but the workhouse," he momentarily believed, or at least felt, what he said. I took it all literally and had the gloomiest anticipation of adult life. In the meantime, the putting on of the school clothes was, I well knew, the assumption of a prison uniform.

We reach the quay and go on board the old "Fleetwood boat"; after some miserable strolling about the deck my father bids us good-by. He is deeply moved; I, alas, am mainly embarrassed and self-conscious. When he has gone ashore we almost, by comparison, cheer up. My brother begins to show me over the ship and tell me about all the other shipping in sight. He is an experienced traveler and a complete man of the world. A certain agreeable excitement steals over me. I like the reflected port and starboard lights on the oily water, the rattle of winches, the warm smell from the engine-room skylight. We cast off. The black space widens between us and the quay; I feel the throb of screws underneath me. Soon we are dropping down the Lough and there is a taste of salt on one's lips, and that cluster of lights astern, receding from us, is everything I have known. Later, when we have gone to our bunks, it begins to blow. It is a rough night and my brother is seasick. I absurdly envy him this accomplishment. He is behaving as experienced travelers should. By great efforts I succeed in vomiting; but it is a poor affair—I was, and am, an obstinately good sailor.

No Englishman will be able to understand my first impressions of England. When we disembarked, I suppose at about six next morning (but it seemed to be midnight), I found myself in a world to which I reacted with immediate hatred. The flats of Lancashire in the early morning are in reality a dismal sight; to me they were like the banks of Styx. The strange English accents with which I was surrounded seemed like the voices of demons. But what was worst was the English landscape from Fleetwood to Euston. Even to my adult eye that main line still appears to run through the dullest and most unfriendly strip in the island. But to a child who had always lived near the sea and in sight of high ridges it appeared as I suppose Russia might appear to an English boy. The flatness! The interminableness! The miles and miles of featureless land, shutting one in from the sea, imprisoning, suffocating! Everything was wrong; wooden fences instead of stone walls and hedges, red brick farmhouses instead of white cottages, the fields too big, haystacks the wrong shape. Well does the *Kalevala* say that in the stranger's house the floor is full of knots. I have made up the quarrel since; but at that moment I conceived a hatred for England which took many years to heal.

Our destination was the little town of—let us call it Belsen—in Hertfordshire. "Green Hertfordshire," Lamb calls it; but it was not green to a boy bred in County Down. It was flat Hertfordshire, flinty Hertfordshire, Hertfordshire of the yellow soil. There is the same difference between the climate of Ireland and of England as between that of England and the Continent. There was far more weather at Belsen than I had ever met before; there I first knew bitter frost and stinging fog, sweltering heat and thunderstorms on the great scale. There, through the curtainless dormitory windows, I first came to know the ghastly beauty of the full moon.

The school, as I first knew it, consisted of some eight or nine boarders and about as many day boys. Organized games, except for endless rounders in the flinty playground, had long been moribund and were finally abandoned not very long after my arrival. There was no bathing except one's weekly bath in the bathroom. I was already doing Latin exercises (as taught by my mother) when I went there in 1908, and I was still doing Latin exercises when I left there in 1910; I had never got in sight of a Roman author. The only stimulating element in the teaching consisted of a few well-used canes which hung on the green iron chimney piece of the single schoolroom. The teaching staff consisted of the headmaster and proprietor (we called him Oldie), his grown-up son (Wee Wee), and an usher. The ushers succeeded one another with great rapidity; one lasted for less than a week. Another was dismissed in the presence of the boys, with a rider from Oldie to the effect that if he were not in Holy Orders he would kick him downstairs. This curious scene took place in the dormitory, though I cannot remember why. All these ushers (except the one who stayed less than a week) were obviously as much in awe of Oldie as we. But there came a time when there were no more ushers, and Oldie's youngest daughter taught the junior pupils. By that time there were only five boarders, and Oldie finally gave up his school and sought a cure of souls. I was one of the last survivors, and left the ship only when she went down under us.

Oldie lived in a solitude of power, like a sea captain in the days of sail. No man or woman in that house spoke to him as an equal. No one except Wee Wee initiated conversation with him at all. At meal times we boys had a glimpse of his family life. His son sat on his right hand; they two had separate food. His wife and three grown-up daughters (silent), the usher (silent), and the boys (silent) munched their inferior messes. His wife, though I think she never addressed Oldie, was allowed to make something of a reply to him; the girls—three tragic figures, dressed summer and winter in the same shabby black—never went beyond an almost whispered "Yes, Papa," or "No, Papa," on the rare occasions when they were addressed. Few visitors entered the house. Beer, which Oldie and Wee Wee drank regularly at dinner, was offered to the usher but he was expected to refuse; the one who accepted got his pint, but was taught his place by being asked a few moments later in a voice of thunderous irony, "Perhaps you would like a little *more* beer, Mr. N.?" Mr. N., a man of spirit, replied casually, "Well, thank you, Mr. C., I think I would." He was the one who did not stay till the end of his first week; and the rest of that day was a black one for us boys.

I myself was rather a pet or mascot of Oldie's — a position which I swear I never sought and of which the advantages were purely negative. Even my brother was not one of his favorite victims. For he had his favorite victims, boys who could do nothing right. I have known Oldie enter the schoolroom after breakfast, cast his eyes round, and remark, "Oh, there you are, Rees, you horrid boy. If I'm not too tired I shall give you a good drubbing this afternoon." He was not angry, nor was he joking. He was a big, bearded man with full lips like an Assyrian king on a monument, immensely strong, physically dirty. Everyone talks of sadism nowadays but I question whether his cruelty had any erotic element in it. I half divined then, and seem to see clearly now, what all his whipping boys had in common. They were the boys who fell below a certain social status, the boys with vulgar accents. Poor P. — dear, honest, hardworking, friendly, healthily pious P. — was flogged incessantly, I now think, for one offense only; he was the son of a dentist. I have seen Oldie make that child bend down at one end of the schoolroom and then take a run of the room's length at each stroke; but P. was the trained sufferer of countless thrashings and no sound escaped him until, toward the end of the torture, there came a noise quite unlike a human utterance. That peculiar croaking or rattling cry, that, and the gray faces of all the other boys, and their deathlike stillness, are among the memories I could willingly dispense with.[1]

The curious thing is that despite all this cruelty we did sur-

---

1. This punishment was for a mistake in a geometrical proof.

prisingly little work. This may have been partly because the cruelty was irrational and unpredictable; but it was partly because of the curious methods employed. Except at geometry (which he really liked) it might be said that Oldie did not teach at all. He called his class up and asked questions. When the replies were unsatisfactory he said in a low, calm voice, "Bring me my cane. I see I shall need it." If a boy became confused Oldie flogged the desk, shouting in a crescendo, "Think—Think—THINK!!" Then, as the prelude to execution, he muttered, "Come out, come out, come out." When really angry he proceeded to antics; worming for wax in his ear with his little finger and babbling, "Aye, aye, aye, aye . . ." I have seen him leap up and dance round and round like a performing bear. Meanwhile, almost in whispers, Wee Wee or the usher, or (later) Oldie's youngest daughter, was questioning us juniors at another desk. "Lessons" of this sort did not take very long; what was to be done with the boys for the rest of the time? Oldie had decided that they could, with least trouble to himself, be made to do arithmetic. Accordingly, when you entered school at nine o'clock you took your slate and began doing sums. Presently you were called up to "say a lesson." When that was finished you went back to your place and did more sums—and so forever. All the other arts and sciences thus appeared as islands (mostly rocky and dangerous islands)

Which like to rich and various gems inlaid
The unadorned bosom of the deep

—the deep being a shoreless ocean of arithmetic. At the end of the morning you had to say how many sums you had done; and it was not quite safe to lie. But supervision was slack and very little assistance was given. My brother—I have told you that he was already a man of the world—soon found the proper solution. He announced every morning with perfect truth that he had done five sums; he did not add that they were the same five every day. It would be interesting to know how many thousand times he did them.

I must restrain myself. I could continue to describe Oldie for many pages; some of the worst is unsaid. But perhaps it would be wicked, and it is certainly not obligatory, to do so. One good thing I can tell of him. Impelled by conscience, a boy once confessed to him an otherwise undetectable lie. The ogre was touched; he only patted the terrified boy's back and said, "Always stick to the truth." I can also say that though he taught geometry cruelly, he taught it well. He forced us to reason, and I have been the better for those geometry lessons all my life. For the rest, there is a possible explanation of his behavior which renders it more forgivable. Years after, my brother met a man who had grown up in the house next door to Oldie's school. That man and his family, and (I think) the neighbors in general, believed Oldie to be insane. Perhaps they were right. And if he had fairly recently become so, it would explain a thing which puzzles me. At that school as I knew it most boys learned nothing and no boy learned much. But Oldie could boast an impressive record of scholarships in the past. His school cannot always have been the swindle it was in our time.

You may ask how our father came to send us there. Certainly not because he made a careless choice. The surviving correspondence shows that he had considered many other schools before fixing on Oldie's; and I know him well enough to be sure that in such a matter he would never have been guided by his first thoughts (which would probably have been right) nor even by his twenty-first (which would at least have been explicable). Beyond doubt he would have prolonged deliberation till his hundred-and-first; and they would be infallibly and invincibly wrong. This is what always happens to the deliberations of a simple man who thinks he is a subtle one. Like Earle's *Scepticke in Religion* he "is always too hard for himself." My father piqued himself on what he called "reading between the lines."

The obvious meaning of any fact or document was always suspect: the true and inner meaning, invisible to all eyes except his own, was unconsciously created by the restless fertility of his imagination. While he thought he was interpreting Oldie's prospectus, he was really composing a school story in his own mind. And all this, I doubt not, with extreme conscientiousness and even some anguish. It might, perhaps, have been expected that this story of his would presently be blown away by the real story which we had to tell after we had gone to Belsen. But this did not happen. I believe it rarely happens. If the parents in each generation always or often knew what really goes on at their sons' schools, the history of education would be very different. At any rate, my brother and I certainly did not succeed in impressing the truth on our father's mind. For one thing (and this will become clearer in the sequel) he was a man not easily informed. His mind was too active to be an accurate receiver. What he thought he had heard was never exactly what you had said. We did not even try very hard. Like other children, we had no standard of comparison; we supposed the miseries of Belsen to be the common and unavoidable miseries of all schools. Vanity helped to tie our tongues. A boy home from school (especially during that first week when the holidays seem eternal) likes to cut a dash. He would rather represent his master as a buffoon than an ogre. He would hate to be thought a coward and a crybaby, and he cannot paint the true picture of his concentration camp without admitting himself to have been for the last thirteen weeks a pale, quivering, tear-stained, obsequious slave. We all like showing scars received in battle; the wounds of the *ergastulum*, less. My father must not bear the blame for our wasted and miserable years at Oldie's; and now, in Dante's words, "to treat of the good that I found there."

First, I learned, if not friendship, at least gregariousness. There had been bullying at the school when my brother first went there. I had my brother's protection for my first few terms (after which he left to go to a school we may call Wyvern) but I doubt if it was necessary. During those last declining years of the school we boarders were too few and too badly treated to do or suffer much in that way. Also, after a certain time, there were no new boys. We had our quarrels, which seemed serious enough at the time; but long before the end we had known one another too long and suffered too much together not to be, at the least, very old acquaintance. That, I think, is why Belsen did me, in the long run, so little harm. Hardly any amount of oppression from above takes the heart out of a boy like oppression from his fellows. We had many pleasant hours alone together, we five remaining boarders. The abandonment of organized games, though a wretched preparation for the public-school life to which most of us were destined, was at the time a great blessing. We were sent out for walks alone on half holidays. We did not do much walking. We bought sweets in drowsy village shops and pottered about on the canal bank or sat at the brow of a railway cutting watching a tunnel mouth for trains. Hertfordshire came to look less hostile. Our talk was not bound down to the narrow interests which satisfy public-school boys; we still had the curiosity of children. I can even remember from those days what must have been the first metaphysical argument I ever took part in. We debated whether the future was like a line you can't see or like a line that is not yet drawn. I have forgotten which side I took though I know that I took it with great zeal. And always there was what Chesterton calls "the slow maturing of old jokes."

The reader will notice that school was thus coming to reflect a pattern I had already encountered in my home life. At home, the bad times had drawn my brother and me closer together; here, where the times were always bad, the fear and hatred of Oldie had something the same effect upon us all. His school was in some ways very like Dr. Grimstone's school in *Vice Versa*; but unlike Dr. Grimstone's it contained no informer. We stood foursquare against the common enemy. I suspect that this pattern, occurring twice and so early in my life, has unduly biased my whole outlook. To this day the vision of the world which comes most naturally to me is one in which "we two" or "we few" (and in a sense "we happy few") stand together against something stronger and larger. England's position in 1940 was to me no surprise; it was the sort of thing that I always expect. Hence while friendship has been by far the chief source of my happiness, acquaintance or general society has always meant little to me, and I cannot quite understand why a man should wish to know more people than he can make real friends of. Hence, too, a very defective, perhaps culpably defective, interest in large impersonal movements, causes and the like. The concern aroused in me by a battle (whether in story or in reality) is almost in an inverse ratio to the number of the combatants.

In another way too Oldie's school presently repeated my home experience. Oldie's wife died; and in term time. He reacted to bereavement by becoming more violent than before; so much so that Wee Wee made a kind of apology for him to the boys. You will remember that I had already learned to fear and hate emotion; here was a fresh reason to do so.

But I have not yet mentioned the most important thing that befell me at Oldie's. There first I became an effective believer. As far as I know, the instrument was the church to which we were taken twice every Sunday. This was high "Anglo-Catholic." On the conscious level I reacted strongly against its peculiarities—was I not an Ulster Protestant, and were not these unfamiliar rituals an essential part of the hated English atmosphere? Unconsciously, I suspect, the candles and incense, the vestments and the hymns sung on our knees, may have had a considerable, and opposite, effect on me. But I do not think they were the important thing. What really mattered was that I here heard the doctrines of Christianity (as distinct from general "uplift") taught by men who obviously believed them. As I had no skepticism, the effect was to bring to life what I would already have said that I believed. In this experience there was a great deal of fear. I do not think there was more than was wholesome or even necessary; but if in my books I have spoken too much of Hell, and if critics want a historical explanation of the fact, they must seek it not in the supposed Puritanism of my Ulster childhood but in the Anglo-Catholicism of the church at Belsen. I feared for my soul; especially on certain blazing moonlit nights in that curtainless dormitory—how the sound of other boys breathing in their sleep comes back! The effect, so far as I can judge, was entirely good. I began seriously to pray and to read my Bible and to attempt to obey my conscience. Religion was among the subjects which we often discussed; discussed, if my memory serves me, in an entirely healthy and profitable way, with great gravity and without hysteria, and without the shamefacedness of older boys. How I went back from this beginning you shall hear later.

Intellectually, the time I spent at Oldie's was almost entirely wasted; if the school had not died, and if I had been left there two years more, it would probably have sealed my fate as a scholar for good. Geometry and some pages in West's *English Grammar* (but even those I think I found for myself) are the only items on the credit side. For the rest, all that rises out of the sea of arithmetic is a jungle of dates, battles, exports, imports and the like, forgotten as soon as learned and perfectly useless had they been remembered. There was also a great decline in my imaginative life. For many years Joy (as I have defined it) was not only absent but forgotten. My reading was now mainly rubbish; but as there was no library at the school we must not make Oldie responsible for that. I read twaddling school stories in *The Captain*. The pleasure here was, in the proper sense, mere wish fulfillment and fantasy; one enjoyed vicariously the triumphs of the hero. When the boy passes from nursery literature to school stories he is going down, not up. *Peter Rabbit* pleases a disinterested imagination, for the child does not want to be a rabbit, though he may like pretend-

ing to be a rabbit as he may later like acting Hamlet; but the
story of the unpromising boy who became captain of the First
Eleven exists precisely to feed his real ambitions. I also developed a great taste for all the fiction I could get about the ancient world: *Quo Vadis, Darkness and Dawn, The Gladiators, Ben
Hur.* It might be expected that this arose out of my new concern for my religion, but I think not. Early Christians came
into many of these stories, but they were not what I was after.
I simply wanted sandals, temples, togas, slaves, emperors, gal-
leys, amphitheaters; the attraction, as I now see, was erotic, and
erotic in rather a morbid way. And they were mostly, as literature, rather bad books. What has worn better, and what I took
to at the same time, is the work of Rider Haggard; and also the
"scientifiction" of H. G. Wells. The idea of other planets ex-
ercised upon me then a peculiar, heady attraction, which was
quite different from any other of my literary interests. Most
emphatically it was not the romantic spell of *Das Ferne.* "Joy"
(in my technical sense) never darted from Mars or the Moon.
This was something coarser and stronger. The interest, when
the fit was upon me, was ravenous, like a lust. This particular
coarse strength I have come to accept as a mark that the interest which has it is psychological, not spiritual; behind such a
fierce tang there lurks, I suspect, a psychoanalytical explanation. I may perhaps add that my own planetary romances have
been not so much the gratification of that fierce curiosity as its
exorcism. The exorcism worked by reconciling it with, or subjecting it to, the other, the more elusive, and genuinely imaginative, impulse. That the ordinary interest in scientifiction is
an affair for psychoanalysts is borne out by the fact that all who
like it, like it thus ravenously, and equally by the fact that those
who do not, are often nauseated by it. The repulsion of the one
sort has the same coarse strength as the fascinated interest of
the other and is equally a telltale.

So much for Oldie's; but the year was not all term. Life at a
vile boarding school is in this way a good preparation for the

Christian life, that it teaches one to live by hope. Even, in a
sense, by faith; for at the beginning of each term, home and the
holidays are so far off that it is as hard to realize them as to realize heaven. They have the same pitiful unreality when con-
fronted with immediate horrors. Tomorrow's geometry blots
out the distant end of term as tomorrow's operation may blot
out the hope of Paradise. And yet, term after term, the unbelievable happened. Fantastical and astronomical figures like
"this time six weeks" shrank into practicable figures like "this
time next week," and then "this time tomorrow," and the almost supernatural bliss of the Last Day punctually appeared.
It was a delight that almost demanded to be stayed with flag-
ons and comforted with apples; a delight that tingled down the
spine and troubled the belly and at moments went near to stopping the breath. Of course this had a terrible and equally relevant reverse side. In the first week of the holidays we might
acknowledge that term would come again — as a young man, in
peacetime, in full health, acknowledges that he will one day die.
But like him we could not even by the grimmest *memento mori*
be brought to realize it. And there too, each time, the unbelievable happened. The grinning skull finally peered through
all disguises; the last hour, held at bay by every device our will
and imaginations knew, came in the end, and once more it was
the bowler hat, the Eton collar, the knickerbockers, and (clop-
clop-clop-clop) the evening drive to the quay. In all seriousness I think that the life of faith is easier to me because of these
memories. To think, in sunny and confident times, that I shall
die and rot, or to think that one day all this universe will slip
away and become memory (as Oldie slipped away into memory
three times a year, and with him the canes and the disgusting
food, the stinking sanitation and the cold beds) — this is easier
to us if we have seen just that sort of thing happening before.
We have learned not to take present things at their face value.

In attempting to give an account of our home life at this
time I am troubled by doubts about chronology. School affairs

can to some extent be dated by surviving records, but the slow,
continuous unfolding of family life escapes them. Our slight
alienation from our father imperceptibly increased. In part no
one was to blame; in a very great part we were to blame. A
temperamental widower, still prostrated by the loss of his wife,
must be a very good and wise man indeed if he makes no mistakes in bringing up two noisy and mischievous schoolboys
who reserve their confidence wholly for each other. And my
father's good qualities as well as his weaknesses incapacitated
him for the task. He was far too manly and generous to strike
a child for the gratification of his anger; and he was too impulsive ever to punish a child in cold blood and on principle. He
therefore relied wholly on his tongue as the instrument of domestic discipline. And here that fatal bent toward dramatiza-
tion and rhetoric (I speak of it the more freely since I inherit
it) produced a pathetic yet comic result. When he opened his
mouth to reprove us he no doubt intended a short well-cho-
sen appeal to our common sense and conscience. But alas, he
had been a public speaker long before he became a father. He
had for many years been a public prosecutor. Words came to
him and intoxicated him as they came. What actually happened
was that a small boy who had walked on damp grass in his slippers or left a bathroom in a pickle found himself attacked with
something like Cicero on Catiline, or Burke on Warren Hast-
ings; simile piled on simile, rhetorical question on rhetorical
question, the flash of an orator's eye and the thundercloud of
an orator's brow, the gestures, the cadences and the pauses. The
pauses might be the chief danger. One was so long that my
brother, quite innocently supposing the denunciation to have
ended, humbly took up his book and resumed his reading; a
gesture which my father (who had after all only made a rhetorical miscalculation of about a second and a half) not unnaturally
took for "cool, premeditated insolence." The ludicrous dispro-
portion between such harangues and their occasions puts me
in mind of the advocate in Martial who thunders about all the

villains of Roman history while meantime *lis est de tribus capel-*
lis—

> *This case, I beg the court to note,*
> *Concerns a trespass by a goat.*

My poor father, while he spoke, forgot not only the offense, but
the capacities, of his audience. All the resources of his immense
vocabulary were poured forth. I can still remember such words
as "abominable," "sophisticated," and "surreptitious." You will
not get the full flavor unless you know an angry Irishman's energy in explosive consonants and the rich growl of his r's. A
worse treatment could hardly have been applied. Up to a certain age these invectives filled me with boundless terror and
dismay. From the wilderness of the adjectives and the welter of
the unintelligible, emerged ideas which I thought I understood
only too well, as I heard with implicit and literal belief that our
Father's ruin was approaching, that we should all soon beg our
bread in the streets, that he would shut up the house and keep
us at school all the year round, that we should be sent to the
colonies and there end in misery the career of crime on which
we had, it seemed, already embarked. All security seemed to
be taken from me; there was no solid ground beneath my feet.
It is significant that at this time if I woke in the night and did
not immediately hear my brother's breathing from the neighboring bed, I often suspected that my father and he had secretly risen while I slept and gone off to America—that I was
finally abandoned. Such was the effect of my father's rhetoric
up to a certain age; then, quite suddenly, it became ridiculous.
I can even remember the moment of the change, and the story
well illustrates both the justice of my father's anger and the unhappy way in which he expressed it. One day my brother decided it would be a good thing to make a tent. Accordingly we
procured a dust sheet from one of the attics. The next step was
to find uprights; the stepladder in the wash house suggested itself. For a boy with a hatchet it was the work of a moment to

reduce this to a number of disconnected poles. Four of these were then planted in the earth and the sheet draped over them. To make sure that the whole structure was really reliable my brother then tried sitting on the top of it. We remembered to put away the ragged remains of the sheet but quite forgot about the uprights. That evening, when my father had come home from work and dined, he went for a stroll in the garden, accompanied by us. The sight of four slender wooden posts rising from the grass moved in him a pardonable Curiosity. Interrogation followed; on this occasion we told the truth. Then the lightnings flashed and the thunder roared; and all would have gone now as it had gone on a dozen previous occasions, but for the climax—"Instead of which I find you have cut up the stepladder. And what for, forsooth? To make a thing like an abortive Punch-and-Judy show." At that moment we both hid our faces; not, alas, to cry.

As will be seen from this anecdote one dominant factor in our life at home was the daily absence of our father from about nine in the morning till six at night. For the rest of the day we had the house to ourselves, except for the cook and housemaid with whom we were sometimes at war and sometimes in alliance. Everything invited us to develop a life that had no connection with our father. The most important of our activities was the endless drama of Animal-Land and India, and this of itself isolated us from him.

But I must not leave the reader under the impression that all the happy hours of the holidays occurred during our father's absence. His temperament was mercurial, his spirits rose as easily as they fell, and his forgiveness was as thoroughgoing as his displeasure. He was often the most jovial and companionable of parents. He could "play the fool" as well as any of us, and had no regard for his own dignity, "conned no state." I could not, of course, at that age see what good company (by adult standards) he was, his humor being of the sort that requires at least some knowledge of life for its full appreciation;

I merely basked in it as in fine weather. And all the time there was the sensuous delight of being at home, the delight of luxury—"civilization," as we called it. I spoke just now of *Vice Versa*. Its popularity was surely due to something more than farce. It is the only truthful school story in existence. The machinery of the Garuda Stone really serves to bring out in their true colors (which would otherwise seem exaggerated) the sensations which every boy had on passing from the warmth and softness and dignity of his home life to the privations, the raw and sordid ugliness, of school. I say "had" not "has"; for perhaps homes have gone down in the world and schools gone up since then.

It will be asked whether we had no friends, no neighbors, no relatives. We had. To one family in particular our debt is so great that it had better be left, with some other matters, to the next chapter.

III

Mountbracken and Campbell

For all these fair people in hall were in their first age;
none happier under the heaven; their king, the man of
noblest temper. It would be a hard task to-day to find so
brave a fellowship in any castle.

GAWAIN AND THE GREEN KNIGHT

TO SPEAK of my nearer relatives is to remind myself
how the contrast of Lewis and Hamilton dominated
my whole early life. It began, for me, with the grandparents.
Grandfather Lewis, deaf, slow-moving, humming his psalm
chants, much concerned for his health and prone to remind
the family that he would not be with them long, is contrasted
with Grandmother Hamilton, the sharp-tongued, sharp-witted
widow, full of heterodox opinions (even, to the scandal of the
whole connection, a Home Ruler), every inch a Warren, indifferent to convention as only an old Southern Irish aristocrat
could be, living alone in a large tumble-down house with half a
hundred cats for company. To how many an innocent conver-
sational gambit did she reply, "You're talking great nonsense"?
Born a little later, she would, I think, have been a Fabian. She
met vague small talk with ruthless statements of ascertainable

44

fact and well-worn maxims with a tart demand for evidence. Naturally, people called her eccentric. Coming down a generation I find the same opposition. My father's elder brother "Uncle Joe," with his family of two boys and three girls, lived very close to us while we were at the Old House. His younger son was my earliest friend, but we drifted apart as we grew older. Uncle Joe was both a clever man and a kind, and especially fond of me. But I remember nothing that was said by our elders in that house; it was simply "grown-up" conversation—about people, business, politics, and health, I suppose. But "Uncle Gussie"—my mother's brother, A. W. Hamilton—talked to me as if we were of an age. That is, he talked about Things. He told me all the science I could then take in, clearly, eagerly, without silly jokes and condescensions, obviously liking it as much as I did. He thus provided the intellectual background for my reading of H. G. Wells. I do not suppose he cared for me as a person half so much as Uncle Joe did; and that (call it an injustice or not) was what I liked. During these talks our attention was fixed not on one another but on the subject. His Canadian wife I have already mentioned. In her also I found what I liked best—an unfailing, kindly welcome without a hint of sentimentality, unruffled good sense, the unobtrusive talent for making all things at all times as cheerful and comfortable as circumstances allowed. What one could not have one did without and made the best of it. The tendency of the Lewises to re-open wounds and to rouse sleeping dogs was unknown to her as to her husband.

But we had other kin who mattered to us far more than our aunts and uncles. Less than a mile from our home stood the largest house I then knew, which I will here call Mountbracken, and there lived Sir W. E. Lady E. was my mother's first cousin and perhaps my mother's dearest friend, and it was no doubt for my mother's sake that she took upon herself the heroic work of civilizing my brother and me. We had a standing invitation to lunch at Mountbracken whenever we were at home; to this, almost entirely, we owe it that we did not grow up savages. The debt is not only to Lady E. ("Cousin Mary") but to her whole family; walks, motor drives (in those days an exciting novelty), picnics, and invitations to the theater were showered on us, year after year, with a kindness which our rawness, our noise, and our unpunctuality never seemed to weary. We were at home there almost as much as in our own house, but with this great difference, that a certain standard of manners had to be kept up. Whatever I know (it is not much) of courtesy and *savoir faire* I learned at Mountbracken.

Sir W. ("Cousin Quartus") was the eldest of several brothers who owned between them one of the most important industrial concerns in Belfast. He belonged in fact to just that class and generation of which the modern man gets his impressions through Galsworthy's Forsytes. Unless Cousin Quartus was very untrue to type (as he may well have been) that impression is grossly unjust. No one less like a Galsworthian character ever existed. He was gracious, childlike, deeply and religiously humble, and abounding in charity. No man could feel more fully his responsibility to dependants. He had a good deal of boyish gaiety about him; at the same time I always felt that the conception of duty dominated his life. His stately figure, his gray beard, and his strikingly handsome profile make up one of the most venerable images in my memory. Physical beauty was indeed common to most of the family. Cousin Mary was the very type of the beautiful old lady, with her silver hair and her sweet Southern Irish voice; foreigners must be warned that this resembles what they call a "brogue" about as little as the speech of a Highland gentleman resembles the jargon of the Glasgow slums. But it was the three daughters whom we knew best. All three were "grown up" but in fact much nearer to us in age than any other grown-ups we knew, and all three were strikingly handsome. H., the eldest and the gravest, was a Juno, a dark queen who at certain moments looked like a Jewess. K. was more like a Valkyrie (though all, I think, were good horsewomen) with her father's profile. There was in her face something of the delicate fierceness of a thoroughbred horse, an indignant fineness of nostril, the possibility of an excellent disdain. She had what the vanity of my own sex calls a "masculine" honesty; no man ever was a truer friend. As for the youngest, G., I can only say that she was the most beautiful woman I have ever seen, perfect in shape and color and voice and every movement—but who can describe beauty? The reader may smile at this as the far-off echo of a precocious calf love, but he will be wrong. There are beauties so unambiguous that they need no lens of that kind to reveal them; they are visible even to the careless and objective eyes of a child. (The first woman who ever spoke to my blood was a dancing mistress at a school that will come in a later chapter.)

In some ways Mountbracken was like our father's house. There too we found the attics, the indoor silences, the endless bookshelves. In the early days, when we were still only a quarter tamed, we often neglected our hostesses and rummaged on our own; it was there that I found Lubbock's *Ants, Bees and Wasps*. But it was also very different. Life there was more spacious and considered than with us, glided like a barge where ours bumped like a cart.

Friends of our own age—boy and girl friends—we had none. In part this is a natural result of boarding school; children grow up strangers to their next-door neighbors. But much more it was the result of our own obstinate choice. One boy who lived near us attempted every now and then to get to know us. We avoided him by every means in our power. Our lives were already full, and the holidays too short for all the reading, writing, playing, cycling, and talking that we wanted to get through. We resented the appearance of any third party as an infuriating interruption. We resented even more bitterly all attempts (excepting the great and successful attempt made by Mountbracken) to show us hospitality. At the period that I am now speaking of this had not yet become a serious nuisance, but as it became gradually and steadily more serious throughout our schooldays I may be allowed to say a word about it here and to get the subject out of our way. It was the custom of the neighborhood to give parties which were really dances for adults but to which, none the less, mere schoolboys and schoolgirls were asked. One sees the advantages of this arrangement from the hostess's point of view; and when the junior guests know each other well and are free from self-consciousness perhaps they enjoy themselves. To me these dances were a torment — of which ordinary shyness made only a part. It was the false position (which I was well able to realize) that tormented me; to know that one was regarded as a child and yet be forced to take part in an essentially grown-up function, to feel that all the adults present were being half-mockingly kind and pretending to treat you as what you were not. Add to this the discomfort of one's Eton suit and stiff shirt, the aching feet and burning head, and the mere weariness of being kept up so many hours after one's usual bedtime. Even adults, I fancy, would not find an evening party very endurable without the attraction of sex and the attraction of alcohol; and how a small boy who can neither flirt nor drink should be expected to enjoy prancing about on a polished floor till the small hours of the morning, is beyond my conception. I had of course no notion of the social nexus. I never realized that certain people were in civility obliged to ask me because they knew my father or had known my mother. To me it was all inexplicable, unprovoked persecution; and when, as often happened, such engagements fell in the last week of the holidays and wrested from us a huge cantle of hours in which every minute was worth gold, I positively felt that I could have torn my hostess limb from limb. Why should she thus pester me? I had never done her any harm, never asked *her* to a party.

My discomforts were aggravated by the totally unnatural

behavior which I thought it my duty to adopt at a dance; and that had come about in a sufficiently amusing way. Reading much and mixing little with children of my own age, I had, before I went to school, developed a vocabulary which must (I now see) have sounded very funny from the lips of a chubby urchin in an Eton jacket. When I brought out my "long words" adults not unnaturally thought I was showing off. In this they were quite mistaken. I used the only words I knew. The position was indeed the exact reverse of what they supposed; my pride would have been gratified by using such schoolboy slang as I possessed, not at all by using the bookish language which (inevitably in my circumstances) came naturally to my tongue. And there were not lacking adults who would egg me on with feigned interest and feigned seriousness—on and on till the moment at which I suddenly knew I was being laughed at. Then, of course, my mortification was intense; and after one or two such experiences I made it a rigid rule that at "social functions" (as I secretly called them) I must never on any account speak of any subject in which I felt the slightest interest nor in any words that naturally occurred to me. And I kept my rule only too well; a giggling and gurgling imitation of the vapidest grown-up chatter, a deliberate concealment of all that I really thought and felt under a sort of feeble jocularity and enthusiasm, was henceforth my party manner, assumed as consciously as an actor assumes his role, sustained with unspeakable weariness, and dropped with a groan of relief the moment my brother and I at last tumbled into our cab and the drive home (the only pleasure of the evening) began. It took me years to make the discovery that any real human intercourse could take place at a mixed assembly of people in their good clothes.

I am here struck by the curious mixture of justice and injustice in our lives. We are blamed for our real faults but usually not on the right occasions. I was, no doubt, and was blamed for being, a conceited boy; but the blame was usually attached to something in which no conceit was present. Adults often accuse a child of vanity without pausing to discover on what points children in general, or that child in particular, are likely to be vain. Thus it was for years a complete mystery to me that my father should stigmatize as "affectation" my complaints about the itching and tickling of new underclothes. I see it all now; he had in mind a social legend associating delicacy of skin with refinement and supposed that I was claiming to be unusually refined. In reality I was in simple ignorance of that social legend, and if vanity had come into the matter would have been much prouder of having a skin like a sailor. I was being accused of an offense which I lacked resources to commit. I was on another occasion called "affected" for asking what "stirabout" was. It is, in fact, a "low" Irish word for porridge. To certain adults it seems obvious that he who claims not to know the Low must be pretending to be High. Yet the real reason why I asked was that I had never happened to hear the word; had I done so I should have piqued myself on using it.

Oldie's school, you will remember, sank unlamented in summer 1910; new arrangements had to be made for my education. My father now hit upon a plan which filled me with delight. About a mile from the New House rose the large redbrick walls and towers of Campbell College, which had been founded for the express purpose of giving Ulster boys all the advantages of a public-school education without the trouble of crossing the Irish Sea. My clever cousin, Uncle Joe's boy, was already there and doing well. It was decided that I should go as a boarder, but I could get an *exeat* to come home every Sunday. I was enchanted. I did not believe that anything Irish, even a school, could be bad; certainly not so bad as all I yet knew of England. To "Campbell" I accordingly went.

I was at this school for so short a time that I shall attempt no criticism of it. It was very unlike any English public school that I have ever heard of. It had indeed prefects, but the prefects were of no importance. It was nominally divided into "houses" on the English pattern, but they were mere legal fictions; except for purposes of games (which were not compulsory) no one took any notice of them. The population was socially much more "mixed" than at most English schools; I rubbed shoulders there with farmers' sons. The boy I most nearly made a friend of was the son of a tradesman who had recently been going the rounds with his father's van because the driver was illiterate and could not keep "the books." I much envied him this pleasant occupation, and he, poor fellow, looked back on it as a golden age. "This time last month, Lewis," he used to say, "I wouldn't have been going in to Preparation. I'd have been coming home from my rounds and a wee tea cloth laid for me at one end of the table and sausages to my tea."

I am always glad, as a historian, to have known Campbell, for I think it was very much what the great English schools had been before Arnold. There were real fights at Campbell, with seconds, and (I think) betting, and a hundred or more roaring spectators. There was bullying, too, though no serious share of it came my way, and there was no trace of the rigid hierarchy which governs a modern English school; every boy held just the place which his fists and mother wit could win for him. From my point of view the great drawback was that one had, so to speak, no home. Only a few very senior boys had studies. The rest of us, except when seated at table for meals or in a huge "preparation room" for evening "Prep," belonged nowhere. In out-of-school hours one spent one's time either evading or conforming to all those inexplicable movements which a crowd exhibits as it thins here and thickens there, now slackens its pace and now sets like a tide in one particular direction, now seems about to disperse and then clots again. The bare brick passages echoed to a continual tramp of feet, punctuated with catcalls, scrimmages, gusty laughter. One was always "moving on" or "hanging about"—in lavatories, in storerooms, in the great hall. It was very like living permanently in a large railway station.

The bullying had this negative merit that it was honest bullying; not bullying conscience-salved and authorized in the *maison tolérée* of the prefectorial system. It was done mainly by gangs; parties of eight or ten boys each who scoured those interminable corridors for prey. Their sorties, though like a whirlwind, were not perceived by the victim till too late; the general, endless confusion and clamor, I suppose, masked them. Sometimes capture involved serious consequences; two boys whom I knew were carried off and flogged in some backwater—flogged in the most disinterested fashion, for their captors had no personal acquaintance with them; art for art's sake. But on the only occasion when I was caught myself my fate was much milder and perhaps odd enough to be worth recording. When I had come to myself after being dragged at headlong speed through a labyrinth of passages which took me beyond all usual landmarks, I found that I was one of several prisoners in a low, bare room, half-lit (I think) by a single gas jet. After a pause to recover their breath two of the brigands led out the first captive. I now noticed that a horizontal row of pipes ran along the opposite wall, about three feet from the floor. I was alarmed but not surprised when the prisoner was forced into a bending position under the lowest pipe, in the very posture for execution. But I was very much surprised a moment later. You will remember that the room was half dark. The two gangsters gave their victim a shove; and instantly no victim was there. He vanished; without trace, without sound. It appeared to be sheer black magic. Another victim was led out; again the posture for a flogging was assumed; again, instead of flogging—dissolution, atomization, annihilation. At last my own turn came. I too received the shove from behind, and found myself falling through a hole or hatch in the wall into what turned out to be a coal cellar. Another small boy came hurtling in after me, the door was slammed and bolted behind us, and our captors with a joyous whoop rushed away for more booty. They were, no doubt, playing against a rival gang with whom they would presently compare "bags." We were let out again presently, very dirty and rather cramped, but otherwise none the worse.

Much the most important thing that happened to me at Campbell was that I there read *Sohrab and Rustum* in form under an excellent master whom we called Octie. I loved the poem at first sight and have loved it ever since. As the wet fog, in the first line, rose out of the Oxus stream, so out of the whole poem there rose and wrapped me round an exquisite, silvery coolness, a delightful quality of distance and calm, a grave melancholy. I hardly appreciated then, as I have since learned to do, the central tragedy; what enchanted me was the artist in Pekin with his ivory forehead and pale hands, the cypress in the queen's garden, the backward glance at Rustum's youth, the pedlars from Khabul, the hushed Chorasmian waste. Arnold gave me at once (and the best of Arnold gives me still) a sense, not indeed of passionless vision, but of a passionate, silent gazing at things a long way off. And here observe how literature actually works. Parrot critics say that *Sohrab* is a poem for classicists, to be enjoyed only by those who recognize the Homeric echoes. But I, in Octie's form room (and on Octie be peace) knew nothing of Homer. For me the relation between Arnold and Homer worked the other way; when I came, years later, to read the *Iliad* I liked it partly because it was for me reminiscent of *Sohrab*. Plainly, it does not matter at what point you first break into the system of European poetry. Only keep your ears open and your mouth shut and everything will lead you to everything else in the end—*ogni parte ad ogni parte splende*.

About halfway through my first and only term at Campbell I fell ill and was taken home. My father, for reasons I do not quite know, had become dissatisfied with the school. He had also been attracted by accounts of a preparatory school in the town of Wyvern, though quite unconnected with Wyvern College; especially by the convenience that if I went there my

brother and I could still do the journey together. Accordingly
I had a blessed six weeks at home, with the Christmas holidays
to look forward to at the end and, after that, a new adventure.
In a surviving letter my father writes to my brother that I think
myself lucky but he "fears I shall be very lonely before the end
of the week." It is strange that having known me all my life he
should have known me so little. During these weeks I slept
in his room and was thus freed from solitude during most of
those dark hours in which alone solitude was dreadful to me.
My brother being absent, he and I could not lead one another
into mischief; there was therefore no friction between my father and myself. I remember no other time in my life of such
untroubled affection; we were famously snug together. And in
the days, when he was out, I entered with complete satisfaction into a deeper solitude than I had ever known. The empty
house, the empty, silent rooms, were like a refreshing bath after the crowded noise of Campbell. I could read, write, and
draw to my heart's content. Curiously enough it is at this time,
not in earlier childhood, that I chiefly remember delighting
in fairy tales. I fell deeply under the spell of Dwarfs—the old
bright-hooded, snowy-bearded dwarfs we had in those days before Arthur Rackham sublimed, or Walt Disney vulgarized, the
earthmen. I visualized them so intensely that I came to the very
frontiers of hallucination; once, walking in the garden, I was
for a second not quite sure that a little man had not run past
me into the shrubbery. I was faintly alarmed, but it was not like
my night fears. A fear that guarded the road to Faerie was one
I could face. No one is a coward at all points.

IV

I Broaden My Mind

I struck the board, and cry'd, 'No more;
                       I will abroad.'
What? shall I ever sigh and pine?
My lines and life are free: free as the rode,
Loose as the winde, as large as store.

HERBERT

IN JANUARY, 1911, just turned thirteen, I set out with my brother to Wyvern, he for the College and I for a preparatory school which we will call Chartres. Thus began what may be called the classic period of our schooldays, the thing we both think of first when boyhood is mentioned. The joint journeys back to school with a reluctant parting at Wyvern station, the hilarious reunion at the same station for the joint journey home, were now the great structural pillars of each year. Growing maturity is marked by the increasing liberties we take with our traveling. At first, on being landed early in the morning at Liverpool, we took the next train south; soon we learned that it was pleasanter to spend the whole morning in the lounge of the Lime Street Hotel with our magazines and cigarettes and to proceed to Wyvern by an afternoon train which brought us there at the latest permitted moment. Soon too we gave up the magazines; we made the discovery (some people never make it) that real books can be taken on a journey and that hours of golden reading can so be added to its other delights. (It is important to acquire early in life the power of reading sense wherever you happen to be. I first read *Tamburlaine* while traveling from Larne to Belfast in a thunderstorm, and first read Browning's *Paracelsus* by a candle which went out and had to be relit whenever a big battery fired in a pit below me, which I think it did every four minutes all that night.) The homeward journey was even more festal. It had an invariable routine: first the supper at a restaurant—it was merely poached eggs and tea but to us the tables of the gods—then the visit to the old Empire (there were still music halls in those days)—and after that the journey to the Landing Stage, the sight of great and famous ships, the departure, and once more the blessed salt on our lips.

The smoking was of course, as my father would have said, "surreptitious"; not so the visit to the Empire. He was no Puritan about such matters, and often of a Saturday night would take us to the Belfast Hippodrome. I recognize now that I never had the taste for vaudeville which he shared with my brother. At the time I supposed myself to be enjoying the show, but I was mistaken. All those antics lie dead in my memory and are incapable of rousing the least vibration even of reminiscent pleasure; whereas the pain of sympathy and vicarious humiliation which I felt when a "turn" failed is still vivid. What I enjoyed was merely the et cetera of the show, the bustle and lights, the sense of having a night out, the good spirits of my father in his holiday mood, and—above all—the admirable cold supper to which we came back at about ten o'clock. For this was also the classical age of our domestic cookery, the age of one Annie Strahan. There were certain "raised pies" set on that table of which a modern English boy has no conception, and which even then would have astonished those who knew only the poor counterfeits sold in shops.

Chartres, a tall, white building further up the hill than the College, was a smallish school with less than twenty boarders; but it was quite unlike Oldie's. Here indeed my education really began. The Headmaster, whom we called Tubbs, was a clever and patient teacher; under him I rapidly found my feet in Latin and English and even began to be looked on as a promising candidate for a scholarship at the College. The food was good (though of course we grumbled at it) and we were well cared for. On the whole I got on well with my school fellows, though we had our full share of those lifelong friendships and irreconcilable factions and deadly quarrels and final settlements and glorious revolutions which made up so much of the life of a small boy, and in which I came out sometimes at the bottom and sometimes at the top.

Wyvern itself healed my quarrel with England. The great blue plain below us and, behind, those green, peaked hills, so mountainous in form and yet so manageably small in size, became almost at once my delight. And Wyvern Priory was the first building that I ever perceived to be beautiful. And at Chartres I made my first real friends. But there, too, something far more important happened to me: I ceased to be a Christian.

The chronology of this disaster is a little vague, but I know for certain that it had not begun when I went there and that the process was complete very shortly after I left. I will try to set down what I know of the conscious causes and what I suspect of the unconscious.

Most reluctantly, venturing no blame, and as tenderly as I would at need reveal some error in my own mother, I must begin with dear Miss C., the Matron. No school ever had a better Matron, more skilled and comforting to boys in sickness, or more cheery and companionable to boys in health. She was one of the most selfless people I have ever known. We all loved her; I, the orphan, especially. Now it so happened that Miss C., who seemed old to me, was still in her spiritual immaturity, still hunting, with the eagerness of a soul that had a touch of angelic quality in it, for a truth and a way of life. Guides were even rarer then than now. She was (as I should now put it) floundering in the mazes of Theosophy, Rosicrucianism, Spiritualism; the whole Anglo-American Occultist tradition. Nothing was further from her intention than to destroy my faith; she could not tell that the room into which she brought this candle was full of gunpowder. I had never heard of such things before; never, except in a nightmare or a fairy tale, conceived of spirits other than God and men. I had loved to read of strange sights and other worlds and unknown modes of being, but never with the slightest belief; even the phantom dwarf had only flashed on my mind for a moment. It is a great mistake to suppose that children believe the things they imagine; and I, long familiar with the whole imaginary world of Animal-Land and India (which I could not possibly believe in since I knew I was one of its creators) was as little likely as any child to make that mistake. But now, for the first time, there burst upon me the idea that there might be real marvels all about us, that the visible world might be only a curtain to conceal huge realms uncharted by my very simple theology. And that started in me something with which, on and off, I have had plenty of trouble since—the desire for the preternatural, simply as such, the passion for the Occult. Not everyone has this disease; those who have will know what I mean. I once tried to describe it in a novel. It is a spiritual lust; and like the lust of the body it has the fatal power of making everything else in the world seem uninteresting while it lasts. It is probably this passion, more even than the desire for power, which makes magicians. But the result of Miss C.'s conversation did not stop there. Little by little, unconsciously, unintentionally, she loosened the whole framework, blunted all the sharp edges, of my belief. The vagueness, the merely speculative character, of all this Occultism began to spread—yes, and to spread *deliciously*—to the stern truths of the creed. The whole thing became a matter of speculation: I was soon (in the famous words) "altering 'I believe' to 'one does feel.'" And oh, the relief of it! Those moonlit nights in the dormitory at Belsen faded far away. From the tyrannous noon of revelation I passed into the cool evening of Higher Thought, where there was nothing to be obeyed, and nothing to be believed except what was either comforting or exciting. I do not mean that Miss C. did this; better say that the Enemy did this in me, taking occasion from things she innocently said.

One reason why the Enemy found this so easy was that, without knowing it, I was already desperately anxious to get rid of my religion; and that for a reason worth recording. By a sheer mistake—and I still believe it to have been an honest mistake—in spiritual technique I had rendered my private practice of that religion a quite intolerable burden. It came about in this way. Like everyone else I had been told as a child that one must not only say one's prayers but think about what one was saying. Accordingly, when (at Oldie's) I came to a serious belief, I tried to put this into practice. At first it seemed plain sailing. But soon the false conscience (St. Paul's "Law," Herbert's "prattler") came into play. One had no sooner reached "Amen" than it whispered, "Yes. But are you sure you were really thinking about what you said?"; then, more subtly, "Were you, for example, thinking about it as well as you did last night?" The answer, for reasons I did not then understand, was nearly always No. "Very well," said the voice, "hadn't you, then, better try it over again?" And one obeyed; but of course with no assurance that the second attempt would be any better.

To these nagging suggestions my reaction was, on the whole, the most foolish I could have adopted. I set myself a standard. No clause of my prayer was to be allowed to pass muster unless it was accompanied by what I called a "realization," by which I meant a certain vividness of the imagination and the affections. My nightly task was to produce by sheer will power a phenomenon which will power could never produce, which was so ill-defined that I could never say with absolute confidence whether it had occurred, and which, even when it did occur, was of very mediocre spiritual value. If only some-one had read to me old Walter Hilton's warning that we must never in prayer strive to extort "by maistry" what God does not give! But no one did; and night after night, dizzy with desire for sleep and often in a kind of despair, I endeavored to pump up my "realizations." The thing threatened to become an infi-nite regress. One began of course by praying for good "realiza-tions." But had that preliminary prayer itself been "realized"? This question I think I still had enough sense to dismiss; oth-erwise it might have been as difficult to begin my prayers as to end them. How it all comes back! The cold oilcloth, the quar-ters chiming, the night slipping past, the sickening, hopeless weariness. This was the burden from which I longed with soul and body to escape. It had already brought me to such a pass that the nightly torment projected its gloom over the whole evening, and I dreaded bedtime as if I were a chronic sufferer from insomnia. Had I pursued the same road much further I think I should have gone mad.

This ludicrous burden of false duties in prayer provided, of course, an unconscious motive for wishing to shuffle off the Christian faith; but about the same time, or a little later, con-scious causes of doubt arose. One came from reading the clas-sics. Here, especially in Virgil, one was presented with a mass of religious ideas; and all teachers and editors took it for granted from the outset that these religious ideas were sheer illusion. No one ever attempted to show in what sense Christianity ful-filled Paganism or Paganism prefigured Christianity. The ac-cepted position seemed to be that religions were normally a mere farrago of nonsense, though our own, by a fortunate ex-ception, was exactly true. The other religions were not even ex-plained, in the earlier Christian fashion, as the work of devils. That I might, conceivably, have been brought to believe. But the impression I got was that religion in general, though ut-terly false, was a natural growth, a kind of endemic nonsense into which humanity tended to blunder. In the midst of a thousand such religions stood our own, the thousand and first, labeled True. But on what grounds could I believe in this exception? It obviously was in some general sense the same kind of thing as all the rest. Why was it so differently treated? Need I, at any rate, continue to treat it differently? I was very anxious not to.

In addition to this, and equally working against my faith, there was in me a deeply ingrained pessimism; a pessimism, by that time, much more of intellect than of temper. I was now by no means unhappy; but I had very definitely formed the opinion that the universe was, in the main, a rather regrettable institution. I am well aware that some will feel disgust and some will laugh, at the idea of a loutish, well-fed boy in an Eton collar, passing an unfavorable judgment on the cosmos. They may be right in either reaction, but no more right because I wore an Eton collar. They are forgetting what boyhood felt like from within. Dates are not so important as people believe. I fancy that most of those who think at all have done a great deal of their thinking in the first fourteen years. As to the sources of my pessimism, the reader will remember that, though in many ways most fortunate, yet I had very early in life met a great dismay. But I am now inclined to think that the seeds of pessimism were sown before my mother's death. Ridiculous as it may sound, I believe that the clumsiness of my hands was at the root of the matter. How could this be? Not, certainly, that a child says, "I can't cut a straight line with a pair of scissors, therefore the universe is evil." Childhood has no such power of generalization and is not (to do it justice) so silly. Nor did my clumsiness produce what is ordinarily called an Inferiority Complex. I was not comparing myself with other boys; my defeats occurred in solitude. What they really bred in me was a deep (and, of course, inarticulate) sense of resistance or opposition on the part of inanimate things. Even that makes it too abstract and adult. Perhaps I had better call it a settled expectation that everything would do what you did not want it to do.

Whatever you wanted to remain straight, would bend; whatever you tried to bend would fly back to the straight; all knots which you wished to be firm would come untied; all knots you wanted to untie would remain firm. It is not possible to put it into language without making it comic, and I have indeed no wish to see it (now) except as something comic. But it is perhaps just these early experiences which are so fugitive and, to an adult, so grotesque, that give the mind its earliest bias, its habitual sense of what is or is not plausible.

There was another predisposing factor. Though the son of a prosperous man—a man by our present tax-ridden standards almost incredibly comfortable and secure—I had heard ever since I could remember, and believed, that adult life was to be an unremitting struggle in which the best I could hope for was to avoid the workhouse by extreme exertion. My father's highly colored statements on such matters had sunk deeply into my mind; and I never thought to check them by the very obvious fact that most of the adults I actually knew seemed to be living very comfortable lives. I remember summing up what I took to be our destiny, in conversation with my best friend at Chartres, by the formula, "Term, holidays, term, holidays, till we leave school, and then work, work, work till we die." Even if I had been free from this delusion, I think I should still have seen grounds for pessimism. One's views, even at that age, are not wholly determined by one's own momentary situation; even a boy can recognize that there is desert all round him though he, for the nonce, sits in an oasis. I was, in my ineffective way, a tenderhearted creature; perhaps the most murderous feelings I ever entertained were toward an under master at Chartres who forbade me to give to a beggar at the school gate. Add to this that my early reading—not only Wells but Sir Robert Ball—had lodged very firmly in my imagination the vastness and cold of space, the littleness of Man. It is not strange that I should feel the universe to be a menacing and unfriendly place.

Several years before I read Lucretius I felt the force of his argument (and it is surely the strongest of all) for atheism—

> *Nequaquam nobis divinitus esse paratam*
> *Naturam rerum; tanta stat praedita culpa*
> *Had God designed the world, it would not be*
> *A world so pail and faulty as we see.*

You may ask how I combined this directly Atheistical thought, this great "Argument from Undesign" with my Occultist fancies. I do not think I achieved any logical connection between them. They swayed me in different moods, and had only this in common, that both made against Christianity. And so, little by little, with fluctuations which I cannot now trace, I became an apostate, dropping my faith with no sense of loss but with the greatest relief.

My stay at Chartres lasted from the spring term of 1911 till the end of the summer term 1913, and, as I have said, I cannot give an accurate chronology, between those dates, of my slow apostasy. In other respects the period is divided into two; about halfway through it a much loved under master, and the even more loved Matron, left at the same time. From that day onward there was a sharp decline; not, indeed, in apparent happiness but in solid good. Dear Miss C. had been the occasion of much good to me as well as of evil. For one thing, by awakening my affections, she had done something to defeat that antisentimental inhibition which my early experience had bred in me. Nor would I deny that in all her "Higher Thought," disastrous though its main effect on me was, there were elements of real and disinterested spirituality by which I benefited. Unfortunately, once her presence was withdrawn, the good effects withered and the bad ones remained. The change of masters was even more obviously for the worse. "Sirrah," as we called him, had been an admirable influence. He was what I would now describe as a wise madcap: a boisterous, boyish, hearty man, well able to keep his authority while yet mixing with us almost as one of ourselves, an untidy, rollicking man without a particle of affectation. He communicated (what I very much needed) a sense of the gusto with which life ought, wherever possible, to be taken. I fancy it was on a run with him in the sleet that I first discovered how bad weather is to be treated—as a rough joke, a romp. He was succeeded by a young gentleman just down from the University whom we may call Pogo. Pogo was a very minor edition of a Saki, perhaps even a Wodehouse, hero. Pogo was a wit, Pogo was a dressy man, Pogo was a man about town, Pogo was even a lad. After a week or so of hesitation (for his temper was uncertain) we fell at his feet and adored. Here was sophistication, glossy all over, and (dared one believe it?) ready to impart sophistication to us.

We became—at least I became—dressy. It was the age of the "knut": of "spread" ties with pins in them, of very low cut coats and trousers worn very high to show startling socks, and brogue shoes with immensely wide laces. Something of all this had already trickled to me from the College through my brother, who was now becoming sufficiently senior to aspire to knuttery. Pogo completed the process. A more pitiful ambition for a lout of an overgrown fourteen-year-old with a shilling a week pocket money could hardly be imagined; the more so since I am one of those on whom Nature has laid the doom that whatever they buy and whatever they wear they will always look as if they had come out of an old clothes shop. I cannot even now remember without embarrassment the concern that I then felt about pressing my trousers and (filthy habit) plastering my hair with oil. A new element had entered my life: Vulgarity. Up till now I had committed nearly every other sin and folly within my power, but I had not yet been flashy.

These hobbledehoy fineries were, however, only a small part of our new sophistication. Pogo was a great theatrical authority. We soon knew all the latest songs. We soon knew all about the famous actresses of that age—Lily Elsie, Gertie Millar,

Zena Dare. Pogo was a fund of information about their private lives. We learned from him all the latest jokes; where we did not understand he was ready to give us help. He explained many things. After a term of Pogo's society one had the feeling of being not twelve weeks but twelve years older.

How gratifying, and how edifying, it would be if I could trace to Pogo all my slips from virtue and wind up by pointing the moral; how much harm a loose-talking young man can do to innocent boys! Unfortunately this would be false. It is quite true that at this time I underwent a violent, and wholly successful, assault of sexual temptation. But this is amply accounted for by the age I had then reached and by my recent, in a sense my deliberate, withdrawal of myself from Divine protection. I do not believe Pogo had anything to do with it. The mere facts of generation I had learned long ago, from another boy, when I was too young to feel much more than a scientific interest in them. What attacked me through Pogo was not the Flesh (I had that of my own) but the World: the desire for glitter, swagger, distinction, the desire to be in the know. He gave little help, if any, in destroying my chastity, but he made sad work of certain humble and childlike and self-forgetful qualities which (I think) had remained with me till that moment. I began to labor very hard to make myself into a fop, a cad, and a snob.

Pogo's communications, however much they helped to vulgarize my mind, had no such electric effect on my senses as the dancing mistress, nor as Bekker's *Charicles*, which was given me for a prize. I never thought that dancing mistress as beautiful as my cousin G., but she was the first woman I ever "looked upon to lust after her"; assuredly through no fault of her own. A gesture, a tone of the voice, may in these matters have unpredictable results. When the schoolroom on the last night of the winter term was decorated for a dance, she paused, lifted a flag, and, remarking, "I love the smell of bunting," pressed it to her face—and I was undone.

You must not suppose that this was a romantic passion. The

passion of my life, as the next chapter will show, belonged to a wholly different region. What I felt for the dancing mistress was sheer appetite; the prose and not the poetry of the Flesh. I did not feel at all like a knight devoting himself to a lady; I was much more like a Turk looking at a Circassian whom he could not afford to buy. I knew quite well what I wanted. It is common, by the way, to assume that such an experience produces a feeling of guilt, but it did not do so in me. And I may as well say here that the feeling of guilt, save where a moral offense happened also to break the code of honor or had consequences which excited my pity, was a thing which at that time I hardly knew. It took me as long to acquire inhibitions as others (they say) have taken to get rid of them. That is why I often find myself at such cross-purposes with the modern world: I have been a converted Pagan living among apostate Puritans.

I would be sorry if the reader passed too harsh a judgment on Pogo. As I now see it, he was not too old to have charge of boys but too young. He was only an adolescent himself, still immature enough to be delightedly "grown up" and naive enough to enjoy our greater naivete. And there was a real friendliness in him. He was moved partly by that to tell us all he knew or thought he knew. And now, as Herodotus would say, "Good-by to Pogo."

Meanwhile, side by side with my loss of faith, of virtue, and of simplicity, something quite different was going on. It will demand a new chapter.

V

Renaissance

*So is there in us a world of love to somewhat, though we
know not what in the world that should be.*

TRAHERNE

I DO NOT much believe in the Renaissance as generally
described by historians. The more I look into the evidence
the less trace I find of that vernal rapture which is supposed to
have swept Europe in the fifteenth century. I half suspect that
the glow in the historians' pages has a different source, that
each is remembering, and projecting, his own personal Renaissance; that wonderful reawakening which comes to most of us
when puberty is complete. It is properly called a rebirth not a
birth, a reawakening not a wakening, because in many of us,
besides being a new thing, it is also the recovery of things we
had in childhood and lost when we became boys. For boyhood
is very like the "dark ages" not as they were but as they are
represented in bad, short histories. The dreams of childhood
and those of adolescence may have much in common; between
them, often, boyhood stretches like an alien territory in which
everything (ourselves included) has been greedy, cruel, noisy,
and prosaic, in which the imagination has slept and the most

unideal senses and ambitions have been restlessly, even mania-
cally, awake.

In my own life it was certainly so. My childhood is at unity
with the rest of my life; my boyhood not so. Many of the books
that pleased me as a child, please me still; nothing but necessity
would make me reread most of the books that I read at Oldie's
or at Campbell. From that point of view it is all a sandy desert.
The authentic "Joy" (as I tried to describe it in an earlier chapter) had vanished from my life: so completely that not even the
memory or the desire of it remained. The reading of *Sohrab*
had not given it to me. Joy is distinct not only from pleasure in
general but even from aesthetic pleasure. It must have the stab,
the pang, the inconsolable longing.

This long winter broke up in a single moment, fairly early
in my time at Chartres. Spring is the inevitable image, but this
was not gradual like Nature's springs. It was as if the Arctic itself, all the deep layers of secular ice, should change not in a
week nor in an hour, but instantly, into a landscape of grass and
primroses and orchards in bloom, deafened with bird songs
and astir with running water. I can lay my hand on the very moment; there is hardly any fact I know so well, though I cannot
date it. Someone must have left in the schoolroom a literary
periodical: *The Bookman*, perhaps, or the *Times Literary Supplement*. My eye fell upon a headline and a picture, carelessly,
expecting nothing. A moment later, as the poet says, "The sky
had turned round."

What I had read was the words *Siegfried and the Twilight of
the Gods*. What I had seen was one of Arthur Rackham's illustrations to that volume. I had never heard of Wagner, nor of
Siegfried. I thought the Twilight of the Gods meant the twilight in which the gods lived. How did I know, at once and beyond question, that this was no Celtic, or silvan, or terrestrial
twilight? But so it was. Pure "Northernness" engulfed me: a
vision of huge, clear spaces hanging above the Atlantic in the

endless twilight of Northern summer, remoteness, severity . . . and almost at the same moment I knew that I had met this before, long, long ago (it hardly seems longer now) in *Tegner's Drapa*, that Siegfried (whatever it might be) belonged to the same world as Balder and the sunward-sailing cranes. And with that plunge back into my own past there arose at once, almost like heartbreak, the memory of Joy itself, the knowledge that I had once had what I had now lacked for years, that I was returning at last from exile and desert lands to my own country; and the distance of the Twilight of the Gods and the distance of my own past Joy, both unattainable, flowed together into a single, unendurable sense of desire and loss, which suddenly became one with the loss of the whole experience, which, as I now stared round that dusty schoolroom like a man recovering from unconsciousness, had already vanished, had eluded me at the very moment when I could first say *It is*. And at once I knew (with fatal knowledge) that to "have it again" was the supreme and only important object of desire.

After this everything played into my hands. One of my father's many presents to us boys had been a gramophone. Thus at the moment when my eyes fell on the words *Siegfried and the Twilight of the Gods*, gramophone catalogues were already one of my favorite forms of reading; but I had never remotely dreamed that the records from Grand Opera with their queer German or Italian names could have anything to do with me. Nor did I for a week or two think so now. But then I was assailed from a new quarter. A magazine called *The Soundbox* was doing synopses of great operas week by week, and it now did the whole *Ring*. I read in a rapture and discovered who Siegfried was and what was the "twilight" of the gods. I could contain myself no longer—I began a poem, a heroic poem on the Wagnerian version of the Niblung story. My only source was the abstracts in *The Soundbox*, and I was so ignorant that I made Alberich rhyme with *ditch* and Mime with *time*. My model was

Pope's *Odyssey* and the poem began (with some mixture of my-thologies)

> *Descend to earth, descend, celestial Nine*
> *And chant the ancient legends of the Rhine....*

Since the fourth book had carried me only as far as the last scene of *The Rheingold*, the reader will not be surprised to hear that the poem was never finished. But it was not a waste of time, and I can still see just what it did for me and where it be-gan to do it. The first three books (I may, perhaps, at this dis-tance of time, say it without vanity) are really not at all bad for a boy. At the beginning of the unfinished fourth it goes all to pieces; and that is exactly the point at which I really began to try to make poetry. Up to then, if my lines rhymed and scanned and got on with the story I asked no more. Now, at the begin-ning of the fourth, I began to try to convey some of the intense excitement I was feeling, to look for expressions which would not merely state but suggest. Of course I failed, lost my prosaic clarity, spluttered, gasped, and presently fell silent; but I had learned what writing means.

All this time I had still not heard a note of Wagner's mu-sic, though the very shape of the printed letters of his name had become to me a magical symbol. Next holidays, in the dark, crowded shop of T. Edens Osborne (on whom be peace), I first heard a record of the *Ride of the Valkyries*. They laugh at it nowadays, and, indeed, wrenched from its context to make a concert piece, it may be a poor thing. But I had this in com-mon with Wagner, that I was thinking not of concert pieces but of heroic drama. To a boy already crazed with "the North-ernness," whose highest musical experience had been Sullivan, the *Ride* came like a thunderbolt. From that moment Wagne-rian records (principally from the *Ring*, but also from *Lohengrin* and *Parsifal*) became the chief drain on my pocket money and the presents I invariably asked for. My general appreciation of music was not, at first, much altered. "Music" was one thing, "Wagnerian music" quite another, and there was no common measure between them; it was not a new pleasure but a new kind of pleasure, if indeed "pleasure" is the right word, rather than trouble, ecstasy, astonishment, "a conflict of sensations without name."

That summer our cousin H. (you remember, I hope, Cousin Quartus's eldest daughter, the dark Juno, the queen of Olympus), who was now married, asked us to spend some weeks with her on the outskirts of Dublin, in Dundrum. There, on her drawing-room table, I found the very book which had started the whole affair and which I had never dared to hope I should see, *Siegfried and the Twilight of the Gods*, illustrated by Arthur Rackham. His pictures, which seemed to me then to be the very music made visible, plunged me a few fathoms deeper into my delight. I have seldom coveted anything as I coveted that book; and when I heard that there was a cheaper edition at fifteen shillings (though the sum was to me almost mythological) I knew I could never rest till it was mine. I got it in the end, largely because my brother went shares with me, purely through kindness, as I now see and then more than half suspected, for he was not enslaved by the Northernness. With a generosity which I was even then half ashamed to accept, he sank in what must have seemed to him a mere picture book seven and sixpence for which he knew a dozen better uses.

Although this affair will already seem to some readers undeserving of the space I have given it, I cannot continue my story at all without noting some of its bearings on the rest of my life.

First, you will misunderstand everything unless you realize that, at the time, Asgard and the Valkyries seemed to me incomparably more important than anything else in my experience—than the Matron Miss C., or the dancing mistress, or my chances of a scholarship. More shockingly, they seemed much more important than my steadily growing doubts about Christianity. This may have been — in part, no doubt was — penal blindness; yet that might not be the whole story. If the Northernness seemed then a bigger thing than my religion, that may partly have been because my attitude toward it contained elements which my religion ought to have contained and did not. It was not itself a new religion, for it contained no trace of belief and imposed no duties. Yet unless I am greatly mistaken there was in it something very like adoration, some kind of quite disinterested self-abandonment to an object which securely claimed this by simply being the object it was. We are taught in the Prayer Book to "give thanks to God for His great glory," as if we owed Him more thanks for being what He necessarily is than for any particular benefit He confers upon us; and so indeed we do and to know God is to know this. But I had been far from any such experience; I came far nearer to feeling this about the Norse gods whom I disbelieved in than I had ever done about the true God while I believed. Sometimes I can almost think that I was sent back to the false gods there to acquire some capacity for worship against the day when the true God should recall me to Himself. Not that I might not have learned this sooner and more safely, in ways I shall now never know, without apostasy, but that Divine punishments are also mercies, and particular good is worked out of particular evil, and the penal blindness made sanative.

Secondly, this imaginative Renaissance almost at once produced a new appreciation of external nature. At first, I think, this was parasitic on the literary and musical experiences. On that holiday at Dundrum, cycling among the Wicklow mountains, I was always involuntarily looking for scenes that might belong to the Wagnerian world, here a steep hillside covered with firs where Mime might meet Sieglinde, there a sunny glade where Siegfried might listen to the bird, or presently a dry valley of rocks where the lithe scaly body of Fafner might emerge from its cave. But soon (I cannot say how soon) nature ceased to be a mere reminder of the books, became herself the medium of the real joy. I do not say she ceased to be a reminder. All Joy reminds. It is never a possession, always a desire for something longer ago or further away or still "about to be." But Nature and the books now became equal reminders, joint reminders, of—well, of whatever it is. I came no nearer to what some would regard as the only genuine love of nature, the studious love which will make a man a botanist or an ornithologist. It was the mood of a scene that mattered to me; and in tasting that mood my skin and nose were as busy as my eyes.

Thirdly, I passed on from Wagner to everything else I could get hold of about Norse mythology, *Myths of the Norsemen*, *Myths and Legends of the Teutonic Race*, Mallet's *Northern Antiquities*. I became knowledgeable. From these books again and again I received the stab of Joy. I did not yet notice that it was, very gradually, becoming rarer. I did not yet reflect on the difference between it and the merely intellectual satisfaction of getting to know the Eddaic universe. If I could at this time have found anyone to teach me Old Norse I believe I would have worked at it hard.

And finally, the change I had undergone introduces a new difficulty into the writing of this present book. From that first moment in the schoolroom at Chartres my secret, imaginative life began to be so important and so distinct from my outer life that I almost have to tell two separate stories. The two lives do not seem to influence each other at all. Where there are hungry wastes, starving for Joy, in the one, the other may be full of cheerful bustle and success; or again, where the outer life is miserable, the other may be brimming over with ecstasy. By the imaginative life I here mean only my life as concerned with Joy—including in the outer life much that would ordinarily be called imagination, as, for example, much of my reading, and all my erotic or ambitious fantasies; for these are self-regarding. Even Animal-Land and India belong to the "Outer."

But they were no longer Animal-Land and India; some time in the late eighteenth century (their eighteenth century, not ours) they had been united into the single state of Boxen, which yields, oddly, an adjective *Boxonian*, not *Boxenian* as you might expect. By a wise provision they retained their separate kings but had a common legislative assembly, the Damerfesk. The electoral system was democratic, but this mattered very much less than in England, for the Damerfesk was never doomed to one fixed meeting place. The joint sovereigns could summon it anywhere, say at the tiny fishing village of Danphabel (the Clovelly of Northern Animal-Land, nestling at the foot of the mountains) or in the island of Piscia; and since the Court knew the sovereigns' choice earlier than anyone else, all local accommodation would be booked before a private member got wind of the matter, nor, if he reached the session, had he the least assurance that it would not be moved elsewhere as soon as he arrived. Hence we hear of a certain member who had never actually sat in the Damerfesk at all except on one fortunate occasion when it met in his home town. The records sometimes call this assembly the Parliament, but that is misleading. It had only a single chamber, and the kings presided. At the period which I know best the effective control, however, was not in their hands but in those of an all-important functionary known as the Littlemaster (you must pronounce this all as one word with the accent on the first syllable—like *Jerrybuilder*). The Littlemaster was a Prime Minister, a judge, and if not always Commander in Chief (the records waver on this point) certainly always a member of the General Staff. Such at least were the powers he wielded when I last visited Boxen. They may have been encroachments, for the office was held at that time by a man—or to speak more accurately, a Frog—of powerful personality. Lord Big brought to his task one rather unfair advantage; he had been the tutor of the two young kings and continued to hold over them a quasi-parental authority. Their spasmodic efforts to break his yoke were, unhappily, more di-

rected to the evasion of his inquiry into their private pleasures
than to any serious political end. As a result Lord Big, immense
in size, resonant of voice, chivalrous (he was the hero of innumerable duels), stormy, eloquent, and impulsive, almost was
the state. The reader will divine a certain resemblance between
the life of the two kings under Lord Big and our own life under
our father. He will be right. But Big was not, in origin, simply
our father first batrachised and then caricatured in some directions and glorified in others. He was in many ways a prophetic
portrait of Sir Winston Churchill as Sir Winston Churchill
came to be during the last war; I have indeed seen photographs
of that great statesman in which, to anyone who has known
Boxen, the frog element was unmistakable. This was not our
only anticipation of the real world. Lord Big's most consistent
opponent, the gadfly that always got inside his armor, was a
certain small brown bear, a lieutenant in the Navy; and believe
me or believe me not, Lieutenant James Bar was almost exactly
like Mr. John Betjeman, whose acquaintance I could not then
have made. Ever since I have done so, I have been playing Lord
Big to his James Bar.

The interesting thing about the resemblance between Lord
Big and my father is that such reflections of the real world had
not been the germ out of which Boxen grew. They were more
numerous as it drew nearer to its end, a sign of over-ripeness or
even the beginning of decay. Go back a little and you will not
find them. The two sovereigns who allowed themselves to be
dominated by Lord Big were King Benjamin VIII of Animal-
Land and Rajah Hawki (I think, VI) of India. They had much
in common with my brother and myself. But their fathers,
the elder Benjamin and the elder Hawki, had not. The Fifth
Hawki is a shadowy figure; but the Seventh Benjamin (a rabbit, as you will have guessed) is a rounded character. I can see
him still—the heaviest-jowled and squarest-built of all rabbits,
very fat in his later years, most shabbily and unroyally clad in
his loose brown coat and baggy checked trousers, yet not with-

out a certain dignity which could, on occasion, take disconcerting forms. His earlier life had been dominated by the belief that he could be both a king and an amateur detective. He never succeeded in the latter role, partly because the chief enemy whom he was pursuing (Mr. Baddlesmere) was not really a criminal at all but a lunatic—a complication which would have thrown out the plans of Sherlock Holmes himself. But he very often got himself kidnaped, sometimes for longish periods, and caused great anxiety to his court (we do not learn that his colleague, Hawki V, shared this). Once, on his return from such a misadventure, he had great difficulty in establishing his identity; Baddlesmere had dyed him and the familiar brown figure reappeared as a piebald rabbit. Finally (what will not boys think of?) he was a very early experimenter with what has since been called artificial insemination. The judgment of history cannot pronounce him either a good rabbit or a good King; but he was not a nonentity. He ate prodigiously.

And now that I have opened the gate, all the Boxonians, like the ghosts in Homer, come clamoring for mention. But they must be denied it. Readers who have built a world would rather tell of their own than hear of mine; those who have not would perhaps be bewildered and repelled. Nor had Boxen any connection with Joy. I have mentioned it at all only because to omit it would have been to misrepresent this period of my life.

One caution must here be repeated. I have been describing a life in which, plainly, imagination of one sort or another played the dominant part. Remember that it never involved the least grain of belief; I never mistook imagination for reality. About the Northernness no such question could arise: it was essentially a desire and implied the absence of its object. And Boxen we never could believe in, for we had made it. No novelist (in that sense) believes in his own characters.

At the end of the Summer Term 1913 I won a classical entrance scholarship to Wyvern College.

VI

Bloodery

Any way for Heaven sake
So I were out of your whispering.

WEBSTER

NOW that we have done with Chartres we may call
Wyvern College simply Wyvern, or more simply still,
as Wyvernians themselves call it, the Coll.

Going to the Coll was the most exciting thing that had yet
happened in my outer life. At Chartres we had lived under the
shadow of the Coll. We were often taken there to see matches
or sports or the finish of the great Goldbury Run. These visits
turned our heads. The crowd of boys older than oneself, their
dazzling air of sophistication, scraps of their esoteric talk overheard, were like Park Lane in the old "Season" to a girl who is
to be a debutante next year. Above all, the Bloods, the adored
athletes and prefects, were an embodiment of all worldly pomp,
power, and glory. Beside them Pogo shrank into insignificance;
what is a Master compared with a Blood? The whole school
was a great temple for the worship of these mortal gods; and
no boy ever went there more prepared to worship them than I.

If you have not been at such a school as Wyvern, you may

ask what a *Blood* is. He is a member of the school aristocracy. Foreign readers must clearly understand that this aristocracy has nothing whatever to do with the social position of the boys in the outer world. Boys of good, or wealthy, family are no more likely to be in it than anyone else; the only nobleman in my House at Wyvern never became a Blood. Shortly before my time there the son of a very queer customer had been at least on the fringe of Bloodery. The qualifying condition for Bloodery is that one should have been at the school for a considerable time. This by itself will not get you in, but newness will certainly exclude you. The most important qualification is athletic prowess. Indeed if this is sufficiently brilliant it makes you a Blood automatically. If it is a little less brilliant, then good looks and personality will help. So, of course, will fashion, as fashion is understood at your school. A wise candidate for Bloodery will wear the right clothes, use the right slang, admire the right things, laugh at the right jokes. And of course, as in the outer world, those on the fringes of the privileged class can, and do, try to worm their way into it by all the usual arts of pleasing.

At some schools, I am told, there is a sort of dyarchy. An aristocracy of Bloods, supported or at least tolerated by popular sentiment, stands over against an official ruling class of prefects appointed by the Masters. I believe they usually appoint it from the highest form, so that it has some claim to be an intelligentsia. It was not so at the Coll. Those who were made prefects were nearly all Bloods and they did not have to be in any particular form. Theoretically (though I do not suppose this would ever happen) the dunce at the bottom of the lowest form could have been made the captain—in our language, the Head—of the Coll. We thus had only a single governing class, in whom every kind of power, privilege, and prestige were united. Those to whom the hero worship of their juniors would in any case have gone, and those whose astuteness and ambition would under any system have enabled them to rise, were the same whom the official power of the Masters supported. Their position was emphasized by special liberties, clothes, priorities, and dignities which affected every side of School life. This, you will see, makes a pretty strong class. But it was strengthened still further by a factor which distinguishes school from ordinary life. In a country governed by an oligarchy, huge numbers of people, and among them some very stirring spirits, know they can never hope to get into that oligarchy; it may therefore be worth their while to attempt a revolution. At the Coll the lowest social class of all were too young, therefore too weak, to dream of revolt. In the middle class—boys who were no longer fags but not yet Bloods—those who alone had physical strength and popularity enough to qualify them as leaders of a revolution were already beginning to hope for Bloodery themselves. It suited them better to accelerate their social progress by courting the existing Bloods than to risk a revolt which, in the unlikely event of its succeeding, would destroy the very prize they were longing to share. And if at last they despaired of ever doing so—why, by that time their schooldays were nearly over. Hence the Wyvernian constitution was unbreakable. Schoolboys have often risen against their Masters; I doubt if there has ever been or ever can be a revolt against Bloods.

It is not, then, surprising if I went to the Coll prepared to worship. Can any adult aristocracy present the World to us in quite such an alluring form as the hierarchy of a public school? Every motive for prostration is brought to bear at once on the mind of the New Boy when he sees a Blood; the natural respect of the thirteen-year-old for the nineteen-year-old, the fan's feeling for a film star, the suburban woman's feeling for a duchess, the newcomer's awe in the presence of the Old Hand, the street urchin's dread of the police.

One's first hours at a public school are unforgettable. Our House was a tall, narrow stone building (and, by the way, the only house in the place which was not an architectural nightmare) rather like a ship. The deck on which we chiefly lived consisted of two very dark stone corridors at right angles to one another. The doors off them opened into the studies — little rooms about six feet square, each shared by two or three boys. The very sight of them was ravishing to a boy from a Prep school who had never before had a *pied-à-terre* of his own. As we were still living (culturally) in the Edwardian period, each study imitated as closely as possible the cluttered appearance of an Edwardian drawing room; the aim was to fill the tiny cell as full as it could hold with bookcases, corner cupboards, knickknacks, and pictures. There were two larger rooms on the same floor; one the "Pres' Room," the synod of Olympus, and the other the New Boys' Study. It was not like a study at all. It was larger, darker, and undecorated; an immovable bench ran round a clamped table. But we knew, we ten or twelve recruits, that not all of us would be left in the New Boys' Study. Some of us would be given "real" studies; the residue would occupy the opprobrious place for a term or so. That was the great hazard of our first evening; one was to be taken and another left.

As we sat round our clamped table, silent for the most part and speaking in whispers when we spoke, the door would be opened at intervals; a boy would look in, smile (not at us but to himself) and withdraw. Once, over the shoulder of the smiler there came another face, and a chuckling voice said, "Ho-ho! I know what *you're* looking for." Only I knew what it was all about, for my brother had played Chesterfield to my Stanhope and instructed me in the manners of the Coll. None of the boys who looked in and smiled was a Blood; they were all quite young and there was something common to the faces of them all. They were, in fact, the reigning or fading Tarts of the House, trying to guess which of us were their destined rivals or successors.

It is possible that some readers will not know what a House Tart was. First, as to the adjective. All life at Wyvern was lived, so to speak, in the two concentric circles of Coll and House. You could be a Coll pre or merely a House pre. You could be a

Coll Blood or merely a House Blood, a Coll Punt (*i.e.*, a pariah, an unpopular person) or merely a House Punt; and of course a Coll Tart or merely a House Tart. A Tart is[1] a pretty and effeminate-looking small boy who acts as a catamite to one or more of his seniors, usually Bloods. Usually, not always. Though our oligarchy kept most of the amenities of life to themselves, they were, on this point, liberal; they did not impose chastity on the middle-class boy in addition to all his other disabilities. Pederasty among the lower classes was not "side," or at least not serious side; not like putting one's hands in one's pockets or wearing one's coat unbuttoned. The gods had a sense of proportion.

The Tarts had an important function to play in making school (what it was advertised to be) a preparation for public life. They were not like slaves, for their favors were (nearly always) solicited, not compelled. Nor were they exactly like prostitutes, for the liaison often had some permanence and, far from being merely sensual, was highly sentimentalized. Nor were they paid (in hard cash, I mean) for their services; though of course they had all the flattery, unofficial influence, favor, and privileges which the mistresses of the great have always enjoyed in adult society. That was where the Preparation for Public Life came in. It would appear from Mr. Arnold Lunn's *Harrovians* that the Tarts at his school acted as informers. None of ours did. I ought to know, for one of my friends shared a study with a minor Tart; and except that he was sometimes turned out of the study when one of the Tart's lovers came in (and that, after all, was only natural) he had nothing to complain of. I was not shocked by these things. For me, at that age, the chief drawback to the whole system was that it bored me considerably. For you will have missed the atmosphere of our House unless you picture the whole place from week's end to week's end buzzing, tittering, hinting, whispering about this subject.

---

1. Here, and throughout this account, I sometimes use the "historic present." Heaven forfend I should be taken to mean that Wyvern is the same today.

After games, gallantry was the principal topic of polite conversation; who had "a case with" whom, whose star was in the
ascendant, who had whose photo, who and when and how often and what night and where. . . . I suppose it might be called
the Greek Tradition. But the vice in question is one to which I
had never been tempted, and which, indeed, I still find opaque
to the imagination. Possibly, if I had only stayed longer at the
Coll, I might, in this respect as in others, have been turned into
a Normal Boy, as the system promises. As things were, I was
bored.

Those first days, like your first days in the army, were spent
in a frantic endeavor to find out what you had to do. One of
my first duties was to find out what "Club" I was in. Clubs were
the units to which we were assigned for compulsory games;
they belonged to the Coll organization, not the House organization, so I had to go to a notice board "Up Coll" to get my
facts. And first to find the place — and then to dare to squeeze
oneself into the crowd of more important boys around the notice board — and then to begin reading through five hundred
names, but always with one eye on your watch, for of course
there is something else to be done within ten minutes. I was
forced away from the board before I had found my name, and
so, sweating, back to the House, in a flurry of anxiety, wonder-
ing how I could find time to do the job tomorrow and what
unheard-of disaster might follow if I could not. (Why, by the
way, do some writers talk as if care and worry were the special
characteristics of adult life? It appears to me that there is more
atra cura in an average schoolboy's week than in a grown man's
average year.)

When I reached the House something gloriously unexpected happened. At the door of the Pres' Room stood one
Fribble; a mere House Blood, it is true, even a minor House
Blood, but to me a sufficiently exalted figure; a youth of the
lean, laughing type, I could hardly believe it when he actually
addressed me. "Oh, I say, Lewis," he bawled, "I can tell you

your Club. You're in the same one as me, B6." What a transition from all but despair to elation I underwent! All my anxiety was laid to rest. And then the graciousness of Fribble, the condescension! If a reigning monarch had asked me to dine, I could hardly have been more flattered. But there was better to follow. On every half-holiday I went dutifully to the B6 notice board to see whether my name was down to play that afternoon or not. And it never was. This was pure joy, for of course I hated games. My native clumsiness, combined with the lack of early training for which Belsen was responsible, had ruled out all possibility of my ever playing well enough to amuse myself, let alone to satisfy other players. I accepted games (quite a number of boys do) as one of the necessary evils of life, comparable to Income Tax or the Dentist. And so, for a week or two, I was in clover.

Then the blow fell. Fribble had lied. I was in a totally different Club. My name had more than once appeared on a notice board I had never seen. I had committed the serious crime of "Skipping Clubs." The punishment was a flogging administered by the Head of the Coll in the presence of the assembled Coll Pres. To the Head of the Coll himself—a redheaded, pimply boy with a name like Borage or Porridge—I can bear no grudge; it was to him a routine matter. But I must give him a name because the real point of the story requires it. The emissary (some Blood a little lower than the Head himself) who summoned me to execution attempted to reveal to me the heinousness of my crime by the words, "Who are you? Nobody. Who is Porridge? THE MOST IMPORTANT PERSON THERE IS."

I thought then, and I still think, that this rather missed the point. There were two perfectly good morals he could have drawn. He might have said, "We are going to teach you never to rely on secondhand information when firsthand is available"—a very profitable lesson. Or he might have said, "What made you think that a Blood could not be a liar?" But, "Who are you? Nobody," however just, seems hardly relevant. The implication is that I have skipped Club in arrogance or defiance. And I puzzle endlessly over the question whether the speaker really believed that. Did he really think it likely that an utterly helpless stranger in a new society, a society governed by an irresistible class on whose favor all his hopes of happiness depended, had set himself in the first week to pull the nose of The Most Important Person There Is? It is a problem which has met me many times in later life. What does a certain type of examiner mean when he says, "To show up work like this is an insult to the examiners"? Does he really think that the plowed candidate has insulted him?

Another problem is Fribble's share in my little catastrophe. Was his lie to me a hoax, a practical joke? Was he paying off some old score against my brother? Or was he (as I now think most likely) simply what our ancestors called a Rattle, a man from whose mouth information, true and false, flows out all day long without consideration, almost without volition? Some might think that, whatever his motive had originally been, he might have come forward and confessed his part when he saw what I was in for. But that, you know, was hardly to be expected. He was a very minor Blood, still climbing up the social stair; Burradge was almost as far above Fribble as Fribble was above me. By coming forward he would have imperiled his social position, in a community where social advancement was the one thing that mattered; school is a preparation for public life.

In justice to Wyvern, I must add that Fribble was not, by our standards, quite a fair representative of Bloodery. He had offended against the rules of gallantry in a manner which (my brother tells me) would have been impossible in his day. I said just now that the Tarts were solicited, not compelled. But Fribble did use all his prefectorial powers for a whole term to persecute a boy called, let us say, Parsley who had refused his suit. This was quite easy for Fribble to do. The innumerable small regulations which a junior boy could break almost unawares enabled a prefect to make sure that a given boy was nearly always in trouble, while the fagging system made it easy to see that he had no leisure at all at any hour of any day. So Parsley learned what it was to refuse even a minor Blood. The story would be more impressive if Parsley had been a virtuous boy and had refused on moral grounds. Unfortunately he was "as common as a barber's chair," had been a reigning toast in my brother's day, and was now almost past his bloom. He drew the line at Fribble. But Fribble's attempt at coercion was the only instance of its kind I ever knew.

Indeed, taking them by and large, and considering the temptations of adolescents, so privileged, so flattered, our Bloods were not a bad lot. The Count was even kindly. The Parrot was nothing worse than a grave fool: "Yards-of-Face" they called him. Stopfish, whom some thought cruel, even had moral principles; in his younger days many (I'm told) had desired him as a Tart, but he had kept his virtue. "Pretty, but no good to anyone; he's *pie*," would be the Wyvernian comment. The hardest to defend, perhaps, is Tennyson. We did not much mind his being a shoplifter; some people thought it rather clever of him to come back from a tour of the town with more ties and socks than he had paid for. We minded more his favorite punishment for us rabble, "a clip." Yet he could truly have pleaded to the authorities that it meant merely a box on the ear. He would not have added that the patient was made to stand with his left ear, temple and cheek almost, but not quite, touching the jamb of a doorway, and then struck with full force on the right. We also grumbled a little in secret when he got up a tournament (either explicitly or virtually compulsory, I think) in a game called Yard Cricket, collected subscriptions, and neither held the tournament nor returned the cash. But you will remember that this happened in the Marconi period, and to be a prefect is a Preparation for Public Life. And for all of them, even Tennyson, one thing can be said; they were never drunk. I was told that their predecessors, a year before I came, were sometimes very drunk indeed in the House corridor at midday. In fact, odd as it would have sounded to an adult, I joined the House when it was in a stern mood of moral rearmament. That was the point of a series of speeches which the prefects addressed to us all in the House Library during my first week. It was explained with a wealth of threatenings that we were to be pulled Up or Together or wherever decadents are pulled by moral reformers. Tennyson was very great on that occasion. He had a fine bass voice and sang solos in the choir. I knew one of his Tarts.

Peace to them all. A worse fate awaited them than the most vindictive fag among us could have wished. Ypres and the Somme ate up most of them. They were happy while their good days lasted.

My flogging by pimply old Ullage was no unmerciful affair in itself. The real trouble was that I think I now became, thanks to Fribble, a marked man; the sort of dangerous New Boy who skips Clubs. At least I think that must have been the main reason why I was an object of dislike to Tennyson. There were probably others. I was big for my age, a great lout of a boy, and that sets one's seniors against one. I was also useless at games. Worst of all, there was my face. I am the kind of person who gets told, "And take that look off your face too." Notice, once more, the mingled justice and injustice of our lives. No doubt in conceit or ill temper I have often intended to look insolent or truculent; but on those occasions people don't appear to notice it. On the other hand, the moments at which I was told to "take that look off" were usually those when I intended to be most abject. Can there have been a freeman somewhere among my ancestors whose expression, against my will, looked out?

As I have hinted before, the fagging system is the chief medium by which the Bloods, without breaking any rule, can make a junior boy's life a weariness to him. Different schools have different kinds of fagging. At some of them, individual Bloods have individual fags. This is the system most often depicted in school stories; it is sometimes represented as—and, for all I

know, sometimes really is—a fruitful relation as of knight and
squire, in which service on the one part is rewarded with some
degree of countenance and protection on the other. But whatever its merits may be, we never experienced them at Wyvern.
Fagging with us was as impersonal as the labor market in Victorian England; in that way, too, the Coll was a preparation
for public life. All boys under a certain seniority constituted
a labor pool, the common property of all the Bloods. When a
Blood wanted his O.T.C. kit brushed and polished, or his boots
cleaned, or his study "done out," or his tea made, he shouted.
We all came running, and of course the Blood gave the work
to the boy he most disliked. The kit cleaning—it took hours,
and then, when you had finished it, your own kit was still to
do—was the most detested *corvée*. Shoe cleaning was a nuisance not so much in itself as in its attendant circumstances. It
came at an hour which was vital for a boy like me who, having
won a scholarship, had been placed in a high form and could
hardly, by all his best efforts, keep up with the work. Hence the
success of one's whole day in Form might depend on the precious forty minutes between breakfast and Morning School,
when one went over the set passages of translation with other
boys in the same Form. This could be done only if one escaped
being fagged as a shoeblack. Not, of course, that it takes forty
minutes to clean a pair of shoes. What takes the time is waiting
in the queue of other fags in the "boot-hole" to get your turn
at the brushes and blacking. The whole look of that cellar, the
darkness, the smell, and (for most of the year) the freezing cold,
are a vivid memory. You must not of course suppose that, in
those spacious days, we lacked servants. There were two official
"bootboys" paid by the Housemaster for cleaning all boots and
shoes, and everyone, including us fags who had cleaned both
our own shoes and the Bloods' shoes daily, tipped the bootboys
at the end of each term for their services.

For a reason which all English readers will understand (others will hear something of it in the next chapter) I am humili-

ated and embarrassed at having to record that as time went on
I came to dislike the fagging system. No true defender of the
Public Schools will believe me if I say that I was tired. But I
was—dog tired, cab-horse tired, tired (almost) like a child in
a factory. Many things besides fagging contributed to it. I was
big and had possibly outgrown my strength. My work in Form
was almost beyond me. I was having a good deal of dental trouble at the time, and many nights of clamorous pain. Never, except in the front-line trenches (and not always there) do I remember such aching and continuous weariness as at Wyvern.
Oh, the implacable day, the horror of waking, the endless desert of hours that separated one from bedtime! And remember
that, even without fagging, a school day contains hardly any
leisure for a boy who does not like games. For him, to pass
from the form room to the playing field is simply to exchange
work in which he can take some interest for work in which he
can take none, in which failure is more severely punished, and
in which (worst of all) he must feign an interest.

I think that this feigning, this ceaseless pretense of interest in matters to me supremely boring, was what wore me out
more than anything else. If the reader will picture himself, unarmed, shut up for thirteen weeks on end, night and day, in a
society of fanatical golfers—or, if he is a golfer himself, let him
substitute fishermen, theosophists, bimetallists, Baconians, or
German undergraduates with a taste for autobiography—who
all carry revolvers and will probably shoot him if he ever seems
to lose interest in their conversation, he will have an idea of
my school life. Even the hardy Chowbok (in *Erewhon*) quailed
at such a destiny. For games (and gallantry) were the only subjects, and I cared for neither. But I must seem to care for both,
for a boy goes to a Public School precisely to be made a normal, sensible boy—a good mixer—to be taken out of himself;
and eccentricity is severely penalized.

You must not, from this, hastily conclude that most boys
liked *playing* games any better than I did. To escape Clubs

was considered by dozens of boys an obvious good. Leave off Clubs required the Housemaster's signature, and that harmless Merovingian's signature was imitable. A competent forger (I knew one member of the profession) by manufacturing and selling forged signatures could make a steady addition to his pocket money. The perpetual talk about games depended on three things. First, on the same sort of genuine (though hardly practical) enthusiasm which sends the crowds to the League Football Matches. Few wanted to play, but many wanted to watch, to participate vicariously in the triumphs of the Coll, or the House, team. Secondly, this natural feeling had the vigilant backing of all the Bloods and nearly all the Masters. To be lukewarm on such matters was the supreme sin. Hence enthusiasm had to be exaggerated where it existed and simulated where it did not. At cricket matches minor Bloods patrolled the crowd of spectators to detect and punish any "slackness" in the applause; it reminds one of the precautions taken when Nero sang. For of course the whole structure of Bloodery would collapse if the Bloods played in the spirit of play, for their recreation; there must be audience and limelight. And this brings us to the third reason. For boys who were not yet Bloods but who had some athletic promise, Games were essentially a *moyen de parvenir*. There was nothing recreational about Clubs for them any more than for me. They went to the playing fields not as men go to the tennis club but as stagestruck girls go to an Audition; tense and anxious, racked with dazzling hopes and sickening fears, never in peace of mind till they had won some notice which would set their feet on the first rung of the social ladder. And not then at peace either; for not to advance is to fall back.

The truth is that organized and compulsory games had, in my day, banished the element of play from school life almost entirely. There was no time to play (in the proper sense of the word). The rivalry was too fierce, the prizes too glittering, the "hell of failure" too severe.

The only boy, almost, who "played" (but not at games) was our Irish earl. But then he was an exception to all rules; not because of his earldom but because he was an untamable Irishman, anarch in grain, whom no society could iron out. He smoked a pipe in his first term. He went off by night on strange expeditions to a neighboring city; not, I believe, for women, but for harmless rowdyism, low life, and adventure. He always carried a revolver. I remember it well, for he had a habit of loading one chamber only, rushing into your study, and then firing off (if that is the right word) all the others at you, so that your life depended on his counting accurately. I felt at the time, and I feel still, that this (unlike the fagging) was the sort of thing no sensible boy could object to. It was done in defiance both of masters and Bloods, it was wholly useless, and there was no malice in it. I liked Ballygunnian; he, too, was killed in France. I do not think he ever became a Blood; if he had, he wouldn't have noticed it. He cared nothing for the limelight or for social success. He passed through the Coll without paying it any attention.

I suppose Popsy—the pretty redhead who was housemaid on "the Private side"—might also rank as an element making for "play." Popsy, when caught and carried bodily into our part of the House (I think by the Count), was all giggles and screams. She was too sensible a girl to surrender her "virtue" to any Blood; but it was rumored that those who found her in the right time and place might induce her to give certain lessons in anatomy. Perhaps they lied.

I have hardly mentioned a Master yet. One master, dearly loved and reverenced, will appear in the next chapter. But other masters are hardly worth speaking of. It is difficult for parents (and more difficult, perhaps, for schoolmasters) to realize the unimportance of most masters in the life of a school. Of the good and evil which is done to a schoolboy masters, in general, do little, and know less. Our own Housemaster must have been an upright man, for he fed us excellently. For the rest, he treated his House in a very gentlemanly, uninquisitive way. He sometimes walked round the dormitories of a night, but he always wore boots, trod heavily and coughed at the door. He was no spy and no kill-joy, honest man. Live and let live.

As I grew more and more tired, both in body and mind, I came to hate Wyvern. I did not notice the real harm it was doing to me. It was gradually teaching me to be a prig; that is, an intellectual prig or (in the bad sense) a Highbrow. But that subject must wait for another chapter. At the tail end of this I must repeat (for this is the over-all impression left by Wyvern) that I was tired. Consciousness itself was becoming the supreme evil; sleep, the prime good. To lie down, to be out of the sound of voices, to pretend and grimace and evade and slink no more, that was the object of all desire—if only there were not another morning ahead—if only sleep could last for ever!

VII

Light and Shade

*No situation, however wretched it seems, but has some
sort of comfort attending it.*

GOLDSMITH

HERE'S a fellow, you say, who used to come before us
as a moral and religious writer, and now, if you please,
he's written a whole chapter describing his old school as a very
furnace of impure loves without one word on the heinousness
of the sin. But there are two reasons. One you shall hear before
this chapter ends. The other is that, as I have said, the sin in
question is one of the two (gambling is the other) which I have
never been tempted to commit. I will not indulge in futile philippics against enemies I never met in battle.

("This means, then, that all the other vices you have so
largely written about . . ." Well, yes, it does, and more's the
pity; but it's nothing to our purpose at the moment.)

I have now to tell you how Wyvern made me a prig. When
I went there, nothing was further from my mind than the idea
that my private taste for fairly good books, for Wagner, for
mythology, gave me any sort of superiority to those who read
nothing but magazines and listened to nothing but the (then
fashionable) Ragtime. The claim might seem unbelievable if

I did not add that I had been protected from this sort of conceit by downright ignorance. Mr. Ian Hay somewhere draws a picture of the reading minority at a Public School in his day as boys who talked about "G. B. S. and G. K. C." in the same spirit in which other boys secretly smoked; both sets were inspired by the same craving for forbidden fruit and the same desire to be grown up. And I suppose boys such as he describes might come from Chelsea or Oxford or Cambridge homes where they heard things about contemporary literature. But my position was wholly different. I was, for example, a great reader of Shaw about the time I went to Wyvern, but I had never dreamed that reading Shaw was anything to be proud of. Shaw was an author on my father's shelves like any other author. I began reading him because his *Dramatic Opinions* contained a good deal about Wagner and Wagner's very name was then a lure to me. Thence I went on to read most of the other Shaws we had. But how his reputation stood in the literary world I neither knew nor cared; I didn't know there was "a literary world." My father told me Shaw was "a mountebank" but that there were some laughs in *John Bull's Other Island*. It was the same with all my other reading; no one (thank God) had ever admired or encouraged it. (William Morris, for some unfathomable reason, my father always referred to as "that whistlepainter.") I might be—no doubt I was—conceited at Chartres for being good at my Latin; this was something recognized as meritorious. But "Eng. Lit." was blessedly absent from the official syllabus, so I was saved from any possibility of conceit about it. Never in my life had I read a work of fiction, poetry, or criticism in my own language except because, after trying the first few pages, I liked the taste of it. I could not help knowing that most other people, boys and grown-ups alike, did not care for the books I read. A very few tastes I could share with my father, a few more with my brother; apart from that, there was no point of contact, and this I accepted as a sort of natural law. If I reflected on it at all, it would have given me, I think, a slight feeling, not of superiority, but of inferiority. The latest popular novel was so obviously a more adult, a more normal, a more sophisticated taste than any of mine. A certain shame or bashfulness attached itself to whatever one deeply and privately enjoyed. I went to the Coll far more disposed to excuse my literary tastes than to plume myself on them.

But this innocence did not last. It was, from the first, a little shaken by all that I soon began to learn from my form master about the glories of literature. I was at last made free of the dangerous secret that others had, like me, found there "enormous bliss" and been maddened by beauty. Among the other New Bugs of my year, too, I met a pair of boys who came from the Dragon School at Oxford (where Naomi Mitchison in her teens had just produced her first play) and from them also I got the dim impression that there was a world I had never dreamed of, a world in which poetry, say, was a thing public and accepted, just as Games and Gallantry were accepted at Wyvern; nay, a world in which a taste for such things was almost meritorious. I felt as Siegfried felt when it first dawned on him that he was not Mime's son. What had been "my" taste was apparently "our" taste (if only I could ever meet the "we" to whom that "our" belonged). And if "our" taste, then — by a perilous transition — perhaps "good" taste or "the right taste." For that transition involves a land of Fall. The moment good taste knows itself, some of its goodness is lost. Even then, however, it is not necessary to take the further downward step of despising the "philistines" who do not share it. Unfortunately I took it. Hitherto, though increasingly miserable at Wyvern, I had been half ashamed of my own misery, still ready (if I were only allowed) to admire the Olympians, still a little overawed, cowed rather than resentful. I had, you see, no standing place against the Wyvernian *ethos*, no side for which I could play against it; it was a bare "I" against what seemed simply the world. But the moment that "I" became, however vaguely, a we — and Wyvern not *the* world but *a* world — the whole thing changed. It was

now possible, at least in thought, to retaliate. I can remember
what may well have been the precise moment of this transition. A prefect called Blugg or Glubb or some such name stood
opposite me, belching in my face, giving me some order. The
belching was not intended as an insult. You can't "insult" a fag
any more than an animal. If Bulb had thought of my reactions
at all, he would have expected me to find his eructations funny.
What pushed me over the edge into pure priggery was his
face—the puffy bloated cheeks, the thick, moist, sagging lower
lip, the yokel blend of drowsiness and cunning. "The lout!" I
thought. "The clod! The dull, crass clown! For all his powers
and privileges, I would not be he." I had become a Prig, a High-
brow.

The interesting thing is that the public-school system had
thus produced the very thing which it was advertised to prevent
or cure. For you must understand (if you have not been dipped
in that tradition yourself) that the whole thing was devised to
"knock the nonsense" out of the smaller boys and "put them in
their place." "If the junior boys weren't fagged," as my brother
once said, "they would become insufferable." That is why I felt
so embarrassed, a few pages ago, when I had to confess that I
got rather tired of perpetual fagging. If you say this, every true
defender of the system will diagnose your case at once, and
they will all diagnose it in the same way. "Ho-ho!" they will
cry, "so *that's* the trouble! Thought yourself too good to black
your betters' boots, did you? That just shows how badly you
needed to be fagged. It's to cure young prigs like you that the
system exists." That any cause except "thinking yourself too
good for it" might awaken discontent with a fag's lot will not be
admitted. You have only to transfer the thing to adult life and
you will, apparently, see the full logic of the position. If some
neighboring V.I.P. had irresistible authority to call on you for
any service he pleased at any hour when you were not in the
office—if, when you came home on a summer evening, tired
from work and with more work to prepare against the morrow,

he could drag you to the links and make you his caddy till the light failed—if at last he dismissed you unthanked with a suitcase full of his clothes to brush and clean and return to him before breakfast, and a hamper full of his foul linen for your wife to wash and mend—and if, under this regime, you were not always perfectly happy and contented; where could the cause lie except in your own vanity? What else, after all, could it be? For, almost by definition, every offense a junior boy commits must be due to "cheek" or "side"; and to be miserable, even to fall short of rapturous enthusiasm, is an offense.

Obviously a certain grave danger was ever present to the minds of those who built up the Wyvernian hierarchy. It seemed to them self-evident that, if you left things to themselves, boys of nineteen who played rugger for the county and boxed for the school would everywhere be knocked down and sat on by boys of thirteen. And that, you know, would be a very shocking spectacle. The most elaborate mechanism, therefore, had to be devised for protecting the strong against the weak, the close corporation of Old Hands against the parcel of newcomers who were strangers to one another and to everyone in the place, the poor, trembling lions against the furious and ravening sheep.

There is, of course, some truth in it. Small boys can be cheeky; and half an hour in the society of a French thirteen-year-old makes most of us feel that there is something to be said for fagging after all. Yet I cannot help thinking that the bigger boys would have been able to hold their own without all the complicated assurances, pattings on the back, and encouragement which the authorities gave them. For, of course, these authorities, not content with knocking the "nonsense" out of the sheep, were always coaxing and petting an at least equal quantity of "nonsense" into the lions; power and privilege and an applauding audience for the games they play. Might not the mere nature of boys have done all, and rather more than all, that needed doing in this direction without assistance?

But whatever the rationality of the design, I contend that it did not achieve its object. For the last thirty years or so England has been filled with a bitter, truculent, skeptical debunking, and cynical *intelligentsia*. A great many of them were at public schools, and I believe very few of them liked it. Those who defend the schools will, of course, say that these Prigs are the cases which the system failed to cure; they were not kicked, mocked, fagged, flogged, and humiliated enough. But surely it is equally possible that they are the products of the system? that they were not Prigs at all when they came to their schools but were made Prigs by their first year, as I was? For, really, that would be a very natural result. Where oppression does not completely and permanently break the spirit, has it not a natural tendency to produce retaliatory pride and contempt? We reimburse ourselves for cuffs and toil by a double dose of self-esteem. No one is more likely to be arrogant than a lately freed slave.

I write, of course, only to neutral readers. With the whole-hearted adherents of the system there is no arguing, for, as we have already seen, they have maxims and logic which the lay mind cannot apprehend. I have even heard them defend compulsory games on the ground that all boys "except a few rotters" like the games; they have to be compulsory because no compulsion is needed. (I wish I had never heard chaplains in the armed forces produce a similar argument in defense of the wicked institution of Church Parades.)

But the essential evil of public-school life, as I see it, did not lie either in the sufferings of the fags or in the privileged arrogance of the Bloods. These were symptoms of something more all-pervasive, something which, in the long run, did most harm to the boys who succeeded best at school and were happiest there. Spiritually speaking, the deadly thing was that school life was a life almost wholly dominated by the social struggle; to get on, to arrive, or, having reached the top, to remain there, was the absorbing preoccupation. It is often, of course, the pre-occupation of adult life as well; but I have not yet seen any adult society in which the surrender to this impulse was so total. And from it, at school as in the world, all sorts of meanness flow; the sycophancy that courts those higher in the scale, the cultivation of those whom it is well to know, the speedy abandonment of friendships that will not help on the upward path, the readiness to join the cry against the unpopular, the secret motive in almost every action. The Wyvernians seem to me in retrospect to have been the least spontaneous, in that sense the least boyish, society I have ever known. It would perhaps not be too much to say that in some boys' lives everything was calculated to the great end of advancement. For this games were played; for this clothes, friends, amusements, and vices were chosen.

And that is why I cannot give pederasty anything like a first place among the evils of the Coll. There is much hypocrisy on this theme. People commonly talk as if every other evil were more tolerable than this. But why? Because those of us who do not share the vice feel for it a certain nausea, as we do, say, for necrophily? I think that of very little relevance to moral judgment. Because it produces permanent perversion? But there is very little evidence that it does. The Bloods would have preferred girls to boys if they could have come by them; when, at a later age, girls were obtainable, they probably took them. Is it then on Christian grounds? But how many of those who fulminate on the matter are in fact Christians? And what Christian, in a society so worldly and cruel as that of Wyvern, would pick out the carnal sins for special reprobation? Cruelty is surely more evil than lust and the World at least as dangerous as the Flesh. The real reason for all the pother is, in my opinion, neither Christian nor ethical. We attack this vice not because it is the worst but because it is, by adult standards, the most disreputable and unmentionable, and happens also to be a crime in English law. The World will lead you only to Hell; but sodomy may lead you to jail and create a scandal, and lose you your job. The World, to do it justice, seldom does that.

If those of us who have known a school like Wyvern dared to speak the truth, we should have to say that pederasty, however great an evil in itself, was, in that time and place, the only foothold or cranny left for certain good things. It was the only counterpoise to the social struggle; the one oasis (though green only with weeds and moist only with fetid water) in the burning desert of competitive ambition. In his unnatural love affairs, and perhaps only there, the Blood went a little out of himself, forgot for a few hours that he was One of the Most Important People There Are. It softens the picture. A perversion was the only chink left through which something spontaneous and uncalculating could creep in. Plato was right after all. Eros, turned upside down, blackened, distorted, and filthy, still bore the traces of his divinity.

What an answer, by the by, Wyvern was to those who derive all the ills of society from economics! For money had nothing to do with its class system. It was not (thank Heaven) the boys with threadbare coats who became Punts, nor the boys with plenty of pocket money who became Bloods. According to some theorists, therefore, it ought to have been entirely free from bourgeois vulgarities and iniquities. Yet I have never seen a community so competitive, so full of snobbery and flunkeyism, a ruling class so selfish and so class-conscious, or a proletariat so fawning, so lacking in all solidarity and sense of corporate honor. But perhaps one hardly needs to cite experience for a truth so obvious a priori. As Aristotle remarked, men do not become dictators in order to keep warm. If a ruling class has some other source of strength, why need it bother about money? Most of what it wants will be pressed upon it by emulous flatterers; the rest can be taken by force.

There were two blessings at Wyvern that wore no disguise; one of them was my form master, Smewgy as we called him. I

spell the name so as to insure the right pronunciation—the
first syllable should rhyme exactly with *Fugue*—though the
Wyvernian spelling was "Smugy."

Except at Oldie's I had been fortunate in my teachers ever
since I was born; but Smewgy was "beyond expectation, beyond hope." He was a gray-head with large spectacles and a
wide mouth which combined to give him a froglike expression, but nothing could be less froglike than his voice. He was
honey-tongued. Every verse he read turned into music on his
lips: something midway between speech and song. It is not the
only good way of reading verse, but it is the way to enchant
boys; more dramatic and less rhythmical ways can be learned
later. He first taught me the right sensuality of poetry, how
it should be savored and mouthed in solitude. Of Milton's
"Thrones, Dominations, Princedoms, Virtues, Powers" he said,
"That line made me happy for a week." It was not the sort of
thing I had heard anyone say before. Nor had I ever met before
perfect courtesy in a teacher. It had nothing to do with softness; Smewgy could be very severe, but it was the severity of a
judge, weighty and measured, without taunting—

> *He never yet no vileinye ne sayde*
> *In all his lyf unto no maner wight.*

He had a difficult team to drive, for our form consisted partly
of youngsters, New Bugs with scholarships, starting there like
myself, and partly of veterans who had arrived there at the end
of their slow journey up the school. He made us a unity by his
good manners. He always addressed us as "gentlemen" and the
possibility of behaving otherwise seemed thus to be ruled out
from the beginning; and in that room at least the distinction
between fags and Bloods never raised its head. On a hot day,
when he had given us permission to remove our coats, he asked
our permission before removing his gown. Once for bad work I
was sent by him to the Headmaster to be threatened and rated.
The Headmaster misunderstood Smewgy's report and thought

there had been some complaint about my manners. Afterward Smewgy got wind of the Head's actual words and at once corrected the mistake, drawing me aside and saying, "There has been some curious misunderstanding. I said nothing of the sort about you. You will have to be whipped if you don't do better at your Greek Grammar next week, but naturally that has nothing to do with your manners or mine." The idea that the tone of conversation between one gentleman and another should be altered by a flogging (any more than by a duel) was ridiculous. His manner was perfect: no familiarity, no hostility, no threadbare humor; mutual respect; decorum. "Never let us live with *amousia*" was one of his favorite maxims: *amousia*, the absence of the Muses. And he knew, as Spenser knew, that courtesy was of the Muses.

Thus, even had he taught us nothing else, to be in Smewgy's form was to be in a measure ennobled. Amidst all the banal ambition and flashy splendors of school life he stood as a permanent reminder of things more gracious, more humane, larger and cooler. But his teaching, in the narrower sense, was equally good. He could enchant but he could also analyze. An idiom or a textual crux, once expounded by Smewgy, became clear as day. He made us feel that the scholar's demand for accuracy was not merely pedantic, still less an arbitrary moral discipline, but rather a niceness, a delicacy, to lack which argued "a gross and swainish disposition." I began to see that the reader who misses syntactical points in a poem is missing aesthetic points as well.

In those days a boy on the classical side officially did almost nothing but classics. I think this was wise; the greatest service we can do to education today is to teach fewer subjects. No one has time to do more than a very few things well before he is twenty, and when we force a boy to be a mediocrity in a dozen subjects we destroy his standards, perhaps for life. Smewgy taught us Latin and Greek, but everything else came in incidentally. The books I liked best under his teaching were Horace's Odes, Aeneid IV, and Euripides' *Bacchae*. I had always in one sense "liked" my classical work, but hitherto this had only been the pleasure that everyone feels in mastering a craft. Now I tasted the classics as poetry. Euripides' picture of Dionysus was closely linked in my mind with the whole mood of Mr. Stephens' *Crock of Gold*, which I had lately read for the first time with great excitement. Here was something very different from the Northernness. Pan and Dionysus lacked the cold, piercing appeal of Odin and Frey. A new quality entered my imagination: something Mediterranean and volcanic, the orgiastic drum beat. Orgiastic, but not, or not strongly, erotic. It was perhaps unconsciously connected with my growing hatred of the public school orthodoxies and conventions, my desire to break and tear it all.

The other undisguised blessing of the Coll was "the Gurney," the school library; not only because it was a library, but because it was sanctuary. As the Negro used to become free on touching English soil, so the meanest boy was "unfaggable" once he was inside the Gurney. It was not, of course, easy to get there. In the winter terms if you were not on the list for "Clubs" you had to go out for a run. In summer you could reach sanctuary of an afternoon only under favorable conditions. You might be put down for Clubs, and that excluded you. Or there might be either a House match or a Coll match which you were compelled to watch. Thirdly, and most probably, on your way to the Gurney you might be caught and fagged for the whole afternoon. But sometimes one succeeded in running the gauntlet of all these dangers; and then—the books, silence, leisure, the distant sound of bat and ball ("Oh the brave music of a *distant* drum"), bees buzzing at the open windows, and freedom. In the Gurney I found *Corpus Poeticum Boreale* and tried, vainly but happily, to hammer out the originals from the translation at the bottom of the page. There too I found Milton, and Yeats, and a book on Celtic mythology, which soon became, if not a rival, yet a humble companion, to Norse. That did me good; to enjoy two mythologies (or three, now that I had begun to love the Greek), fully aware of their differing flavors, is a balancing thing, and makes for catholicity. I felt keenly the difference between the stony and fiery sublimity of Asgard, the green, leafy, amorous, and elusive world of Cruachan and the Red Branch and Tir-nan-Og, the harder, more defiant, sun-bright beauty of Olympus. I began (presumably in the holidays) an epic on Cuchulain and another on Finn, in English hexameters and in fourteeners respectively. Luckily they were abandoned before these easy and vulgar metres had time to spoil my ear.

But the Northernness still came first and the only work I completed at this time was a tragedy, Norse in subject and Greek in form. It was called *Loki Bound* and was as classical as any Humanist could have desired, with Prologos, Parodos, Epeisodia, Stasima, Exodos, Stichomythia, and (of course) one passage in trochaic *septenarii*—with rhyme. I never enjoyed anything more. The content is significant. My Loki was not merely malicious. He was against Odin because Odin had created a world though Loki had clearly warned him that this was a wanton cruelty. Why should creatures have the burden of existence forced on them without their consent? The main contrast in my play was between the sad wisdom of Loki and the brutal orthodoxy of Thor. Odin was partly sympathetic; he could at least see what Loki meant and there had been old friendship between those two before cosmic politics forced them apart. Thor was the real villain, Thor with his hammer and his threats, who was always egging Odin on against Loki and always complaining that Loki did not sufficiently respect the major gods; to which Loki replied

I pay respect to wisdom not to strength.

Thor was, in fact, the symbol of the Bloods; though I see that more clearly now than I did at the time. Loki was a projection of myself; he voiced that sense of priggish superiority whereby I was, unfortunately, beginning to compensate myself for my unhappiness.

The other feature in *Loki Bound* which may be worth commenting on is the pessimism. I was at this time living, like so many Atheists or Antitheists, in a whirl of contradictions. I maintained that God did not exist. I was also very angry with God for not existing. I was equally angry with Him for creating a world.

How far was this pessimism, this desire not to have been, sincere? Well, I must confess that this desire quite slipped out of my mind during the seconds when I was covered by the wild Earl's revolver. By the Chestertonian test, then, the test of *Manalive*, it was not sincere at all. But I am still not convinced by Chesterton's argument. It is true that when a pessimist's life is threatened he behaves like other men; his impulse to preserve life is stronger than his judgment that life is not worth preserving. But how does this prove that the judgment was insincere or even erroneous? A man's judgment that whisky is bad for him is not invalidated by the fact that when the bottle is at hand he finds desire stronger than reason and succumbs. Having once tasted life, we are subjected to the impulse of self-preservation. Life, in other words, is as habit-forming as cocaine. What then? If I still held creation to be "a great injustice" I should hold that this impulse to retain life aggravates the injustice. If it is bad to be forced to drink the potion, how does it mend matters that the potion turns out to be an addiction drug? Pessimism cannot be answered so. Thinking as I then thought about the universe, I was reasonable in condemning it. At the same time I now see that my view was closely connected with a certain lopsidedness of temperament. I had always been more violent in my negative than in my positive demands. Thus, in personal relations, I could forgive much neglect more easily than the least degree of what I regarded as interference. At table I could forgive much insipidity in my food more easily than the least suspicion of what seemed to me excessive or inappropriate seasoning. In the course of life I could put up with any amount of monotony far more patiently than even the smallest disturbance, bother, bustle, or what the Scotch call *kurfuffle*. Never at any age did I clamor to be amused; always and at all ages (where I dared) I hotly demanded not to be interrupted. The pessimism, or Cowardice, which would prefer non-existence itself to even the mildest unhappiness was thus merely the generalization of all these pusillanimous preferences. And it remains true that I have, almost all my life, been quite unable to feel that horror of nonentity, of annihilation, which, say, Dr. Johnson felt so strongly. I felt it for the first time only in 1947. But that was after I had long been reconverted and thus begun to know what life really is and what would have been lost by missing it.

VIII

Release

As Fortune is wont, at her chosen hour,
Whether she sends us solace or sore,
The wight to whom she shows her power
Will find that he gets still more and more.

PEARL

A FEW chapters ago I warned the reader that the return of Joy had introduced into my life a duality which makes it difficult to narrate. Reading through what I have just written about Wyvern, I find myself exclaiming, "Lies, lies! This was really a period of ecstasy. It consisted chiefly of moments when you were too happy to speak, when the gods and heroes rioted through your head, when satyrs danced and Maenads roared on the mountains, when Brynhild and Sieglinde, Deirdre, Maeve and Helen were all about you, till sometimes you felt that it might break you with mere richness." And all that is true. There were more Leprechauns than fags in that House. I have seen the victories of Cuchulain more often than those of the first eleven. Was Borage the Head of the Coll? or was it Conachar MacNessa? And the world itself—can I have been unhappy, living in Paradise? What keen, tingling sunlight there was! The mere smells were enough to make a man tipsy—cut grass, dew-dabbled mosses, sweet pea, autumn woods, wood burning, peat, salt water. The sense ached. I was sick with desire; that sickness better than health. All this is true, but it does not make the other version a lie. I am telling a story of two lives. They have nothing to do with each other: oil and vinegar, a river running beside a canal, Jekyll and Hyde. Fix your eye on either and it claims to be the sole truth. When I remember my outer life I see clearly that the other is but momentary flashes, seconds of gold scattered in months of dross, each instantly swallowed up in the old, familiar, sordid, hopeless weariness. When I remember my inner life I see that everything mentioned in the last two chapters was merely a coarse curtain which at any moment might be drawn aside to reveal all the heavens I then knew. The same duality perplexes the story of my home life, to which I must now turn.

Once my brother had left Wyvern and I had gone to it, the classic period of our boyhood was at an end. Something not so good succeeded it, but this had long been prepared by slow development within the classic age itself. All began, as I have said, with the fact that our father was out of the house from nine in the morning till six at night. From the very first we built up for ourselves a life that excluded him. He on his part demanded a confidence even more boundless, perhaps, than a father usually, or wisely, demands. One instance of this, early in my life, had far-reaching effects. Once when I was at Oldie's and had just begun to try to live as a Christian I wrote out a set of rules for myself and put them in my pocket. On the first day of the holidays, noticing that my pockets bulged with all sorts of papers and that my coat was being pulled out of all shape, he plucked out the whole pile of rubbish and began to go through it. Boylike, I would have died rather than let him see my list of good resolutions. I managed to keep them out of his reach and get them into the fire. I do not see that either of us was to blame;

but never from that moment until the hour of his death did I enter his house without first going through my own pockets and removing anything that I wished to keep private.

A habit of concealment was thus bred before I had anything guilty to conceal. By now I had plenty. And even what I had no wish to hide I could not tell. To have told him what Wyvern or even Chartres was really like would have been risky (he might write to the Headmaster) and intolerably embarrassing. It would also have been impossible; and here I must touch on one of his strangest characteristics.

My father—but these words, at the head of a paragraph, will carry the reader's mind inevitably to *Tristram Shandy*. On second thoughts I am content that they should. It is only in a Shandean spirit that my matter can be approached. I have to describe something as odd and whimsical as ever entered the brain of Sterne; and if I could, I would gladly lead you to the same affection for my father as you have for Tristram's. And now for the thing itself. You will have grasped that my father was no fool. He had even a streak of genius in him. At the same time he had—when seated in his own arm chair after a heavy midday dinner on an August afternoon with all the windows shut—more power of confusing an issue or taking up a fact wrongly than any man I have ever known. As a result it was impossible to drive into his head any of the realities of our school life, after which (nevertheless) he repeatedly enquired. The first and simplest barrier to communication was that, having earnestly asked, he did not "stay for an answer" or forgot it the moment it was uttered. Some facts must have been asked for and told him, on a moderate computation, once a week, and were received by him each time as perfect novelties. But this was the simplest barrier. Far more often he retained something, but something very unlike what you had said. His mind so bubbled over with humor, sentiment, and indignation that, long before he had understood or even listened to your words, some accidental hint had set his imagination to work, he had produced his own version of the facts, and believed that he was getting it from you. As he invariably got proper names wrong (no name seemed to him less probable than another) his *textus receptus* was often almost unrecognizable. Tell him that a boy called Churchwood had caught a field mouse and kept it as a pet, and a year, or ten years later, he would ask you, "Did you ever hear what became of poor Chickweed who was so afraid of the rats?" For his own version, once adopted, was indelible, and attempts to correct it only produced an incredulous "Hm! Well, that's not the story you *used* to tell." Sometimes, indeed, he took in the facts you had stated; but truth fared none the better for that. What are facts without interpretation? It was axiomatic to my father (in theory) that nothing was said or done from an obvious motive. Hence he who in his real life was the most honorable and impulsive of men, and the easiest victim that any knave or imposter could hope to meet, became a positive Machiavel when he knitted his brows and applied to the behavior of people he had never seen the spectral and labyrinthine operation which he called "reading between the lines." Once embarked upon that, he might make his landfall anywhere in the wide world: and always with unshakable conviction. "I see it all"—"I understand it perfectly"—"It's as plain as a pikestaff," he would say; and then, as we soon learned, he would believe till his dying day in some deadly quarrel, some slight, some secret sorrow or some immensely complex machination, which was not only improbable but impossible. Dissent on our part was attributed, with kindly laughter, to our innocence, gullibility, and general ignorance of life. And besides all these confusions, there were the sheer *non sequiturs* when the ground seemed to open at one's feet. "Did Shakespeare spell his name with an e at the end?" asked my brother. "I believe," said I—but my father interrupted: "I very much doubt if he used the Italian calligraphy *at all*." A certain church in Belfast has both a Greek inscription over the door and a curious tower. "That church is a great landmark," said I, "I can pick it out from all sorts of places—even from the top of Cave Hill." "Such nonsense," said my father, "how could you make out Greek letters three or four miles away?"

One conversation, held several years later, may be recorded as a specimen of these continual cross-purposes. My brother had been speaking of a reunion dinner for the officers of the Nth Division which he had lately attended. "I suppose your friend Collins was there," said my father.

B. Collins? Oh no. He wasn't in the Nth, you know.

F. (After a pause.) Did these fellows not like Collins then?

B. I don't quite understand. What fellows?

F. The Johnnies that got up the dinner.

B. Oh no, not at all. It was nothing to do with liking or not liking. You see, it was a purely Divisional affair. There'd be no question of asking anyone who hadn't been in the Nth.

F. (After a long pause.) Hm! Well, I'm sure poor Collins was very much hurt.

There are situations in which the very genius of Filial Piety would find it difficult not to let some sign of impatience escape him.

I would not commit the sin of Ham. Nor would I, as historian, reduce a complex character to a false simplicity. The man who, in his armchair, sometimes appeared not so much incapable of understanding anything as determined to misunderstand everything, was formidable in the police court and, I presume, efficient in his office. He was a humorist, even on occasion, a wit. When he was dying, the pretty nurse, rallying him, said, "What an old pessimist you are! You're just like my father." "I suppose," replied her patient, "he has *several* daughters."

The hours my father spent at home were thus hours of perplexity for us boys. After an evening of the sort of conversation I have been describing one felt as if one's head were spinning like a top. His presence put an end to all our innocent as well as to all our forbidden occupations. It is a hard thing—nay, a wicked thing—when a man is felt to be an intruder in his own house. And yet, as Johnson said, "Sensation is sensation." I am sure it was not his fault, I believe much of it was ours; what is certain is that I increasingly found it oppressive to be with him. One of his most amiable qualities helped to make it so. I have said before that he "conned no state"; except during his Philippics he treated us as equals. The theory was that we lived together more like three brothers than like a father and two sons. That, I say, was the theory. But of course it was not and could not be so; indeed ought not to have been so. That relation cannot really exist between schoolboys and a middle-aged man of overwhelming personality and of habits utterly unlike theirs. And the pretense that it does ends by putting a curious strain on the juniors. Chesterton has laid his finger on the weak point of all such factitious equality: "If a boy's aunts are his pals, will it not soon follow that a boy needs no pals but his aunts?" That was not, of course, the question for us; we wanted no pals. But we did want liberty, if only liberty to walk about the house. And my father's theory that we were three boys together actually meant that while he was at home we were as closely bound to his presence as if the three of us had been chained together; and all our habits were frustrated. Thus if my father came home unexpectedly at midday, having allowed himself an extra half-holiday, he might, if it were summer, find us with chairs and books in the garden. An austere parent, of the formal school, would have gone in to his own adult occupations. Not so my father. Sitting in the garden? An excellent idea. But would not all three of us be better on the summer seat? Thither, after he had assumed one of his "light spring overcoats," we would go. (I do not know how many overcoats he had; I am still wearing two of them.) After sitting for a few minutes, thus clad, on a shadeless seat where the noonday sun was blistering the paint, he not unnaturally began to perspire. "I don't know what you two think," he would say, "but I'm finding this almost *too*

hot. What about moving indoors?" That meant an adjourn-
ment to the study, where even the smallest chink of open window was rather grudgingly allowed. I say "allowed," but there
was no question of authority. In theory, everything was decided
by the general Will. "Liberty Hall, boys, Liberty Hall," as he
delighted to quote. "What time would you like lunch?" But we
knew only too well that the meal which would otherwise have
been at one had already been shifted, in obedience to his lifelong preference, to two or even two-thirty; and that the cold
meats which we liked had already been withdrawn in favor of
the only food our father ever voluntarily ate—hot butcher's
meat, boiled, stewed or roast . . . and this to be eaten in mid-
afternoon in a dining room that faced south. For the whole of
the rest of the day, whether sitting or walking, we were insep-
arable; and the speech (you see that it could hardly be called
conversation), the speech with its cross-purposes, with its tone
(inevitably) always set by him, continued intermittently till
bedtime. I should be worse than a dog if I blamed my lonely
father for thus desiring the friendship of his sons; or even if
the miserable return I made him did not to this day lie heavy
on my conscience. But "sensation is sensation." It was extraor-
dinarily tiring. And in my own contributions to these endless
talks—which were indeed too adult for me, too anecdotal, too
prevailingly jocular—I was increasingly aware of an artificiality. The anecdotes were, indeed, admirable in their kind: business stories, Mahaffy stories (many of which I found attached
to Jowett at Oxford), stories of ingenious swindles, social blunders, police-court "drunks." But I was acting when I responded
to them. Drollery, whimsicality, the kind of humor that borders
on the fantastic, was my line. I had to act. My father's geniality
and my own furtive disobediences both helped to drive me into
hypocrisy. I could not "be myself" while he was at home. God
forgive me, I thought Monday morning, when he went back to
his work, the brightest jewel in the week.

Such was the situation which developed during the clas-

sic period. Now, when I had gone to Wyvern and my brother
to a tutor to prepare for Sandhurst, there came a change. My
brother had liked Wyvern as much as I loathed it. There were
many reasons for this: his more adaptable temper, his face
which bore no such smack-inviting signature as mine, but most
of all the fact that he had gone there straight from Oldie's and
I from preparatory school where I had been happy. No school
in England but would have appeared a heaven on earth after Oldie's. Thus in one of his first letters from Wyvern my
brother communicated the startling fact that you could really
eat as much (or as little) as you wanted at table. To a boy fresh
from the school at Belsen, this alone would have outweighed
almost everything else. But by the time I went to Wyvern I had
learned to take decent feeding for granted. And now a terrible
thing happened. My reaction to Wyvern was perhaps the first
great disappointment my brother had ever experienced. Loving the place as he did, he had looked forward to the days when
this too could be shared between us—an *idem sentire* about
Wyvern succeeding an *idem sentire* about Boxen. Instead he
heard, from me, blasphemies against all his gods; from Wyvern,
that his young brother looked like becoming a Coll Punt. The
immemorial league between us was strained, all but broken.

All this was cruelly complicated by the fact that relations between my father and my brother were never before or since so
bad as at this time; and Wyvern was behind that too. My brother's reports had grown worse and worse; and the tutor to whom
he had now been sent confirmed them to the extent of saying that he seemed to have learned almost nothing at school.
Nor was that all. Sentences savagely underlined in my father's
copy of *The Lanchester Tradition* reveal his thoughts. They are
passages about a certain glazed insolence, an elaborate, heartless flippancy, which the reforming Headmaster in that story
encountered in the Bloods of the school he wished to reform.
That was how my father envisaged my brother at this period:
flippant, languid, emptied of the intellectual interests which

had appeared in his earlier boyhood, immovable, indifferent to all real values, and urgent in his demand for a motor bicycle.

It was, of course, to turn us into public-school boys that my father had originally sent us to Wyvern; the finished product appalled him. It is a familiar tragicomedy and you can study it in Lockhart; Scott labored hard to make his son a hussar, but when the actual hussar was presented to him, Scott sometimes forgot the illusion of being an aristocrat and became once more a respectable Edinburgh lawyer with strong views about Puppyism. So in our family. Mispronunciation was one of my father's favorite rhetorical weapons. He now always sounded the first syllable of Wyvern wrongly. I can still hear him growl, "Wyvernian affectation." In proportion as my brother's tone became languid and urbanely weary, so my father's voice became more richly and energetically Irish, and all manner of strange music from his boyhood in Cork and Dublin forced its way up through the more recent Belfastian crust.

During these miserable debates I occupied a most unfortunate position. To have been on my father's side and against my brother I should have had to unmake myself; it was a state of parties outside my whole philosophy of domestic politics. It was all very disagreeable.

Yet out of this "unpleasantness" (a favorite word of my father's) there sprang what I still reckon, by merely natural standards, the most fortunate thing that ever happened to me. The tutor (in Surrey) to whom my brother had been sent was one of my father's oldest friends. He had been headmaster of Lurgan when my father was a boy there. In a surprisingly short time he so rebuilt and extended the ruins of my brother's education that he not only passed into Sandhurst but was placed among those very few candidates at the top of the list who received prize cadetships. I do not think my father ever did justice to my brother's achievement; it came at a time when the gulf between them was too wide, and when they were friends again it had become ancient history. But he saw very clearly what it proved about the exceptional powers of his teacher. At the same time, he was almost as sick as I of the very name of Wyvern. And I never ceased, by letter and by word of mouth, to beg that I might be taken away. All these factors urged him to the decision which he now made. Might it not after all be best to give me my desire? to have done with school for good and send me also to Surrey to read for the University with Mr. Kirkpatrick? He did not form this plan without much doubt and hesitation. He did his best to put all the risks before me: the dangers of solitude, the sudden change from the life and bustle of a great school (which change I might not like so much as I anticipated), the possibly deadening effect of living with only an old man and his old wife for company. Should I really be happy with no companions of my own age? I tried to look very grave at these questions. But it was all imposture. My heart laughed. Happy without other boys? Happy without toothache, without chilblains, happy without pebbles in my shoes? And so the arrangement was made. If it had had nothing else to recommend it, the mere thought, "Never, never, never, shall I have to play games again," was enough to transport me. If you want to know how I felt, imagine your own feelings on waking one morning to find that income tax or unrequited love had somehow vanished from the world.

I should be sorry if I were understood to think, or if I encouraged any reader in thinking, that this invincible dislike of doing things with a bat or a ball were other than a misfortune. Not, indeed, that I allow to games any of the moral and almost mystical virtues which schoolmasters claim for them; they seem to me to lead to ambition, jealousy, and embittered partisan feeling, quite as often as to anything else. Yet not to like them is a misfortune, because it cuts you off from companionship with many excellent people who can be approached in no other way. A misfortune, not a vice; for it is involuntary. I had tried to like games and failed. That impulse had been left out of my make-up; I was to games, as the proverb has it, like an ass to the harp.

It is a curious truth, noticed by many writers, that good fortune is nearly always followed by more good fortune, and bad, by more bad. About the same time that my father decided to send me to Mr. Kirkpatrick, another great good came to me. Many chapters ago I mentioned a boy who lived near us and who had tried, quite unsuccessfully, to make friends with my brother and myself. His name was Arthur and he was my brother's exact contemporary; he and I had been at Campbell together though we never met. I think it was shortly before the beginning of my last term at Wyvern that I received a message saying that Arthur was in bed, convalescent, and would welcome a visit. I can't remember what led me to accept this invitation, but for some reason I did.

I found Arthur sitting up in bed. On the table beside him lay a copy of *Myths of the Norsemen*.

"Do *you* like that?" said I.

"Do *you* like that?" said he.

Next moment the book was in our hands, our heads were bent close together, we were pointing, quoting, talking — soon almost shouting — discovering in a torrent of questions that we liked not only the same thing, but the same parts of it and in the same way; that both knew the stab of Joy and that, for both, the arrow was shot from the North. Many thousands of people have had the experience of finding the first friend, and it is none the less a wonder; as great a wonder (*pace* the novelists) as first love, or even a greater. I had been so far from thinking such a friend possible that I had never even longed for one; no more than I longed to be King of England. If I had found that Arthur had independently built up an exact replica of the Boxonian world I should not really have been much more surprised. Nothing, I suspect, is more astonishing in any man's life than the discovery that there do exist people very, very like himself.

During my last few weeks at Wyvern strange stories began to appear in the papers, for this was the summer of 1914. I remember how a friend and I puzzled over a column that bore the headline "Can England keep out of it?" "Keep out of it?" said he, "I don't see how she can get into it." Memory paints the last hours of that term in slightly apocalyptic colors, and perhaps memory lies. Or perhaps for me it was apocalyptic enough to know that I was leaving, to see all those hated things for the last time; yet not simply (at that moment) to hate them. There is a "rumness," a ghostliness, about even a Windsor chair when it says, "You will not see me again." Early in the holidays we declared war. My brother, then on leave from Sandhurst, was recalled. Some weeks later I went to Mr. Kirkpatrick at Great Bookham in Surrey.

IX

The Great Knock

*You will often meet with characters in nature so
extravagant that a discreet poet would not venture to
set them upon the stage.*

LORD CHESTERFIELD

O N A September day, having crossed to Liverpool and
reached London, I made my way to Waterloo and ran
down to Great Bookham. I had been told that Surrey was "suburban," and the landscape that actually flitted past the windows astonished me. I saw steep little hills, watered valleys, and
wooded commons which ranked by my Wyvernian and Irish
standards as forest; bracken everywhere; a world of red and
russet and yellowish greens. Even the sprinkling of suburban
villas (much rarer then than now) delighted me. These timbered and red-tiled houses, embosomed in trees, were wholly
unlike the stuccoed monstrosities which formed the suburbs of
Belfast. Where I had expected gravel drives and iron gates and
interminable laurels and monkey puzzlers, I saw crooked paths
running up or down hill from wicket gates, between fruit trees
and birches. By a severer taste than mine these houses would all
be mocked perhaps; yet I cannot help thinking that those who
designed them and their gardens achieved their object, which

was to suggest Happiness. They filled me with a desire for that domesticity which, in its full development, I had never known; they set one thinking of tea trays.

At Bookham I was met by my new teacher—"Kirk" or "Knock" or the Great Knock as my father, my brother, and I all called him. We had heard about him all our lives and I therefore had a very clear impression of what I was in for. I came prepared to endure a perpetual lukewarm shower bath of sentimentality. That was the price I was ready to pay for the infinite blessedness of escaping school; but a heavy price. One story of my father's, in particular, gave me the most embarrassing forebodings. He had loved to tell how once at Lurgan, when he was in some kind of trouble or difficulty, the Old Knock, or the dear Old Knock, had drawn him aside and there "quietly and naturally" slid his arm round him and rubbed his dear old whiskers against my father's youthful cheek and whispered a few words of comfort. . . . And here was Bookham at last, and there was the arch-sentimentalist himself waiting to meet me.

He was over six feet tall, very shabbily dressed (like a gardener, I thought), lean as a rake, and immensely muscular. His wrinkled face seemed to consist entirely of muscles, so far as it was visible; for he wore mustache and side whiskers with a clean-shaven chin like the Emperor Franz Joseph. The whiskers, you will understand, concerned me very much at that moment. My cheek already tingled in anticipation. Would he begin at once? There would be tears for certain; perhaps worse things. It is one of my lifelong weaknesses that I never could endure the embrace or kiss of my own sex. (An unmanly weakness, by the way; Aeneas, Beowulf, Roland, Launcelot, Johnson, and Nelson knew nothing of it.)

Apparently, however, the old man was holding his fire. We shook hands, and though his grip was like iron pincers it was not lingering. A few minutes later we were walking away from the station.

"You are now," said Kirk, "proceeding along the principal artery between Great and Little Bookham."

I stole a glance at him. Was this geographical exordium a heavy joke? Or was he trying to conceal his emotions? His face, however, showed only an inflexible gravity. I began to "make conversation" in the deplorable manner which I had acquired at those evening parties and indeed found increasingly necessary to use with my father. I said I was surprised at the "scenery" of Surrey; it was much "wilder" than I had expected.

"Stop!" shouted Kirk with a suddenness that made me jump. "What do you mean by wildness and what grounds had you for not expecting it?"

I replied I don't know what, still "making conversation." As answer after answer was torn to shreds it at last dawned upon me that he really wanted to know. He was not making conversation, nor joking, nor snubbing me; he wanted to know. I was stung into attempting a real answer. A few passes sufficed to show that I had no clear and distinct idea corresponding to the word "wildness," and that, in so far as I had any idea at all, "wildness" was a singularly inept word. "Do you not see, then," concluded the Great Knock, "that your remark was meaningless?" I prepared to sulk a little, assuming that the subject would now be dropped. Never was I more mistaken in my life. Having analyzed my terms, Kirk was proceeding to deal with my proposition as a whole. On what had I based (but he pronounced it *baized*) my expectations about the Flora and Geology of Surrey? Was it maps, or photographs, or books? I could produce none. It had, heaven help me, never occurred to me that what I called my thoughts needed to be "baized" on anything. Kirk once more drew a conclusion—without the slightest sign of emotion, but equally without the slightest concession to what I thought good manners: "Do you not see, then, that you had no right to have any opinion whatever on the subject?"

By this time our acquaintance had lasted about three and a half minutes; but the tone set by this first conversation was preserved without a single break during all the years I spent at Bookham. Anything more grotesquely unlike the "dear Old Knock" of my father's reminiscences could not be conceived. Knowing my father's invariable intention of veracity and also knowing what strange transformations every truth underwent when once it entered his mind, I am sure he did not mean to deceive us. But if Kirk at any time of his life took a boy aside and there "quietly and naturally" rubbed the boy's face with his whiskers, I shall as easily believe that he sometimes varied the treatment by quietly and naturally standing on his venerable and egg-bald head.

If ever a man came near to being a purely logical entity, that man was Kirk. Born a little later, he would have been a Logical Positivist. The idea that human beings should exercise their vocal organs for any purpose except that of communicating or discovering truth was to him preposterous. The most casual remark was taken as a summons to disputation. I soon came to know the differing values of his three openings. The loud cry of "Stop!" was flung in to arrest a torrent of verbiage which could not be endured a moment longer; not because it fretted his patience (he never thought of that) but because it was wasting time, darkening counsel. The hastier and quieter "Excuse!" (i.e., "Excuse me") ushered in a correction or distinction merely parenthetical and betokened that, thus set right, your remark might still, without absurdity, be allowed to reach completion. The most encouraging of all was, "I hear you." This meant that your remark was significant and only required refutation; it had risen to the dignity of error. Refutation (when we got so far) always followed the same lines. Had I read this? Had I studied that? Had I any statistical evidence? Had I any evidence in my own experience? And so to the almost inevitable conclusion, "Do you not see then that you had no right, etc."

Some boys would not have liked it; to me it was red beef and strong beer. I had taken it for granted that my leisure hours at Bookham would be passed in "grown-up conversation." And that, as you know already, I had no taste for. In my experience it meant conversation about politics, money, deaths, and digestion. I assumed that a taste for it, as for eating mustard or reading newspapers, would develop in me when I grew older (so far, all three expectations have been disappointed). The only two kinds of talk I wanted were the almost purely imaginative and the almost purely rational; such talk as I had about Boxen with my brother or about Valhalla with Arthur, on the one hand, or such talk as I had had with my uncle Gussie about astronomy on the other. I could never have gone far in any science because on the path of every science the lion Mathematics lies in wait for you. Even in Mathematics, whatever could be done by mere reasoning (as in simple geometry) I did with delight; but the moment calculation came in I was helpless. I grasped the principles but my answers were always wrong. Yet though I could never have been a scientist, I had scientific as well as imaginative impulses, and I loved ratiocination. Kirk excited and satisfied one side of me. Here was talk that was really about something. Here was a man who thought not about you but about what you said. No doubt I snorted and bridled a little at some of my tossings; but, taking it all in all, I loved the treatment. After being knocked down sufficiently often I began to know a few guards and blows, and to put on intellectual muscle. In the end, unless I flatter myself, I became a not contemptible sparring partner. It was a great day when the man who had so long been engaged in exposing my vagueness at last cautioned me against the dangers of excessive subtlety.

If Kirk's ruthless dialectic had been merely a pedagogic instrument I might have resented it. But he knew no other way of talking. No age or sex was spared the elenchus. It was a continuous astonishment to him that anyone should not desire to be clarified or corrected. When a very dignified neighbor, in the course of a Sunday call, observed with an air of finality, "Well, well, Mr. Kirkpatrick, it takes all sorts to make a world. You are a Liberal and I am a Conservative; we naturally look at the facts from different angles," Kirk replied, "What do you mean? Are you asking me to picture Liberals and Conservatives playing peep-bo at a rectangular Fact from opposite sides of a table?" If an unwary visitor, hoping to waive a subject, observed, "Of course, I know opinions differ—" Kirk would raise both his hands and exclaim, "Good heavens! I have no *opinions* on any subject whatsoever." A favorite maxim was, "You can have enlightenment for ninepence but you prefer ignorance." The commonest metaphors would be questioned till some bitter truth had been forced from its hiding place. "These fiendish German atrocities—" "But are not fiends a figment of the imagination?"—"Very well, then; these brutal atrocities—" "But none of the brutes does anything of the kind!"—"Well, what am I to call them?" "Is it not plain that we must call them simply *Human?*" What excited his supreme contempt was the conversation of other Headmasters, which he had sometimes had to endure at conferences when he himself was Head of Lurgan. "They would come and ask me, 'What attitude do you adopt to a boy who does so-and-so?' Good Heavens! As if I ever adopted an attitude to anybody or anything!" Sometimes, but rarely, he was driven to irony. On such occasions his voice became even weightier than usual and only the distention of his nostrils betrayed the secret to those who knew him. It was in such fashion that he produced his *dictum*, "The Master of Balliol is one of the most important beings in the universe."

It will be imagined that Mrs. Kirkpatrick led a somewhat uneasy life: witness the occasion on which her husband by some strange error found himself in the drawing room at the beginning of what his lady had intended to be a bridge party. About half an hour later she was observed to leave the room with a remarkable expression on her face; and many hours later still the Great Knock was discovered sitting on a stool in the midst of seven elderly ladies ("ful drery was hire chere") begging them to clarify their terms.

I have said that he was almost wholly logical; but not quite.

He had been a Presbyterian and was now an Atheist. He spent Sunday, as he spent most of his time on weekdays, working in his garden. But one curious trait from his Presbyterian youth survived. He always, on Sundays, gardened in a different, and slightly more respectable, suit. An Ulster Scot may come to disbelieve in God, but not to wear his weekday clothes on the Sabbath.

Having said that he was an Atheist, I hasten to add that he was a "Rationalist" of the old, high and dry nineteenth-century type. For Atheism has come down in the world since those days, and mixed itself with politics and learned to dabble in dirt. The anonymous donor who now sends me anti-God magazines hopes, no doubt, to hurt the Christian in me; he really hurts the ex-Atheist. I am ashamed that my old mates and (which matters much more) Kirk's old mates should have sunk to what they are now. It was different then; even McCabe wrote like a man. At the time when I knew him, the fuel of Kirk's Atheism was chiefly of the anthropological and pessimistic kind. He was great on *The Golden Bough* and Schopenhauer.

The reader will remember that my own Atheism and Pessimism were fully formed before I went to Bookham. What I got there was merely fresh ammunition for the defense of a position already chosen. Even this I got indirectly from the tone of his mind or independently from reading his books. He never attacked religion in my presence. It is the sort of fact that no one would infer from an outside knowledge of my life, but it is a fact.

I arrived at Gastons (so the Knock's house was called) on a Saturday, and he announced that we would begin Homer on Monday. I explained that I had never read a word in any dialect but the Attic, assuming that when he knew this he would approach Homer through some preliminary lessons on the Epic language. He replied merely with a sound very frequent in his conversation which I can only spell "Huh." I found this rather disquieting; and I woke on Monday saying to myself, "Now for Homer. Golly!" The name struck awe into my soul. At nine o'clock we sat down to work in the little upstairs study which soon became so familiar to me. It contained a sofa (on which we sat side by side when he was working with me), a table and chair (which I used when I was alone), a bookcase, a gas stove, and a framed photograph of Mr. Gladstone. We opened our books at *Iliad*, Book I. Without a word of introduction Knock read aloud the first twenty lines or so in the "new" pronunciation, which I had never heard before. Like Smewgy, he was a chanter; less mellow in voice, yet full gutturals and rolling r's and more varied vowels seemed to suit the Bronze Age epic as well as Smewgy's honey tongue had suited Horace. For Kirk, even after years of residence in England, spoke the purest Ulster. He then translated, with a few, a very few explanations, about a hundred lines. I had never seen a classical author taken in such large gulps before. When he had finished he handed me over Crusius' *Lexicon* and, having told me to go through again as much as I could of what he had done, left the room. It seems an odd method of teaching, but it worked. At first I could travel only a very short way along the trail he had blazed, but every day I could travel further. Presently I could travel the whole way. Then I could go a line or two beyond his furthest North. Then it became a kind of game to see how far beyond. He appeared at this stage to value speed more than absolute accuracy. The great gain was that I very soon became able to understand a great deal without (even mentally) translating it; I was beginning to think in Greek. That is the great Rubicon to cross in learning any language. Those in whom the Greek word lives only while they are hunting for it in the lexicon, and who then substitute the English word for it, are not reading the Greek at all; they are only solving a puzzle. The very formula, "*Naus* means a ship," is wrong. *Naus* and *ship* both mean a thing, they do not mean one another. Behind *Naus*, as behind *navis* or *naca*, we want to have a picture of a dark, slender mass with sail or oars, climbing the ridges, with no officious English word intruding.

We now settled into a routine which has ever since served in my mind as an archetype, so that what I still mean when I speak of a "normal" day (and lament that normal days are so rare) is a day of the Bookham pattern. For if I could please myself I would always live as I lived there. I would choose always to breakfast at exactly eight and to be at my desk by nine, there to read or write till one. If a cup of good tea or coffee could be brought me about eleven, so much the better. A step or so out of doors for a pint of beer would not do quite so well; for a man does not want to drink alone and if you meet a friend in the taproom the break is likely to be extended beyond its ten minutes. At one precisely lunch should be on the table; and by two at the latest I would be on the road. Not, except at rare intervals, with a friend. Walking and talking are two very great pleasures, but it is a mistake to combine them. Our own noise blots out the sounds and silences of the outdoor world; and talking leads almost inevitably to smoking, and then farewell to nature as far as one of our senses is concerned. The only friend to walk with is one (such as I found, during the holidays, in Arthur) who so exactly shares your taste for each mood of the countryside that a glance, a halt, or at most a nudge, is enough to assure us that the pleasure is shared. The return from the walk, and the arrival of tea, should be exactly coincident, and not later than a quarter past four. Tea should be taken in solitude, as I took it at Bookham on those (happily numerous) occasions when Mrs. Kirkpatrick was out; the Knock himself disdained this meal. For eating and reading are two pleasures that combine admirably. Of course not all books are suitable for mealtime reading. It would be a kind of blasphemy to read poetry at table. What one wants is a gossipy, formless book which can be opened anywhere. The ones I learned so to use at Bookham were Boswell, and a translation of Herodotus, and Lang's *His-*

tory of English Literature. Tristram Shandy, Elia and the *Anatomy of Melancholy* are all good for the same purpose. At five a man should be at work again, and at it till seven. Then, at the evening meal and after, comes the time for talk, or, failing that, for lighter reading; and unless you are making a night of it with your cronies (and at Bookham I had none) there is no reason why you should ever be in bed later than eleven. But when is a man to write his letters? You forget that I am describing the happy life I led with Kirk or the ideal life I would live now if I could. And it is an essential of the happy life that a man would have almost no mail and never dread the postman's knock. In those blessed days I received, and answered, only two letters a week; one from my father, which was a matter of duty, and one from Arthur which was the high light of the week, for we poured out to each other on paper all the delight that was intoxicating us both. Letters from my brother, now on active service, were longer and rarer, and so were my replies.

Such is my ideal, and such then (almost) was the reality, of "settled, calm, Epicurean life." It is no doubt for my own good that I have been so generally prevented from leading it, for it is a life almost entirely selfish. Selfish, not self-centered: for in such a life my mind would be directed toward a thousand things, not one of which is myself. The distinction is not unimportant. One of the happiest men and most pleasing companions I have ever known was intensely selfish. On the other hand I have known people capable of real sacrifice whose lives were nevertheless a misery to themselves and to others, because self-concern and self-pity filled all their thoughts. Either condition will destroy the soul in the end. But till the end, give me the man who takes the best of everything (even at my expense) and then talks of other things, rather than the man who serves me and talks of himself, and whose very kindnesses are a continual reproach, a continual demand for pity, gratitude, and admiration.

Kirk did not, of course, make me read nothing but Homer.

The Two Great Bores (Demosthenes and Cicero) could not be avoided. There were (oh glory!) Lucretius, Catullus, Tacitus, Herodotus. There was Virgil, for whom I still had no true taste. There were Greek and Latin compositions. (It is a strange thing that I have contrived to reach my late fifties without ever reading one word of Caesar.) There were Euripides, Sophocles, Aeschylus. In the evenings there was French with Mrs. Kirkpatrick, treated much as her husband treated Homer. We got through a great many good novels in this way and I was soon buying French books on my own. I had hoped there would be English essays, but whether because he felt he could not endure mine or because he soon guessed that I was already only too proficient in that art (which he almost certainly despised) Kirk never set me one. For the first week or so he gave me directions about my English reading, but when he discovered that, left to myself, I was not likely to waste my time, he gave me absolute freedom. Later in my career we branched out into German and Italian. Here his methods were the same. After the very briefest contact with Grammars and Exercises I was plunged into *Faust* and the *Inferno*. In Italian we succeeded. In German I have little doubt that we should equally have succeeded if I had stayed with him a little longer. But I left too soon and my German has remained all my life that of a schoolboy. Whenever I have set about rectifying this, some other and more urgent task has always interrupted me.

But Homer came first. Day after day and month after month we drove gloriously onward, tearing the whole *Achilleid* out of the *Iliad* and tossing the rest on one side, and then reading the *Odyssey* entire, till the music of the thing and the clear, bitter brightness that lives in almost every formula had become part of me. Of course my appreciation was very romanticized—the appreciation of a boy soaked in William Morris. But this slight error saved me from that far deeper error of "classicism" with which the Humanists have hoodwinked half the world. I cannot therefore deeply regret the days when I called Circe a "wise-wife" and every marriage a "high-tide." That has all burned itself out and left no snuff, and I can now enjoy the *Odyssey* in a maturer way. The wanderings mean as much as ever they did; the great moment of "eucatastrophe" (as Professor Tolkien would call it) when Odysseus strips off his rags and bends the bow, means more; and perhaps what now pleases me best of all is those exquisite, Charlotte M. Yonge families at Pylos and elsewhere. How rightly Sir Maurice Powicke says, "There have been civilised people in all ages." And let us add, "In all ages they have been surrounded by barbarism."

Meanwhile, on afternoons and on Sundays, Surrey lay open to me. County Down in the holidays and Surrey in the term—it was an excellent contrast. Perhaps, since their beauties were such that even a fool could not force them into competition, this cured me once and for all of the pernicious tendency to compare and to prefer—an operation that does little good even when we are dealing with works of art and endless harm when we are dealing with nature. Total surrender is the first step toward the fruition of either. Shut your mouth; open your eyes and ears. Take in what is there and give no thought to what might have been there or what is somewhere else. That can come later, if it must come at all. (And notice here how the true training for anything whatever that is good always prefigures and, if submitted to, will always help us in, the true training for the Christian life. That is a school where they can always use your previous work whatever subject it was on.) What delighted me in Surrey was its intricacy. My Irish walks commanded large horizons and the general lie of land and sea could be taken in at a glance; I will try to speak of them later. But in Surrey the contours were so tortuous, the little valleys so narrow, there was so much timber, so many villages concealed in woods or hollows, so many field paths, sunk lanes, dingles, copses, such an unpredictable variety of cottage, farmhouse, villa, and country seat, that the whole thing could never lie clearly in my mind, and to walk in it daily gave one the same sort of pleasure that there is in the labyrinthine complexity of Malory or the *Faerie Queene*. Even where the prospect was tolerably open, as when I sat looking down on the Leatherhead and Dorking valley from Polesdan Lacey, it always lacked the classic comprehensibility of the Wyvern landscape. The valley twisted away southward into another valley, a train thudded past invisible in a wooded cutting, the opposite ridge concealed its bays and promontories. This, even on a summer morning. But I remember more dearly autumn afternoons in bottoms that lay intensely silent under old and great trees, and especially the moment, near Friday Street, when our party (that time I was not alone) suddenly discovered, from recognizing a curiously shaped stump, that we had traveled round in a circle for the last half-hour; or one frosty sunset over the Hog's Back at Guildford. On a Saturday afternoon in winter, when nose and fingers might be pinched enough to give an added relish to the anticipation of tea and fireside, and the whole weekend's reading lay ahead, I suppose I reached as much happiness as is ever to be reached on earth. And especially if there were some new, long-coveted book awaiting me.

For I had forgotten. When I spoke of the post I forgot to tell you that it brought parcels as well as letters. Every man of my age has had in his youth one blessing for which our juniors may well envy him: we grew up in a world of cheap and abundant books. Your *Everyman* was then a bare shilling, and, what is more, always in stock; your *World's Classic*, *Muses' Library*, *Home University Library*, *Temple Classic*, Nelson's French series, Bohn, and Longman's Pocket Library, at proportionate prices. All the money I could spare went in postal orders to Messrs. Denny of the Strand. No days, even at Bookham, were happier than those on which the afternoon post brought me a neat little parcel in dark gray paper. Milton, Spenser, Malory, *The High History of the Holy Grail*, the *Laxdale Saga*, Ronsard, Chénier, Voltaire, *Beowulf* and *Gawain and the Green Knight* (both in translations), Apuleius, the *Kalevala*, Herrick, Walton,

Sir John Mandeville, Sidney's *Arcadia*, and nearly all of Morris, came volume by volume into my hands. Some of my purchases proved disappointments and some went beyond my hopes, but the undoing of the parcel always remained a delicious moment. On my rare visits to London I looked at Messrs. Denny in the Strand with a kind of awe; so much pleasure had come from it.

Smewgy and Kirk were my two greatest teachers. Roughly, one might say (in medieval language) that Smewgy taught me Grammar and Rhetoric and Kirk taught me Dialectic. Each had, and gave me, what the other lacked. Kirk had none of Smewgy's graciousness or delicacy, and Smewgy had less humor than Kirk. It was a saturnine humor. Indeed he was very like Saturn—not the dispossessed King of Italian legend, but grim old Cronos, Father Time himself with scythe and hourglass. The bitterest, and also funniest, things came out when he had risen abruptly from table (always before the rest of us) and stood ferreting in a villainous old tobacco jar on the mantelpiece for the dottles of former pipes which it was his frugal habit to use again. My debt to him is very great, my reverence to this day undiminished.

X

Fortune's Smile

The fields, the floods, the heavens, with one consent
Did seeme to laugh on me, and favour mine intent.

SPENSER

A T THE same time that I exchanged Wyvern for Bookham I also exchanged my brother for Arthur as my chief
companion. My brother, as you know, was serving in France.
From 1914 to 1916, which is the Bookham period, he becomes
a figure that at rare intervals appears unpredicted on leave, in
all the glory of a young officer, with what then seemed unlimited wealth at his command, and whisks me off to Ireland.
Luxuries hitherto unknown to me, such as first-class railway
carriages and sleeping cars, glorify these journeys. You will understand that I had been crossing the Irish sea six times a year
since I was nine. My brother's leaves now often added journeys
extraordinary. That is why my memory is stored with ship's-
side images to a degree unusual for such an untraveled man.
I have only to close my eyes to see if I choose, and sometimes
whether I choose or no, the phosphorescence of a ship's wash,
the mast unmoving against the stars though the water is rushing past us, the long salmon-colored rifts of dawn or sunset on

the horizon of cold gray-green water, or the astonishing behavior of land as you approach it, the promontories that walk out to meet you, the complex movements and final disappearance of the mountains further inland.

These leaves were of course a great delight. The strains that had been developing (thanks to Wyvern) before my brother went to France were forgotten. There was a tacit determination on both sides to revive, for the short time allowed us, the classic period of our boyhood. As my brother was in the R.A.S.C., which in those days was reckoned a safe place to be, we did not feel that degree of anxiety about him which most families were suffering at this time. There may have been more anxiety in the unconscious than came out in fully waking thought. That, at least, would explain an experience I had, certainly once, and perhaps more often; not a belief, nor quite a dream, but an impression, a mental image, a haunting, which on a bitter winter night at Bookham represented my brother hanging about the garden and calling — or rather trying to call, but as in Virgil's Hell *inceptus clamor frustratur hiantem*, a bat's cry is all that comes. There hung over this image an atmosphere which I dislike as much as any I ever breathed, a blend of the macabre and the weakly, wretchedly, hopelessly pathetic — the dreary miasma of the Pagan Hades.

Though my friendship with Arthur began from an identity of taste on a particular point, we were sufficiently different to help one another. His home life was almost the opposite of mine. His parents were members of the Plymouth Brothers, and he was the youngest of a large family; his home, nevertheless, was almost as silent as ours was noisy. He was at this time working in the business of one of his brothers, but his health was delicate and after an illness or two he was withdrawn from it. He was a man of more than one talent: a pianist and, in hope, a composer, and also a painter. One of our earliest schemes was that he should make an operatic score for *Loki Bound* — a project which, of course, after an extremely short and happy life, died a painless death. In literature he influenced me more, or more permanently, than I did him. His great defect was that he cared very little for verse. Something I did to mend this, but less than I wished. He, on the other hand, side by side with his love for myth and marvel, which I fully shared, had another taste which I lacked till I met him and with which, to my great good, he infected me for life. This was the taste for what he called "the good, solid, old books," the classic English novelists. It is astonishing how I had avoided them before I met Arthur. I had been persuaded by my father to read *The Newcomes* when I was rather too young for it and never tried Thackeray again till I was at Oxford. He is still antipathetic to me, not because he preaches but because he preaches badly. Dickens I looked upon with a feeling of horror, engendered by long poring over the illustrations before I had learned to read. I still think them depraved. Here, as in Walt Disney, it is not the ugliness of the ugly figures but the simpering dolls intended for our sympathy which really betray the secret (not that Walt Disney is not far superior to the illustrators of Dickens). Of Scott I knew only a few of the medieval, that is, the weakest, novels. Under Arthur's influence I read at this time all the best Waverleys, all the Brontës, and all the Jane Austens. They provided an admirable complement to my more fantastic reading, and each was the more enjoyed for its contrast to the other. The very qualities which had previously deterred me from such books Arthur taught me to see as their charm. What I would have called their "stodginess" or "ordinariness" he called "Homeliness"—a key word in his imagination. He did not mean merely Domesticity, though that came into it. He meant the rooted quality which attaches them to all our simple experiences, to weather, food, the family, the neighborhood. He could get endless enjoyment out of the opening sentence of *Jane Eyre*, or that other opening sentence in one of Hans Andersen's stories, "How it did rain, to be sure." The mere word "beck" in the Brontës was a feast to him; and so were the schoolroom and kitchen scenes. This love of the "Homely" was not confined to literature; he looked for it in out-of-door scenes as well and taught me to do the same.

Hitherto my feelings for nature had been too narrowly romantic. I attended almost entirely to what I thought awe-inspiring, or wild, or eerie, and above all to distance. Hence mountains and clouds were my especial delight; the sky was, and still is, to me one of the principal elements in any land-scape, and long before I had seen them all named and sorted out in *Modern Painters* I was very attentive to the different qual-ities, and different heights, of the cirrus, the cumulus, and the raincloud. As for the Earth, the country I grew up in had every-thing to encourage a romantic bent, had indeed done so ever since I first looked at the unattainable Green Hills through the nursery window. For the reader who knows those parts it will be enough to say that my main haunt was the Holy-wood Hills—the irregular polygon you would have described if you drew a line from Stormont to Comber, from Comber to Newtownards, from Newtownards to Scrabo, from Scrabo to Craigantlet, from Craigantlet to Holywood, and thence through Knocknagonney back to Stormont. How to suggest it all to a foreigner I hardly know.

First of all, it is by Southern English standards bleak. The woods, for we have a few, are of small trees, rowan and birch and small fir. The fields are small, divided by ditches with ragged sea-nipped hedges on top of them. There is a good deal of gorse and many outcroppings of rock. Small abandoned quarries, filled with cold-looking water, are surprisingly nu-merous. There is nearly always a wind whistling through the grass. Where you see a man plowing there will be gulls follow-ing him and pecking at the furrow. There are no field paths or rights of way, but that does not matter for everyone knows you—or if they do not know you, they know your kind and understand that you will shut gates and not walk over crops. Mushrooms are still felt to be common property, like the air. The soil has none of the rich chocolate or ocher you find in parts of England: it is pale—what Dyson calls "the ancient, bitter earth." But the grass is soft, rich, and sweet, and the cottages, always whitewashed and single storied and roofed with blue slate, light up the whole landscape.

Although these hills are not very high, the expanse seen from them is huge and various. Stand at the northeastern extremity where the slopes go steeply down to Holywood. Beneath you is the whole expanse of the Lough. The Antrim coast twists sharply to the north and out of sight; green, and humble in comparison, Down curves away southward. Between the two the Lough merges into the sea, and if you look carefully on a good day you can even see Scotland, phantom-like on the horizon. Now come further to the south and west. Take your stand at the isolated cottage which is visible from my father's house and overlooks our whole suburb, and which everyone calls the Shepherd's Hut, though we are not really a shepherd country. You are still looking down on the Lough, but its mouth and the sea are now hidden by the shoulder you have just come from, and it might (for all you see) be a landlocked lake. And here we come to one of those great contrasts which have bitten deeply into my mind—Niflheim and Asgard, Britain and Logres, Handramit and Harandra, air and ether, the low world and the high. Your horizon from here is the Antrim Mountains, probably a uniform mass of grayish blue, though if it is a sunny day you may just trace on the Cave Hill the distinction between the green slopes that climb two-thirds of the way to the summit and the cliff wall that perpendicularly accomplishes the rest. That is one beauty; and here where you stand is another, quite different and even more dearly loved—sunlight and grass and dew, crowing cocks and gaggling ducks. In between them, on the flat floor of the Valley at your feet, a forest of factory chimneys, gantries, and giant cranes rising out of a welter of mist, lies Belfast. Noises come up from it continually, whining and screeching of trams, clatter of horse traffic on uneven sets, and, dominating all else, the continual throb and stammer of the great shipyards. And because we have heard this all our lives it does not, for us, violate the peace of the hilltop; rather, it emphasizes it, enriches the contrast, sharpens the dualism. Down in that "smoke and stir" is the hated office to which Arthur, less fortunate than I, must return tomorrow: for it is only one of his rare holidays that allows us to stand here together on a weekday morning. And down there too are the barefoot old women, the drunken men stumbling in and out of the "spirit grocers" (Ireland's horrible substitute for the kindly English "pub"), the straining, overdriven horses, the hard-faced rich women — all the world which Alberich created when he cursed love and twisted the gold into a ring.

Now step a little way — only two fields and across a lane and up to the top of the bank on the far side — and you will see, looking south with a little east in it, a different world. And having seen it, blame me if you can for being a romantic. For here is the thing itself, utterly irresistible, the way to the world's end, the land of longing, the breaking and blessing of hearts. You are looking across what may be called, in a certain sense, the plain of Down, and seeing beyond it the Mourne Mountains.

It was K. — that is, Cousin Quartus' second daughter, the Valkyrie — who first expounded to me what this plain of Down is really like. Here is the recipe for imagining it. Take a number of medium-sized potatoes and lay them down (one layer of them only) in a flat-bottomed tin basin. Now shake loose earth over them till the potatoes themselves, but not the shape of them, is hidden; and of course the crevices between them will now be depressions of earth. Now magnify the whole thing till those crevices are large enough to conceal each its stream and its huddle of trees. And then, for coloring, change your brown earth into the checkered pattern of fields, always small fields (a couple of acres each), with all their normal variety of crop, grass, and plow. You have now got a picture of the "plain" of Down, which is a plain only in the sense that if you were a very large giant you would regard it as level but very ill to walk on—like cobbles. And now remember that every cottage is white. The whole expanse laughs with these little white dots; it is like nothing so much as the assembly of white foam caps when a fresh breeze is on a summer sea. And the roads are white too; there is no tarmac yet. And because the whole country is a turbulent democracy of little hills, these roads shoot in every direction, disappearing and reappearing. But you must not spread over this landscape your hard English sunlight; make it paler, make it softer, blur the edges of the white cumuli, cover it with watery gleams, deepening it, making all unsubstantial. And beyond all this, so remote that they seem fantastically abrupt, at the very limit of your vision, imagine the mountains. They are no stragglers. They are steep and compact and pointed and toothed and jagged. They seem to have nothing to do with the little hills and cottages that divide you from them. And sometimes they are blue, sometimes violet; but quite often they look transparent—as if huge sheets of gauze had been cut out into mountainous shapes and hung up there, so that you could see through them the light of the invisible sea at their backs.

I number it among my blessings that my father had no car, while yet most of my friends had, and sometimes took me for a drive. This meant that all these distant objects could be visited just enough to clothe them with memories and not impossible desires, while yet they remained ordinarily as inaccessible as the Moon. The deadly power of rushing about wherever I pleased had not been given me. I measured distances by the standard of man, man walking on his two feet, not by the standard of the internal combustion engine. I had not been allowed to deflower the very idea of distance; in return I possessed "infinite riches" in what would have been to motorists "a little room." The truest and most horrible claim made for modern transport is that it "annihilates space." It does. It annihilates one of the most glorious gifts we have been given. It is a vile inflation which lowers the value of distance, so that a modern boy travels a hundred miles with less sense of liberation and pilgrimage and adventure than his grandfather got from traveling ten. Of course if a man hates space and wants it to be annihilated, that is another matter. Why not creep into his coffin at once? There is little enough space there.

Such were my outdoor delights before I met Arthur, and all these he shared and confirmed. And in his search for the Homely he taught me to see other things as well. But for him I should never have known the beauty of the ordinary vegetables that we destine to the pot. "Drills," he used to say. "Just ordinary drills of cabbages—what can be better?" And he was right. Often he recalled my eyes from the horizon just to look through a hole in a hedge, to see nothing more than a farmyard in its mid-morning solitude, and perhaps a gray cat squeezing its way under a barn door, or a bent old woman with a wrinkled, motherly face coming back with an empty bucket from the pigsty. But best of all we liked it when the Homely and the unhomely met in sharp juxtaposition; if a little kitchen garden ran steeply up a narrowing enclave of fertile ground surrounded by outcroppings and furze, or some shivering quarry pool under a moonrise could be seen on our left, and on our right the smoking chimney and lamp-lit window of a cottage that was just settling down for the night.

Meanwhile, on the Continent, the unskilled butchery of the first German War went on. As it did so and as I began to foresee that it would probably last till I reached military age, I was compelled to make a decision which the law had taken out of the hands of English boys of my own age; for in Ireland we had no conscription. I did not much plume myself even then for deciding to serve, but I did feel that the decision absolved me from taking any further notice of the war. For Arthur, whose heart hopelessly disqualified him, there was no such question. Accordingly I put the war on one side to a degree which some people will think shameful and some incredible. Others will call it a flight from reality. I maintain that it was rather a treaty with reality, the fixing of a frontier. I said to my country, in effect, "You shall have me on a certain date, not before. I will die in your wars if need be, but till then I shall live my own life. You may have my body, but not my mind. I will take part in battles but not read about them." If this attitude needs excusing I must say that a boy who is unhappy at school inevitably learns the habit of keeping the future in its place; if once he began to allow infiltrations from the coming term into the present holidays he would despair. Also, the Hamilton in me was always on guard against the Lewis; I had seen enough of the self-torturing temperament.

No doubt, even if the attitude was right, the quality in me which made it so easy to adopt is somewhat repellent. Yet, even so, I can hardly regret having escaped the appalling waste of time and spirit which would have been involved in reading the war news or taking more than an artificial and formal part in conversations about the war. To read without military knowledge or good maps accounts of fighting which were distorted before they reached the Divisional general and further distorted before they left him and then "written up" out of all recognition by journalists, to strive to master what will be contradicted the next day, to fear and hope intensely on shaky evidence, is surely an ill use of the mind. Even in peacetime I think those are very wrong who say that schoolboys should be encouraged to read the newspapers. Nearly all that a boy reads there in his teens will be known before he is twenty to have been false in emphasis and interpretation, if not in fact as well, and most of it will have lost all importance. Most of what he remembers he will therefore have to unlearn; and he will probably have acquired an incurable taste for vulgarity and sensationalism and the fatal habit of fluttering from paragraph to paragraph to learn how an actress has been divorced in California, a train derailed in France, and quadruplets born in New Zealand.

I was now happier than I had ever been. All the sting had been drawn from the beginning of term. Yet the homecoming at its end remained almost as joyful as before. The holidays grew better and better. Our grown-up friends, and especially my cousins at Mountbracken, now seemed less grown up—for one's immediate elders grow downward or backward to meet one at that age. There were many merry meetings, much good talk. I discovered that other people besides Arthur loved books that I loved. The horrible old "social functions," the dances, were at an end, for my father now allowed me to refuse the invitations. All my engagements were now pleasant ones, within a small circle of people who were all intermarried, or very old neighbors, or (the women anyway) old school fellows. I am shy of mentioning them. Of Mountbracken I have had to speak because the story of my life could not be told without it; beyond that I hesitate to go. Praise of one's friends is near impertinence. I cannot tell you here of Janie M. nor of her mother, nor of Bill and Mrs. Bill. In novels, provincial-suburban society is usually painted gray to black. I have not found it so. I think we Strandtown and Belmont people had among us as much kindness, wit, beauty, and taste as any circle of the same size that I have ever known.

At home the real separation and apparent cordiality between my father and myself continued. Every holidays I came back from Kirk with my thoughts and my speech a little clearer, and this made it progressively less possible to have any real conversation with my father. I was far too young and raw to appreciate the other side of the account, to weigh the rich (if vague) fertility, the generosity and humor of my father's mind against the dryness, the rather deathlike lucidity, of Kirk's. With the cruelty of youth I allowed myself to be irritated by traits in my father which, in other elderly men, I have since regarded as lovable foibles. There were so many unbridgeable misunderstandings. Once I received a letter from my brother in my father's presence which he immediately demanded to see. He objected to some expressions in it about a third person. In defense of them I pleaded that they had not been addressed to him. "What nonsense!" answered my father. "He knew you would show me the letter, and intended you to show me the letter." In reality, as I well knew, my brother had foolishly gambled on the chance that it would arrive when my father was out. But this my father could not conceive. He was not overriding by authority a claim to privacy which he disallowed; he could not imagine anyone making such a claim.

My relations to my father help to explain (I am not suggesting that they excuse) one of the worst acts of my life. I allowed myself to be prepared for confirmation, and confirmed, and to make my first Communion, in total disbelief, acting a part, eating and drinking my own condemnation. As Johnson points out, where courage is not, no other virtue can survive except by accident. Cowardice drove me into hypocrisy and hypocrisy into blasphemy. It is true that I did not and could not then know the real nature of the thing I was doing: but I knew very well that I was acting a lie with the greatest possible solemnity. It seemed to me impossible to tell my father my real views. Not that he would have stormed and thundered like the traditional orthodox parent. On the contrary, he would (at first) have responded with the greatest kindness. "Let's talk the whole thing over," he would have said. But it would have been quite impossible to drive into his head my real position. The thread would have been lost almost at once, and the answer implicit in all the quotations, anecdotes, and reminiscences which would have poured over me would have been one I then valued not a straw—the beauty of the Authorized Version, the beauty of the Christian tradition and sentiment and character. And later, when this failed, when I still tried to make my exact points clear, there would have been anger between us, thunder from him and a thin, peevish rattle from me. Nor could the subject, once raised, ever have been dropped again. All this, of course, ought to have been dared rather than the thing I did. But at the time it seemed to me impossible. The Syrian captain was forgiven for bowing in the house of Rimmon. I am one of many who have bowed in the house of the real God when I believed Him to be no more than Rimmon.

During the week ends and evenings I was closely tethered to my father and felt this something of a hardship, since these were the times when Arthur was most often accessible. My weekdays continued to supply me with a full ration of solitude. I had, to be sure, the society of Tim, who ought to have been mentioned far sooner. Tim was our dog. He may hold a record for longevity among Irish terriers since he was already with us when I was at Oldie's and did not die till 1922. But Tim's society did not amount to much. It had long since been agreed between him and me that he should not be expected to accompany me on walks. I went a good deal further than he liked, for his shape was already that of a bolster, or even a barrel, on four legs. Also, I went to places where other dogs might be met; and though Tim was no coward (I have seen him fight like a demon on his home ground) he hated dogs. In his walking days he had been known, on seeing a dog far ahead, to disappear behind the hedge and re-emerge a hundred yards later. His mind had been formed during our schooldays and he had perhaps learned his attitude to other dogs from our attitude to other boys. By now he and I were less like master and dog than like two friendly visitors in the same hotel. We met constantly, passed the time of day, and parted with much esteem to follow our own paths. I think he had one friend of his own species, a neighboring red setter; a very respectable, middle-aged dog. Perhaps a good influence; for poor Tim, though I loved him, was the most undisciplined, unaccomplished, and dissipated-looking creature that ever went on four legs. He never exactly obeyed you; he sometimes agreed with you.

The long hours in the empty house passed delightfully in reading and writing. I was in the midst of the Romantics now. There was a humility in me (as a reader) at that time which I shall never recapture. Some poems I could not enjoy as well as others. It never occurred to me that these might be the inferior ones; I merely thought that I was getting tired of my author or was not in the right mood. The *longueurs* of Endymion I attributed wholly to myself. The "swoony" element in Keats' sensuality (as when Porphyro grows "faint") I tried hard to like, and failed. I thought — though I have forgotten why — that Shelley must be better than Keats and was sorry I liked him less. But my great author at this period was William Morris. I had met him first in quotation in books on Norse Mythology; that led me to *Sigurd the Volsung*. I did not really like this as much as I tried to, and I think I now know why: the metre does not satisfy my ear. But then, in Arthur's bookcase, I found *The Well at the World's End*. I looked — I read chapter headings — I dipped — and next day I was off into town to buy a copy of my own. Like so many new steps it appeared to be partly a revival — "Knights in Armor" returning from a very early period of my childhood. After that I read all the Morris I could get, *Jason*, *The Earthly Paradise*, the prose romances. The growth of the new delight is marked by my sudden realization, almost with a sense of disloyalty, that the letters WILLIAM MORRIS were coming to have at least as potent a magic in them as WAGNER.

One other thing that Arthur taught me was to love the bodies of books. I had always respected them. My brother and I might cut up stepladders without scruple; to have thumb-marked or dog's-eared a book would have filled us with shame. But Arthur did not merely respect, he was enamored; and soon, I too. The set up of the page, the feel and smell of the paper, the differing sounds that different papers make as you turn the

leaves, became sensuous delights. This revealed to me a flaw in
Kirk. How often have I shuddered when he took a new classical text of mine in his gardener's hands, bent back the boards
till they creaked, and left his sign on every page.

"Yes, I remember," said my father. "That was old Knock's
one fault."

"A bad one," said I.

"An all but unforgivable one," said my father.

XI

Check

When bale is at highest, boote hat next.

SIR ALDINGAR

THE history of Joy, since it came riding back to me on huge waves of Wagnerian music and Norse and Celtic mythology several chapters ago, must now be brought up to date.

I have already hinted how my first delight in Valhalla and Valkyries began to turn itself imperceptibly into a scholar's interest in them. I got about as far as a boy who knew no old Germanic language could get. I could have faced a pretty stiff examination in my subject. I would have laughed at popular bunglers who confused the late mythological Sagas with the classic Sagas, or the Prose with the Verse Edda, or even, more scandalously, Edda with Saga. I knew my way about the Eddaic cosmos, could locate each of the roots of the Ash and knew who ran up and down it. And only very gradually did I realize that all this was something quite different from the original Joy. And I went on adding detail to detail, progressing toward the moment when "I should know most and should least enjoy." Finally I woke from building the temple to find that the God had flown. Of course I did not put it that way. I would have said simply that I didn't get the old thrill. I was in the Wordsworthian predicament, lamenting that "a glory" had passed away.

Thence arose the fatal determination to recover the old thrill, and at last the moment when I was compelled to realize that all such efforts were failures. I had no lure to which the bird would come. And now, notice my blindness. At that very moment there arose the memory of a place and time at which I had tasted the lost Joy with unusual fullness. It had been a particular hill walk on a morning of white mist. The other volumes of the *Ring* (*The Rheingold* and *The Valkyrie*) had just arrived as a Christmas present from my father, and the thought of all the reading before me, mixed with the coldness and loneliness of the hillside, the drops of moisture on every branch, and the distant murmur of the concealed town, had produced a longing (yet it was also fruition) which had flowed over from the mind and seemed to involve the whole body. That walk I now remembered. It seemed to me that I had tasted heaven then. If only such a moment could return! But what I never realized was that it had returned—that the remembering of that walk was itself a new experience of just the same kind. True, it was desire, not possession. But then what I had felt on the walk had also been desire, and only possession in so far as that kind of desire is itself desirable, is the fullest possession we can know on earth; or rather, because the very nature of Joy makes nonsense of our common distinction between having and wanting. There, to have is to want and to want is to have. Thus, the very moment when I longed to be so stabbed again, was itself again such a stabbing. The Desirable which had once alighted on Valhalla was now alighting on a particular moment of my own past; and I would not recognize him there because, being an idolater and a formalist, I insisted that he ought to appear in the temple I had built him; not knowing that he cares only for temples building and not at all for temples built. Wordsworth,

I believe, made this mistake all his life. I am sure that all that
sense of the loss of vanished vision which fills *The Prelude* was
itself vision of the same kind, if only he could have believed it.

In my scheme of thought it is not blasphemous to compare
the error which I was making with that error which the angel at
the Sepulchre rebuked when he said to the women, "Why seek
ye the living among the dead? He is not here, He is risen." The
comparison is of course between something of infinite moment and something very small; like comparison between the
Sun and the Sun's reflection in a dewdrop. Indeed, in my view,
very like it, for I do not think the resemblance between the
Christian and the merely imaginative experience is accidental. I think that all things, in their way, reflect heavenly truth,
the imagination not least. "Reflect" is the important word. This
lower life of the imagination is not[1] a beginning of, nor a step
toward, the higher life of the spirit, merely an image. In me, at
any rate, it contained no element either of belief or of ethics;
however far pursued, it would never have made me either wiser
or better. But it still had, at however many removes, the shape
of the reality it reflected.

If nothing else suggests this resemblance it is at least suggested by the fact that we can make exactly the same mistakes
on both levels. You will remember how, as a schoolboy, I had
destroyed my religious life by a vicious subjectivism which
made "realizations" the aim of prayer; turning away from God
to seek states of mind, and trying to produce those states of
mind by "maistry." With unbelievable folly I now proceeded
to make exactly the same blunder in my imaginative life; or
rather the same pair of blunders. The first was made at the
very moment when I formulated the complaint that the "old
thrill" was becoming rarer and rarer. For by that complaint I
smuggled in the assumption that what I wanted was a "thrill,"

1. *I.e.*, not necessarily and by its own nature. God can cause it to be such
a beginning.

a state of my own mind. And there lies the deadly error. Only when your whole attention and desire are fixed on something else—whether a distant mountain, or the past, or the gods of Asgard—does the "thrill" arise. It is a byproduct. Its very existence presupposes that you desire not it but something other and outer. If by any perverse askesis or the use of any drug it could be produced from within, it would at once be seen to be of no value. For take away the object, and what, after all, would be left?—a whirl of images, a fluttering sensation in the diaphragm, a momentary abstraction. And who could want that? This, I say, is the first and deadly error, which appears on every level of life and is equally deadly on all, turning religion into a self-caressing luxury and love into auto-eroticism. And the second error is, having thus falsely made a state of mind your aim, to attempt to produce it. From the fading of the Northernness I ought to have drawn the conclusion that the Object, the Desirable, was further away, more external, less subjective, than even such a comparatively public and external thing as a system of mythology—had, in fact, only shone through that system. Instead, I concluded that it was a mood of state within myself which might turn up in any context. To "get it again" became my constant endeavor; while reading every poem, hearing every piece of music, going for every walk, I stood anxious sentinel at my own mind to watch whether the blessed moment was beginning and to endeavor to retain it if it did. Because I was still young and the whole world of beauty was opening before me, my own officious obstructions were often swept aside and, startled into self-forgetfulness, I again tasted Joy. But far more often I frightened it away by my greedy impatience to snare it, and, even when it came, instantly destroyed it by introspection, and at all times vulgarized it by my false assumption about its nature.

One thing, however, I learned, which has since saved me from many popular confusions of mind. I came to know by experience that it is not a disguise of sexual desire. Those who think that if adolescents were all provided with suitable mistresses we should soon hear no more of "immortal longings" are certainly wrong. I learned this mistake to be a mistake by the simple, if discreditable, process of repeatedly making it. From the Northernness one could not easily have slid into erotic fantasies without noticing the difference; but when the world of Morris became the frequent medium of Joy, this transition became possible. It was quite easy to think that one desired those forests for the sake of their female inhabitants, the garden of Hesperus for the sake of his daughters, Hylas' river for the river nymphs. I repeatedly followed that path—to the end. And at the end one found pleasure; which immediately resulted in the discovery that pleasure (whether that pleasure or any other) was not what you had been looking for. No moral question was involved; I was at this time as nearly nonmoral on that subject as a human creature can be. The frustration did not consist in finding a "lower" pleasure instead of a "higher." It was the irrelevance of the conclusion that marred it. The hounds had changed scent. One had caught the wrong quarry. You might as well offer a mutton chop to a man who is dying of thirst as offer sexual pleasure to the desire I am speaking of. I did not recoil from the erotic conclusion with chaste horror, exclaiming, "Not that!" My feelings could rather have been expressed in the words, "Quite. I see. But haven't we wandered from the real point?" Joy is not a substitute for sex; sex is very often a substitute for Joy. I sometimes wonder whether all pleasures are not substitutes for Joy.

Such, then, was the state of my imaginative life; over against it stood the life of my intellect. The two hemispheres of my mind were in the sharpest contrast. On the one side a many-islanded sea of poetry and myth; on the other a glib and shallow "rationalism." Nearly all that I loved I believed to be imaginary; nearly all that I believed to be real I thought grim and meaningless. The exceptions were certain people (whom I loved and believed to be real) and nature herself. That is, nature as she appeared to the senses. I chewed endlessly on the problem: "How can it be so beautiful and also so cruel, wasteful and futile?" Hence at this time I could almost have said with Santayana, "All that is good is imaginary; all that is real is evil." In one sense nothing less like a "flight from reality" could be conceived. I was so far from wishful thinking that I hardly thought anything true unless it contradicted my wishes.

Hardly, but not quite. For there was one way in which the world, as Kirk's rationalism taught me to see it, gratified my wishes. It might be grim and deadly but at least it was free from the Christian God. Some people (not all) will find it hard to understand why this seemed to me such an overwhelming advantage. But you must take into account both my history and my temperament. The period of faith which I had lived through at Oldie's had contained a good deal of fear. And by now, looking back on that fear, and egged on by Shaw and Voltaire and Lucretius with his *Tantum religio*, I greatly exaggerated that element in my memory and forgot the many other elements which had been combined with it. At all costs I was anxious that those full-moonlit nights in the dormitory should never come again. I was also, as you may remember, one whose negative demands were more violent than his positive, far more eager to escape pain than to achieve happiness, and feeling it something of an outrage that I had been created without my own permission. To such a craven the materialist's universe had the enormous attraction that it offered you limited liabilities. No strictly infinite disaster could overtake you in it. Death ended all. And if ever finite disasters proved greater than one wished to bear, suicide would always be possible. The horror of the Christian universe was that it had no door marked *Exit*. It was also perhaps not unimportant that the externals of Christianity made no appeal to my sense of beauty. Oriental imagery and style largely repelled me; and for the rest, Christianity was mainly associated for me with ugly architecture, ugly music, and bad poetry. Wyvern Priory and Milton's verse were almost the only points at which Christianity and beauty had overlapped in my experience. But, of course, what mattered most of all was my deep-seated hatred of authority, my monstrous individualism, my lawlessness. No word in my vocabulary expressed deeper hatred than the word *Interference*. But Christianity placed at the center what then seemed to me a transcendental Interferer. If its picture were true then no sort of "treaty with reality" could ever be possible. There was no region even in the innermost depth of one's soul (nay, there least of all) which one could surround with a barbed wire fence and guard with a notice No Admittance. And that was what I wanted; some area, however small, of which I could say to all other beings, "This is my business and mine only."

In this respect, and this only at first, I may have been guilty of wishful thinking. Almost certainly I was. The materialist conception would not have seemed so immensely probable to me if it had not favored at least one of my wishes. But the difficulty of explaining even a boy's thought entirely in terms of his wishes is that on such large questions as these he always has wishes on both sides. Any conception of reality which a sane mind can admit must favor some of its wishes and frustrate others. The materialistic universe had one great, negative attraction to offer me. It had no other. And this had to be accepted; one had to look out on a meaningless dance of atoms (remember, I was reading Lucretius), to realize that all the apparent beauty was a subjective phosphorescence, and to relegate everything one valued to the world of mirage. That price I tried loyally to pay. For I had learned something from Kirk about the honor of the intellect and the shame of voluntary inconsistency. And, of course, I exulted with youthful and vulgar pride in what I though my enlightenment. In argument with Arthur I was a very swashbuckler. Most of it, as I now see, was incredibly crude and silly. I was in that state of mind in which a boy thinks it extremely telling to call God *Jahveh* and Jesus *Yeshua*.

Looking back on my life now, I am astonished that I did not progress into the opposite orthodoxy—did not become a Leftist, Atheist, satiric Intellectual of the type we all know so well. All the conditions seem to be present. I had hated my public school. I hated whatever I knew or imagined of the British Empire. And though I took very little notice of Morris's socialism (there were too many things in him that interested me far more), continual reading of Shaw had brought it about that such embryonic political opinions as I had were vaguely socialistic. Ruskin had helped me in the same direction. My lifelong fear of sentimentalism ought to have qualified me to become a vigorous "debunker." It is true that I hated the Collective as much as any man can hate anything; but I certainly did not then realize its relations to socialism. I suppose that my Romanticism was destined to divide me from the orthodox Intellectuals as soon as I met them; and also that a mind so little sanguine as mine about the future and about common action could only with great difficulty be made revolutionary.

Such, then, was my position: to care for almost nothing but the gods and heroes, the garden of the Hesperides, Launcelot and the Grail, and to believe in nothing but atoms and evolution and military service. At times the strain was severe, but I think this was a wholesome severity. Nor do I believe that the intermittent wavering in my materialistic "faith" (so to call it) which set in toward the end of the Bookham period would ever have arisen simply from my wishes. It came from another source.

Among all the poets whom I was reading at this time (I read *The Faerie Queene* and *The Earthly Paradise* entire) there was one who stood apart from the rest. Yeats was this poet. I had been reading him for a long time before I discovered the difference, and perhaps I should never have discovered it if I had not read his prose as well: things like *Rosa Alchemica* and *Per Amica Silentia Lunae*. The difference was that Yeats believed. His "ever living ones" were not merely feigned or merely desired. He really thought that there was a world of beings more or less like them, and that contact between that world and ours was possible. To put it quite plainly, he believed seriously in Magic. His later career as a poet has somewhat obscured that phase in popular estimates of him, but there is no doubt about the fact—as I learned when I met him some years later. Here was a pretty kettle of fish. You will understand that my rationalism was inevitably based on what I believed to be the findings of the sciences, and those findings, not being a scientist, I had to take on trust—in fact, on authority. Well, here was an opposite authority. If he had been a Christian I should have discounted his testimony, for I thought I had the Christians "placed" and disposed of forever. But I now learned that there were people, not traditionally orthodox, who nevertheless rejected the whole Materialist philosophy out of hand. And I was still very ingenuous. I had no conception of the amount of nonsense written and printed in the world. I regarded Yeats as a learned, responsible writer: what he said must be worthy of consideration. And after Yeats I plunged into Maeterlinck; quite innocently and naturally since everyone was reading him at that time and since I made a point of including a fair amount of French in my diet. In Maeterlinck I came up against Spiritualism, Theosophy, and Pantheism. Here once more was a responsible adult (and not a Christian) who believed in a world behind, or around, the material world. I must do myself the justice of saying that I did not give my assent categorically. But a drop of disturbing doubt fell into my Materialism. It was merely a "Perhaps." Perhaps (oh joy!) there was, after all, "something else"; and (oh reassurance!) perhaps it had nothing to do with Christian Theology. And as soon as I paused on that "Perhaps," inevitably all the old Occultist lore, and all the old excitement which the Matron of Chartres had innocently aroused in me, rose out of the past.

Now the fat was in the fire with a vengeance. Two things hitherto widely separated in my mind rushed together: the imaginative longing for Joy, or rather the longing which *was*

Joy, and the ravenous, quasi-prurient desire for the Occult, the Preternatural as such. And with these there came (less welcome) some stirring of unease, some of the immemorial fear we have all known in the nursery, and (if we are honest) long after the nursery age. There is a kind of gravitation in the mind whereby good rushes to good and evil to evil. This mingled repulsion and desire drew toward them everything else in me that was bad. The idea that if there were Occult knowledge it was known to very few and scorned by the many became an added attraction: "we few," you will remember, was an evocative expression for me. That the means should be Magic—the most exquisitely unorthodox thing in the world, unorthodox both by Christian and by Rationalist standards—of course appealed to the rebel in me. I was already acquainted with the more depraved side of Romanticism; had read *Anactoria*, and Wilde, and pored upon Beardsley, not hitherto attracted, but making no moral judgment. Now I thought I began to see the point of it. In a word, you have already had in this story the World and the Flesh; now came the Devil. If there had been in the neighborhood some elder person who dabbled in dirt of the Magical kind (such have a good nose for potential disciples) I might now be a Satanist or a maniac.

In actual fact I was wonderfully protected, and this spiritual debauch had in the end one rather good result. I was protected, first, by ignorance and incapacity. Whether Magic were possible or not, I at any rate had no teacher to start me on the path. I was protected also by cowardice; the reawakened terrors of childhood might add a spice to my greed and curiosity as long as it was daylight. Alone, and in darkness, I used my best endeavors to become a strict Materialist again; not always with success. A "Perhaps" is quite enough for the nerves to work upon. But my best protection was the known nature of Joy. This ravenous desire to break the bounds, to tear the curtain, to be in the secret, revealed itself, more and more clearly the longer I indulged it, to be quite different from the longing that is Joy. Its coarse strength betrayed it. Slowly, and with many relapses, I came to see that the magical conclusion was just as irrelevant to Joy as the erotic conclusion has been. Once again one had changed scents. If circles and pentangles and the Tetragrammaton had been tried and had in fact raised, or seemed to raise, a spirit, that might have been—if a man's nerves could stand it—extremely interesting; but the real Desirable would have evaded one, the real Desire would have been left saying, "What is this to me?"

What I like about experience is that it is such an honest thing. You may take any number of wrong turnings; but keep your eyes open and you will not be allowed to go very far before the warning signs appear. You may have deceived yourself, but experience is not trying to deceive you. The universe rings true wherever you fairly test it.

The other results of my glance into the dark room were as follows. First, I now had both a fresh motive for wishing Materialism to be true and a decreased confidence that it was. The fresh motive came, as you have divined, from those fears which I had so wantonly stirred up from their sleeping place in the memories of childhood; behaving like a true Lewis who will not leave well alone. Every man who is afraid of spooks will have a reason for wishing to be a Materialist; that creed promises to exclude the bogies. As for my shaken confidence, it remained in the form of a "Perhaps," stripped of its directly and grossly magical "affect"—a pleasing possibility that the Universe might combine the snugness of Materialism here and now with . . . well, with I didn't know what; somewhere or something beyond, "the unimaginable lodge for solitary thinkings." This was very bad. I was beginning to try to have it both ways: to get the comforts both of a materialist and of a spiritual philosophy without the rigors of either. But the second result was better. I had learned a wholesome antipathy to everything occult and magical which was to stand me in good stead when, at Oxford, I came to meet Magicians, Spiritualists, and the like.

Not that the ravenous lust was never to tempt me again but that I now knew it for a temptation. And above all, I now knew that Joy did not point in that direction.

You might sum up the gains of this whole period by saying that henceforward the Flesh and the Devil, though they could still tempt, could no longer offer me the supreme bribe. I had learned that it was not in their gift. And the World had never even pretended to have it.

And then, on top of this, in superabundance of mercy, came that event which I have already more than once attempted to describe in other books. I was in the habit of walking over to Leatherhead about once a week and sometimes taking the train back. In summer I did so chiefly because Leatherhead boasted a tiny swimming bath; better than nothing to me who had learned to swim almost before I can remember and who, till middle age and rheumatism crept upon me, was passionately fond of being in water. But I went in winter, too, to look for books and to get my hair cut. The evening that I now speak of was in October. I and one porter had the long, timbered platform of Leatherhead station to ourselves. It was getting just dark enough for the smoke of an engine to glow red on the underside with the reflection of the furnace. The hills beyond the Dorking Valley were of a blue so intense as to be nearly violet and the sky was green with frost. My ears tingled with the cold. The glorious week end of reading was before me. Turning to the bookstall, I picked out an Everyman in a dirty jacket, *Phantastes, a faerie Romance*, George MacDonald. Then the train came in. I can still remember the voice of the porter calling out the village names, Saxon and sweet as a nut—"Bookham, Effingham, Horsley train." That evening I began to read my new book.

The woodland journeyings in that story, the ghostly enemies, the ladies both good and evil, were close enough to my habitual imagery to lure me on without the perception of a change. It is as if I were carried sleeping across the frontier, or

as if I had died in the old country and could never remember
how I came alive in the new. For in one sense the new country was exactly like the old. I met there all that had already
charmed me in Malory, Spenser, Morris, and Yeats. But in another sense all was changed. I did not yet know (and I was long
in learning) the name of the new quality, the bright shadow,
that rested on the travels of Anodos. I do now. It was Holi-
ness. For the first time the song of the sirens sounded like the
voice of my mother or my nurse. Here were old wives' tales;
there was nothing to be proud of in enjoying them. It was as
though the voice which had called to me from the world's end
were now speaking at my side. It was with me in the room, or
in my own body, or behind me. If it had once eluded me by its
distance, it now eluded me by proximity—something too near
to see, too plain to be understood, on this side of knowledge.
It seemed to have been always with me; if I could ever have
turned my head quick enough I should have seized it. Now for
the first time I felt that it was out of reach not because of something I could not do but because of something I could not stop
doing. If I could only leave off, let go, unmake myself, it would
be there. Meanwhile, in this new region all the confusions
that had hitherto perplexed my search for Joy were disarmed.
There was no temptation to confuse the scenes of the tale with
the light that rested upon them, or to suppose that they were
put forward as realities, or even to dream that if they had been
realities and I could reach the woods where Anodos journeyed
I should thereby come a step nearer to my desire. Yet, at the
same time, never had the wind of Joy blowing through any
story been less separable from the story itself. Where the god
and the *idolon* were most nearly one there was least danger of
confounding them. Thus, when the great moments came I did
not break away from the woods and cottages that I read of to
seek some bodiless light shining beyond them, but gradually,
with a swelling continuity (like the sun at mid-morning burning through a fog) I found the light shining on those woods

and cottages, and then on my own past life, and on the quiet room where I sat and on my old teacher where he nodded above his little *Tacitus*. For I now perceived that while the air of the new region made all my erotic and magical perversions of Joy look like sordid trumpery, it had no such disenchanting power over the bread upon the table or the coals in the grate. That was the marvel. Up till now each visitation of Joy had left the common world momentarily a desert—"The first touch of the earth went nigh to kill." Even when real clouds or trees had been the material of the vision, they had been so only by re-minding me of another world; and I did not like the return to ours. But now I saw the bright shadow coming out of the book into the real world and resting there, transforming all common things and yet itself unchanged. Or, more accurately, I saw the common things drawn into the bright shadow. *Unde hoc mihi?* In the depth of my disgraces, in the then invincible ignorance of my intellect, all this was given me without asking, even with-out consent. That night my imagination was, in a certain sense, baptized; the rest of me, not unnaturally, took longer. I had not the faintest notion what I had let myself in for by buying *Phan-tastes*.

XII

Guns and Good Company

La compagnie, de tant d'hommes vous plaist, nobles,
jeunes, actifs; la liberté de cette conversation sans art, et
une façon de vie masle et sans cérémonie.

MONTAIGNE

THE old pattern began to repeat itself. The Bookham days, like a longer and more glorious holidays, drew to their end; a scholarship examination and, after that, the army, loomed behind them like a grimmer term. The good time had never been better than in its last months. I remember, in particular, glorious hours of bathing in Donegal. It was surf bathing: not the formal affair with boards that you have now, but mere rough and tumble, in which the waves, the monstrous, emerald, deafening waves, are always the winner, and it is at once a joke, a terror, and a joy to look over your shoulder and see (too late) one breaker of such sublime proportions that you would have avoided him had you known he was coming. But they gather themselves up, pre-eminent above their fellows, as suddenly and unpredictably as a revolution.

It was late in the winter term of 1916 that I went to Oxford to sit for my scholarship examination. Boys who have faced this ordeal in peacetime will not easily imagine the indifference with which I went. This does not mean that I underestimated the importance (in one sense) of succeeding. I knew very well by now that there was hardly any position in the world save that of a don in which I was fitted to earn a living, and that I was staking everything on a game in which few won and hundreds lost. As Kirk had said of me in a letter to my father (I did not, of course, see it till many years later), "You may make a writer, or a scholar of him, but you'll not make anything else. You may make up your mind to *that*." And I knew this myself; sometimes it terrified me. What blunted the edge of it now was that whether I won a scholarship or no I should next year go into the army; and even a temper more sanguine than mine could feel in 1916 that an infantry subaltern would be insane to waste anxiety on anything so hypothetical as his postwar life. I once tried to explain this to my father; it was one of the attempts I often made (though doubtless less often than I ought) to break through the artificiality of our intercourse and admit him to my real life. It was a total failure. He replied at once with fatherly counsels about the necessity of hard work and concentration, the amount that he had already spent in educating me, the very moderate, nay negligible, assistance he would be able to give me in later life. Poor man! He misjudged me sadly if he thought that idleness at my book was among my many vices. And how, I asked myself, could he expect the winning or losing of a scholarship to lose none of its importance when life and death were the real issues? The truth is, I think, that while death (mine, his, everyone's) was often vividly present to him as a subject of anxiety and other emotions, it had no place in his mind as a sober, matter-of-fact contingency from which consequences could be drawn. At any rate the conversation was a failure. It shipwrecked on the old rock. His intense desire for my total confidence coexisted with an inability to listen (in any strict sense) to what I said. He could never empty, or silence, his own mind to make room for an alien thought.

My first taste of Oxford was comical enough. I had made

no arrangements about quarters and, having no more luggage than I could carry in my hand, I sallied out of the railway station on foot to find either a lodging house or a cheap hotel; all agog for "dreaming spires" and "last enchantments." My first disappointment at what I saw could be dealt with. Towns always show their worst face to the railway. But as I walked on and on I became more bewildered. Could this succession of mean shops really be Oxford? But I still went on, always expecting the next turn to reveal the beauties, and reflecting that it was a much larger town than I had been led to suppose. Only when it became obvious that there was very little town left ahead of me, that I was, in fact, getting to open country, did I turn round and look. There, behind me, far away, never more beautiful since, was the fabled cluster of spires and towers. I had come out of the station on the wrong side and been all this time walking into what was even then the mean and sprawling suburb of Botley. I did not see to what extent this little adventure was an allegory of my whole life. I merely walked back to the station, somewhat footsore, took a hansom, and asked to be driven to "some place where I can get rooms for a week, please." The method, which I should now think hazardous, was a complete success, and I was soon at tea in comfortable lodgings. The house is still there, the first on the right as you turn into Mansfield Road out of Holywell. I shared the sitting room with another candidate, a man from Cardiff College, which he pronounced to be architecturally superior to anything in Oxford. His learning terrified me, but he was an agreeable man. I have never seen him since.

It was very cold and the next day snow began to fall, turning pinnacles into wedding-cake decorations. The examination was held in the Hall of Oriel, and we all wrote in greatcoats and mufflers and wearing at least our left-hand gloves. The Provost, old Phelps, gave out the papers. I remember very little about them, but I suppose I was outshone in pure classics by many of my rivals and succeeded on my general knowledge and dialectics. I had the impression that I was doing badly. Long years (or years that seemed long) with the Knock had cured me of my defensive Wyvernian priggery, and I no longer supposed other boys to be ignorant of what I knew. Thus the essay was on a quotation from Johnson. I had read several times the Boswellian conversation in which it occurred and was able to replace the whole question in that context; but I never thought that this (any more than a fairish knowledge of Schopenhauer) would gain me any particular credit. It was a blessed state to be in, but for the moment depressing. As I left the Hall after that essay I heard one candidate say to his friend, "I worked in all my stuff about Rousseau and the Social Contract." That struck dismay into my soul, for though I had dabbled (not to my good) in the *Confessions* I knew nothing of the *Contrat Social*. At the beginning of the morning a nice Harrovian had whispered to me, "I don't even know if it's Sam or Ben." In my innocence I explained to him that it was Sam and could not be Ben because Ben was spelled without an h. I did not think there could be any harm in giving away such information.

When I arrived home I told my father that I had almost certainly failed. It was an admission calculated to bring out all his tenderness and chivalry. The man who could not understand a boy's taking his own possible, or probable, death into account could very well understand a child's disappointment. Not a word was now heard of expenses and difficulties; nothing but consolation, reassurance and affection. Then, almost on Christmas Eve, we heard that "Univ" (University College) had elected me.

Though I was now a scholar of my College I still had to pass "Responsions," which involved elementary mathematics. To prepare for this I returned after Christmas for one last term with Kirk—a golden term, poignantly happy under the approaching shadow. At Easter I was handsomely plowed in Responsions, having been unable as usual to get my sums right. "Be more careful," was the advice that everyone gave me, but

I found it useless. The more care I took the more mistakes I made; just as, to this day, the more anxiously I fair copy a piece of writing the more certain I am to make a ghastly clerical error in the very first line.

In spite of this I came into residence in the summer (Trinity) term of 1917; for the real object now was simply to enter the University Officers' Training Corps as my most promising route into the army. My first studies at Oxford, nevertheless, still had Responsions in view. I read algebra (devil take it!) with old Mr. Campbell of Hertford who turned out to be a friend of our dear friend Janie M. That I never passed Responsions is certain, but I cannot remember whether I again sat for it and was again plowed. The question became unimportant after the war, for a benevolent decree exempted ex-servicemen from taking it. Otherwise, no doubt, I should have had to abandon the idea of going to Oxford.

I was less than a term at Univ when my papers came through and I enlisted; and the conditions made it a most abnormal term. Half the College had been converted into a hospital and was in the hands of the R.A.M.C. In the remaining portion lived a tiny community of undergraduates — two of us not yet of military age, two unfit, one a Sinn-Feiner who would not fight for England, and a few other oddments which I never quite placed. We dined in the little lecture room which is now a passage between Common Room and Hall. Small though our numbers were (about eight) we were rather distinguished, for we included E. V. Gordon, afterward Professor of English at Manchester, and A. C. Ewing, the Cambridge philosopher; also that witty and kindly man, Theobald Butler, skilled in turning the most lurid limericks into Greek verse. I enjoyed myself greatly; but it bore little resemblance to normal undergraduate life and was for me an unsettled, excited, and generally useless period. Then came the army. By a remarkable turn of fate this did not mean removal from Oxford. I was drafted into a Cadet Battalion whose billet was Keble.

I passed through the ordinary course of training (a mild affair in those days compared with that of the recent war) and was commissioned as a Second Lieutenant in the Somerset Light Infantry, the old XIIIth Foot. I arrived in the front line trenches on my nineteenth birthday (November 1917), saw most of my service in the villages before Arras—Fampoux and Monchy—and was wounded at Mt. Bernenchon, near Lillers, in April, 1918.

I am surprised that I did not dislike the army more. It was, of course, detestable. But the words "of course" drew the sting. That is where it differed from Wyvern. One did not expect to like it. Nobody said you ought to like it. Nobody pretended to like it. Everyone you met took it for granted that the whole thing was an odious necessity, a ghastly interruption of rational life. And that made all the difference. Straight tribulation is easier to bear than tribulation which advertises itself as pleasure. The one breeds camaraderie and even (when intense) a kind of love between the fellow sufferers; the other, mutual distrust, cynicism, concealed and fretting resentment. And secondly, I found my military elders and betters incomparably nicer than the Wyvern Bloods. This is no doubt because Thirty is naturally kinder to Nineteen than Nineteen is to Thirteen: it is really grown up and does not need to reassure itself. But I am inclined to think that my face had altered. That "look" which I had so often been told to "take off it" had apparently taken itself off—perhaps when I read *Phantastes*. There is even some evidence that it had been succeeded by a look which excited either pity or kindly amusement. Thus, on my very first night in France, in a vast marquee or drill hall where about a hundred officers were to sleep on plank beds, two middle-aged Canadians at once took charge of me and treated me, not like a son (that might have given offence) but like a long-lost friend. Blessings upon them! Once, too, in the Officers' Club at Arras where I was dining alone, and quite happy with my book and my wine (a bottle of Heidsieck then cost 8 francs, and a bottle of Perrier Jouet, 12) two immensely senior officers, all covered with ribbons and red tabs, came over to my table toward the end of the meal, and hailing me as "Sunny Jim" carried me off to their own for brandy and cigars. They weren't drunk either; nor did they make me drunk. It was pure good will. And though exceptional, this was not so very exceptional. There were nasty people in the army; but memory fills those months with pleasant, transitory contacts. Every few days one seemed to meet a scholar, an original, a poet, a cheery buffoon, a raconteur, or at the least a man of good will.

Some time in the middle of that winter I had the good luck to fall sick with what the troops called "trench fever" and the doctors P.U.O. (Pyrexia, unknown origin) and was sent for a wholly delightful three weeks to hospital at Le Treport. Perhaps I ought to have mentioned before that I had had a weak chest ever since childhood and had very early learned to make a minor illness one of the pleasures of life, even in peacetime. Now, as an alternative to the trenches, a bed and a book were "very heaven." The hospital was a converted hotel and we were two in a room. My first week was marred by the fact that one of the night nurses was conducting a furious love affair with my roommate. I had too high a temperature to be embarrassed, but the human whisper is a very tedious and unmusical noise; especially at night. After that my fortune mended. The amorous man was sent elsewhere and replaced by a musical misogynist from Yorkshire, who on our second morning together said to me, "Eh, lad, if we make beds ourselves dom b—s won't stay in room so long" (or words to that effect). Accordingly, we made our own beds every day, and every day when the two V.A.D.'s looked in they said, "Oh, they've made their beds! Aren't these two good?" and rewarded us with their brightest smiles. I think they attributed our action to gallantry.

It was here that I first read a volume of Chesterton's essays. I had never heard of him and had no idea of what he stood for; nor can I quite understand why he made such an immediate conquest of me. It might have been expected that my pessimism, my atheism, and my hatred of sentiment would have made him to me the least congenial of all authors. It would almost seem that Providence, or some "second cause" of a very obscure kind, quite overrules our previous tastes when it decides to bring two minds together. Liking an author may be as involuntary and improbable as failing in love. I was by now a sufficiently experienced reader to distinguish liking from agreement. I did not need to accept what Chesterton said in order to enjoy it. His humor was of the kind which I like best—not "jokes" imbedded in the page like currants in a cake, still less (what I cannot endure), a general tone of flippancy and jocularity, but the humor which is not in any way separable from the argument but is rather (as Aristotle would say) the "bloom" on dialectic itself. The sword glitters not because the swordsman set out to make it glitter but because he is fighting for his life and therefore moving it very quickly. For the critics who think Chesterton frivolous or "paradoxical" I have to work hard to feel even pity; sympathy is out of the question. Moreover, strange as it may seem, I liked him for his goodness. I can attribute this taste to myself freely (even at that age) because it was a liking for goodness which had nothing to do with any attempt to be good myself. I have never felt the dislike of goodness which seems to be quite common in better men than me. "Smug" and "smugness" were terms of disapprobation which had never had a place in my critical vocabulary. I lacked the cynic's nose, the *odora canum vis* or bloodhound sensitivity for hypocrisy or Pharisaism. It was a matter of taste: I felt the "charm" of goodness as a man feels the charm of a woman he has no intention of marrying. It is, indeed, at that distance that its "charm" is most apparent.

In reading Chesterton, as in reading MacDonald, I did not know what I was letting myself in for. A young man who wishes to remain a sound Atheist cannot be too careful of his reading. There are traps everywhere—"Bibles laid open, millions of surprises," as Herbert says, "fine nets and stratagems." God is, if I may say it, very unscrupulous.

In my own battalion also I was assailed. Here I met one Johnson (on whom be peace) who would have been a lifelong friend if he had not been killed. He was, like me, already a scholar of an Oxford college (Queen's) who hoped to take up his scholarship after the war, but a few years my senior and at that time in command of a company. In him I found dialectical sharpness such as I had hitherto known only in Kirk, but coupled with youth and whim and poetry. He was moving toward Theism and we had endless arguments on that and every other topic whenever we were out of the line. But it was not this that mattered. The important thing was that he was a man of conscience. I had hardly till now encountered principles in anyone so nearly of my own age and my own sort. The alarming thing was that he took them for granted. It crossed my mind for the first time since my apostasy that the severer virtues might have some relevance to one's own life. I say "the severer virtues" because I already had some notion of kindness and faithfulness to friends and generosity about money—as who has not till he meets the temptation which gives all their opposite vices new and more civil names? But it had not seriously occurred to me that people like ourselves, people like Johnson and me who wanted to know whether beauty was objective or how Aeschylus handled the reconciliation of Zeus and Prometheus, should be attempting strict veracity, chastity, or devotion to duty. I had taken it that they were not our subjects. There was no discussion between us on the point and I do not think he ever suspected the truth about me. I was at no pains to display it. If this is hypocrisy, then I must conclude that hypocrisy can do a man good. To be ashamed of what you were about to say, to pretend that something which you had meant seriously was only a joke—this is an ignoble part. But it is better than not to be ashamed at all. And the distinction between pretending you are better than you are and beginning to be better in reality is finer than moral sleuthhounds conceive. I was, in intention, concealing only a part: I accepted his principles at once, made no attempt internally to defend my own "unexamined life." When a boor first enters the society of courteous people what can he do, for a while, except imitate the motions? How can he learn except by imitation?

You will have divined that ours was a very nice battalion; a minority of good regulars ruling a pleasantly mixed population of promoted rankers (west country farmers, these), barristers, and university men. You could get as good talk there as anywhere. Perhaps the best of us all was our butt, Wallie. Wallie was a farmer, a Roman Catholic, a passionate soldier (the only man I met who really longed for fighting) and gullible to any degree by the rawest subaltern. The technique was to criticize the Yeomanry. Poor Wallie knew that it was the bravest, the most efficient, the hardest and cleanest corps that ever sat on horses. He knew all that inside, having learned it from an uncle in the Yeomanry when he was a child. But he could not get it out. He stammered and contradicted himself and always came at last to his trump card: "I wish my Uncle Ben was here to talk to you. Uncle Ben'd talk to you. He'd tell you." Mortals must not judge; but I doubt whether any man fought in France who was more likely to go straight to Heaven if he were killed. I would have been better employed cleaning his boots than laughing at him. I may add that I did not enjoy the short time I spent in the company he commanded. Wallie had a genuine passion for killing Germans and a complete disregard of his own or anyone else's safety. He was always striking out bright ideas at which the hair of us subalterns stood on end. Luckily he could be very easily dissuaded by any plausible argument that occurred to us. Such was his valor and innocence that he never for a moment suspected us of any but a military motive. He could never grasp the neighborly principles which, by the tacit agreement of the troops, were held to govern trench warfare, and to which I was introduced at once by my sergeant. I had suggested "pooping" a rifle grenade into a German post where we had seen heads moving. "Just as 'ee like, zir," said the sergeant, scratching his head, "but once 'ee start doing that kind of thing, 'ee'll get zummit back, zee?"

I must not paint the wartime army all gold. I met there both the World and the great goddess Nonsense. The world presented itself in a very ridiculous form on that night (my nineteenth birthday) when I first arrived "up the line." As I emerged from the shaft into the dugout and blinked in the candlelight I noticed that the Captain to whom I was reporting was a master whom I had liked more than I had respected at one of my schools. I ventured to claim acquaintance. He admitted in a low, hurried voice that he had once been a schoolmaster, and the topic was never raised between us again. The impact of the Great Goddess was even funnier, and I met it long before I had reached my own battalion. The troop train from Rouen—that interminable, twelve-mile-an-hour train, in which no two coaches were alike—left at about ten in the evening. Three other officers and I were allotted a compartment. There was no heating; for light we brought our own candles; for sanitation there were the windows. The journey would last about fifteen hours. It was freezing hard. In the tunnel just outside Rouen (all my generation remember it) there was a sudden wrenching and grating noise and one of our doors dropped off bodily into the dark. We sat with chattering teeth till the next stop, where the officer commanding the train came bustling up and demanded what we had done with our door. "It came off, sir," said we. "Don't talk nonsense," said he, "it wouldn't have come off if there hadn't been some horseplay!"—as if nothing were more natural than that four officers (being, of course, provided with screwdrivers) should begin a night journey in midwinter by removing the door of their carriage.

The war itself has been so often described by those who saw more of it than I that I shall here say little about it. Until the great German attack came in the Spring we had a pretty quiet time. Even then they attacked not us but the Canadians on our right, merely "keeping us quiet" by pouring shells into our line about three a minute all day. I think it was that day I noticed how a greater terror overcomes a less: a mouse that I met (and a poor shivering mouse it was, as I was a poor shivering man) made no attempt to run from me. Through the winter, weariness and water were our chief enemies. I have gone to sleep marching and woken again and found myself marching still. One walked in the trenches in thigh gum boots with water above the knee; one remembers the icy stream welling up inside the boot when you punctured it on concealed barbed wire. Familiarity both with the very old and the very recent dead confirmed that view of corpses which had been formed the moment I saw my dead mother. I came to know and pity and reverence the ordinary man: particularly dear Sergeant Ayres, who was (I suppose) killed by the same shell that wounded me. I was a futile officer (they gave commissions too easily then), a puppet moved about by him, and he turned this ridiculous and painful relation into something beautiful, became to me almost like a father. But for the rest, the war—the frights, the cold, the smell of H.E., the horribly smashed men still moving like half-crushed beetles, the sitting or standing corpses, the landscape of sheer earth without a blade of grass, the boots worn day and night till they seemed to grow to your feet—all this shows rarely and faintly in memory. It is too cut off from the rest of my experience and often seems to have happened to someone else. It is even in a way unimportant. One imaginative moment seems now to matter more than the realities that followed. It was the first bullet I heard—so far from me that it "whined" like a journalist's or a peacetime poet's bullet. At that moment there was something not exactly like fear, much less like indifference: a little quavering signal that said, "This is War. This is what Homer wrote about."

XIII

The New Look

*This wall I was many a weary month in finishing,
and yet never thought myself safe till it was done.*

DEFOE, *Robinson Crusoe*

THE rest of my war experiences have little to do with this story. How I "took" about sixty prisoners—that is, discovered to my great relief that the crowd of field-gray figures who suddenly appeared from nowhere, all had their hands up—is not worth telling, save as a joke. Did not Falstaff "take" Sir Colville of the Dale? Nor does it concern the reader to know how I got a sound "Blighty" from an English shell, or how the exquisite Sister N. in the C.C.S. has ever since embodied my idea of Artemis. Two things stand out. One is the moment, just after I had been hit, when I found (or thought I found) that I was not breathing and concluded that this was death. I felt no fear and certainly no courage. It did not seem to be an occasion for either. The proposition "Here is a man dying" stood before my mind as dry, as factual, as unemotional as something in a textbook. It was not even interesting. The fruit of this experience was that when, some years later, I met Kant's distinction between the Noumenal and the Phenomenal self, it was more to me than an abstraction. I had tasted it; I had proved that there was a fully conscious "I" whose connections with the "me" of introspection were loose and transitory. The other momentous experience was that of reading Bergson in a Convalescent Camp on Salisbury Plain. Intellectually this taught me to avoid the snares that lurk about the word *Nothing*. But it also had a revolutionary effect on my emotional outlook. Hitherto my whole bent had been toward things pale, remote, and evanescent; the water-color world of Morris, the leafy recesses of Malory,[1] the twilight of Yeats. The word "life" had for me pretty much the same associations it had for Shelley in *The Triumph of Life*. I would not have understood what Goethe meant by *des Lebens goldnes Baum*. Bergson showed me. He did not abolish my old loves, but he gave me a new one. From him I first learned to relish energy, fertility, and urgency; the resource, the triumphs, and even the insolence, of things that grow. I became capable of appreciating artists who would, I believe, have meant nothing to me before; all the resonant, dogmatic, flaming, unanswerable people like Beethoven, Titian (in his mythological pictures), Goethe, Dunbar, Pindar, Christopher Wren, and the more exultant Psalms.

I returned to Oxford—"demobbed"—in January 1919. But before I say anything of my life there I must warn the reader that one huge and complex episode will be omitted. I have no choice about this reticence. All I can or need say is that my earlier hostility to the emotions was very fully and variously avenged. But even were I free to tell the story, I doubt if it has much to do with the subject of the book.

The first lifelong friend I made at Oxford was A. K. Hamilton Jenkin, since known for his books on Cornwall. He continued (what Arthur had begun) my education as a seeing, listening, smelling, receptive creature. Arthur had had his preference for the Homely. But Jenkin seemed to be able to enjoy every-

---

1. The iron in Malory, the tragedy of contrition, I did not yet at all perceive.

thing; even ugliness. I learned from him that we should attempt a total surrender to whatever atmosphere was offering itself at the moment; in a squalid town to seek out those very places where its squalor rose to grimness and almost grandeur, on a dismal day to find the most dismal and dripping wood, on a windy day to seek the windiest ridge. There was no Betjemannic irony about it; only a serious, yet gleeful, determination to rub one's nose in the very quiddity of each thing, to rejoice in its being (so magnificently) what it was.

My next was Owen Barfield. There is a sense in which Arthur and Barfield are the types of every man's First Friend and Second Friend. The First is the *alter ego*, the man who first reveals to you that you are not alone in the world by turning out (beyond hope) to share all your most secret delights. There is nothing to be overcome in making him your friend; he and you join like raindrops on a window. But the Second Friend is the man who disagrees with you about everything. He is not so much the *alter ego* as the antiself. Of course he shares your interests; otherwise he would not become your friend at all. But he has approached them all at a different angle. He has read all the right books but has got the wrong thing out of every one. It is as if he spoke your language but mispronounced it. How can he be so nearly right and yet, invariably, just not right? He is as fascinating (and infuriating) as a woman. When you set out to correct his heresies, you find that he forsooth has decided to correct yours! And then you go at it, hammer and tongs, far into the night, night after night, or walking through fine country that neither gives a glance to, each learning the weight of the other's punches, and often more like mutually respectful enemies than friends. Actually (though it never seems so at the time) you modify one another's thought; out of this perpetual dogfight a community of mind and a deep affection emerge. But I think he changed me a good deal more than I him. Much of the thought which he afterward put into *Poetic Diction* had already become mine before that important little book appeared. It would be strange if it had not. He was of course not so learned then as he has since become; but the genius was already there.

Closely linked with Barfield of Wadham was his friend (and soon mine), A. C. Harwood of The House, later a pillar of Michael Hall, the Steinerite school at Kidbrooke. He was different from either of us; a wholly imperturbable man. Though poor (like most of us) and wholly without "prospects," he wore the expression of a nineteenth-century gentleman with something in the Funds. On a walking tour when the last light of a wet evening had just revealed some ghastly error in map-reading (probably his own) and the best hope was "Five miles to Mudham (if we could find it) and we *might* get beds there," he still wore that expression. In the heat of argument he wore it still. You would think that he, if anyone, would have been told to "take that look off his face." But I don't believe he ever was. It was no mask and came from no stupidity. He has been tried since by all the usual sorrows and anxieties. He is the sole Horatio known to me in this age of Hamlets; no "stop for Fortune's finger."

There is one thing to be said about these and other friends whom I made at Oxford. They were all, by decent Pagan standards (much more, by so low a standard as mine), "good." That is, they all, like my friend Johnson, believed, and acted on the belief, that veracity, public spirit, chastity, and sobriety were obligatory—"to be attempted," as the examiners say, "by all candidates." Johnson had prepared me to be influenced by them. I accepted their standards in principle and perhaps (this part I do not very well remember) tried to act accordingly.

During my first two years at Oxford I was busily engaged (apart from "doing Mods" and "beginning Greats") in assuming what we may call an intellectual "New Look." There was to be no more pessimism, no more self-pity, no flirtations with any idea of the supernatural, no romantic delusions. In a word, like the heroine of *Northanger Abbey*, I formed the resolution "of always judging and acting in future with the greatest good sense." And good sense meant, for me at that moment, a retreat, almost a panic-stricken flight, from all that sort of romanticism which had hitherto been the chief concern of my life. Several causes operated together.

For one thing, I had recently come to know an old, dirty, gabbling, tragic, Irish parson who had long since lost his faith but retained his living. By the time I met him his only interest was the search for evidence of "human survival." On this he read and talked incessantly, and, having a highly critical mind, could never satisfy himself. What was especially shocking was that the ravenous desire for personal immortality co-existed in him with (apparently) a total indifference to all that could, on a sane view, make immortality desirable. He was not seeking the Beatific Vision and did not even believe in God. He was not hoping for more time in which to purge and improve his own personality. He was not dreaming of reunion with dead friends or lovers; I never heard him speak with affection of anybody. All he wanted was the assurance that something he could call "himself" would, on almost any terms, last longer than his bodily life. So, at least, I thought. I was too young and hard to suspect that what secretly moved him was a thirst for the happiness which had been wholly denied him on earth. And his state of mind appeared to me the most contemptible I had ever encountered. Any thoughts or dreams which might lead one into that fierce monomania were, I decided, to be utterly shunned. The whole question of immortality became rather disgusting to me. I shut it out. All one's thought must be confined to

> the very world, which is the world
> Of all of us—the place where, in the end,
> We find our happiness, or not at all.

Secondly, it had been my chance to spend fourteen days, and most of the fourteen nights as well, in close contact with a man who was going mad. He was a man whom I had dearly loved, and well he deserved love. And now I helped to hold him while he kicked and wallowed on the floor, screaming out that devils were tearing him and that he was that moment falling down into Hell. And this man, as I well knew, had not kept the beaten track. He had flirted with Theosophy, Yoga, Spiritualism, Psychoanalysis, what not? Probably these things had in fact no connection with his insanity, for which (I believe) there were physical causes. But it did not seem so to me at the time. I thought I had seen a warning; it was to this, this raving on the floor, that all romantic longings and unearthly speculations led a man in the end—

> *Be not too wildly amorous of the far*
> *Nor lure thy fantasy to its utmost scope.*

Safety first, thought I: the beaten track, the approved road, the center of the road, the lights on. For some months after that nightmare fortnight, the words "ordinary" and "humdrum" summed up everything that appeared to me most desirable.

Thirdly, the new Psychology was at that time sweeping through us all. We did not swallow it whole (few people then did) but we were all influenced. What we were most concerned about was "Fantasy" or "wishful thinking." For (of course) we were all poets and critics and set a very great value on "Imagination" in some high Coleridgean sense, so that it became important to distinguish Imagination, not only (as Coleridge did) from Fancy, but also from Fantasy as the psychologists understand that term. Now what, I asked myself, were all my delectable mountains and western gardens but sheer Fantasies? Had they not revealed their true nature by luring me, time and again, into undisguisedly erotic reverie or the squalid nightmare of Magic? In reality, of course, as previous chapters have told, my own experience had repeatedly shown that these romantic images had never been more than a sort of flash, or even slag, thrown off by the occurrence of Joy, that those mountains and gardens had never been what I wanted but only symbols which professed themselves to be no more, and that every effort to treat them as the real Desirable soon honestly proved itself to be a failure. But now, busy with my New Look, I managed to forget this. Instead of repenting my idolatry I vilified the unoffending images on which I had lavished it. With the confidence of a boy I decided I had done with all that. No more Avalon, no more Hesperides. I had (this was very precisely the opposite of the truth) "seen through" them. And I was never going to be taken in again.

Finally, there was of course Bergson. Somehow or other (for it does not seem very clear when I reopen his books today) I found in him a refutation of the old haunting idea, Schopenhauer's idea, that the universe "might not have existed." In other words one Divine attribute, that of necessary existence, rose above my horizon. It was still, and long after, attached to the wrong subject; to the universe, not to God. But the mere attribute was itself of immense potency. When once one has dropped the absurd notion that reality is an arbitrary alternative to "nothing," one gives up being a pessimist (or even an optimist). There is no sense in blaming or praising the Whole, nor, indeed, in saying anything about it. Even if you persist in hurling Promethean or Hardyesque defiances at it, then, since you are part of it, it is only that same Whole which through you "quietly declaims the cursings of itself"—a futility which seems to me to vitiate Lord Russell's stirring essay on "The Worship of a Free Man." Cursings were as futile, and as immature, as dreams about the western garden. One must (like Carlyle's lady) "accept" the universe; totally, with no reservations, loyally. This sort of Stoical Monism was the philosophy of my New Look. And it gave me a great sense of peace. It was perhaps the nearest thing to a religious experience which I had had since my prep-school days. It ended (I hope forever) any idea of a treaty or compromise with reality. So much the perception of even one Divine attribute can do.

As for Joy, I labeled it "aesthetic experience" and talked

much about it under that name and said it was very "valuable." But it came very seldom and when it came it didn't amount to much.

Those early days of the New Look were on the whole happy ones. Very gradually the sky changed. There came to be more unhappiness and anxiety in my own life; and Barfield was living through

> *that whole year of youth*
> *When life ached like an aching tooth.*

Our generation, the generation of the returned soldiers, began to pass. Oxford was full of new faces. Freshmen began to make historical allowances for our warped point of view. The problem of one's career loomed larger and grimmer.

It was then that a really dreadful thing (dreadful to me) happened. First Harwood (still without changing his expression), and then Barfield, embraced the doctrines of Steiner and became Anthroposophists. I was hideously shocked. Everything that I had labored so hard to expel from my own life seemed to have flared up and met me in my best friends. Not only my best friends but those whom I would have thought safest; the one so immovable, the other brought up in a free-thinking family and so immune from all "superstition" that he had hardly heard of Christianity itself until he went to school. (The gospel first broke on Barfield in the form of a dictated list of Parables Peculiar to St. Matthew.) Not only in my seeming-safest friends but at a moment when we all had most need to stand together. And as I came to learn (so far as I ever have learned) what Steiner thought, my horror turned into disgust and resentment. For here, apparently, were all the abominations; none more abominable than those which had once attracted me. Here were gods, spirits, afterlife and pre-existence, initiates, occult knowledge, meditation. "Why—damn it—it's *medieval*," I exclaimed; for I still had all the chronological snobbery of my period and used the names of earlier periods as terms of abuse. Here was everything which the New Look had been designed to exclude; everything that might lead one off the main road into those dark places where men wallow on the floor and scream that they are being dragged down into Hell. Of course it was all arrant nonsense. There was no danger of *my* being taken in. But then, the loneliness, the sense of being deserted.

Naturally, I attributed to my friends the same desires which, had I become an Anthroposophist, would have been operative in me. I thought they were falling under that ravenous, salt lust for the occult. I now see that, from the very first, all the evidence was against this. They were not that sort. Nor does Anthroposophy, so far as I can see, cater for that sort. There is a difficulty and (to me) a reassuring Germanic dullness about it which would soon deter those who were looking for thrills. Nor have I ever seen that it had a deleterious effect on the character of those who embraced it; I have once known it to have a very good one.

I say this, not because I ever came within a hundred miles of accepting the thing myself, but in common fairness, and also as a tardy amends for the many hard, unjust and bitter things I once said about it to my friends. For Barfield's conversion to Anthroposophy marked the beginning of what I can only describe as the Great War between him and me. It was never, thank God, a quarrel, though it could have become one in a moment if he had used to me anything like the violence I allowed myself to him. But it was an almost incessant disputation, sometimes by letter and sometimes face to face, which lasted for years. And this Great War was one of the turning points of my life.

Barfield never made me an Anthroposophist, but his counterattacks destroyed forever two elements in my own thought. In the first place he made short work of what I have called my "chronological snobbery," the uncritical acceptance of the intellectual climate common to our own age and the assumption that whatever has gone out of date is on that account discredited. You must find why it went out of date. Was it ever refuted (and if so by whom, where, and how conclusively) or did it merely die away as fashions do? If the latter, this tells us nothing about its truth or falsehood. From seeing this, one passes to the realization that our own age is also "a period," and certainly has, like all periods, its own characteristic illusions. They are likeliest to lurk in those widespread assumptions which are so ingrained in the age that no one dares to attack or feels it necessary to defend them. In the second place he convinced me that the positions we had hitherto held left no room for any satisfactory theory of knowledge. We had been, in the technical sense of the term, "realists"; that is, we accepted as rock-bottom reality the universe revealed by the senses. But at the same time we continued to make for certain phenomena of consciousness all the claims that really went with a theistic or idealistic view. We maintained that abstract thought (if obedient to logical rules) gave indisputable truth, that our moral judgment was "valid," and our aesthetic experience not merely pleasing but "valuable." The view was, I think, common at the time; it runs through Bridges' *Testament of Beauty*, the work of Gilbert Murray, and Lord Russell's "Worship of a Free Man." Barfield convinced me that it was inconsistent. If thought were a purely subjective event, these claims for it would have to be abandoned. If one kept (as rock-bottom reality) the universe of the senses, aided by instruments and co-ordinated so as to form "science," then one would have to go much further—as many have since gone—and adopt a Behavioristic theory of logic, ethics, and aesthetics. But such a theory was, and is, unbelievable to me. I am using the word "unbelievable," which many use to mean "improbable" or even "undesirable," in a quite literal sense. I mean that the act of believing what the behaviorist believes is one that my mind simply will not perform. I cannot force my thought into that shape any more than I can scratch my ear with my big toe or pour wine out of a bottle into the cavity at the base of that same bottle. It is as final as a physi-

cal impossibility. I was therefore compelled to give up realism.
I had been trying to defend it ever since I began reading philosophy. Partly, no doubt, this was mere "cussedness." Idealism was then the dominant philosophy at Oxford and I was by
nature "against Government." But partly, too, realism satisfied
an emotional need. I wanted Nature to be quite independent
of our observation; something other, indifferent, self-existing.
(This went with the Jenkinian zest for rubbing one's nose in
the mere quiddity.) But now, it seemed to me, I had to give that
up. Unless I were to accept an unbelievable alternative, I must
admit that mind was no late-come epiphenomenon; that the
whole universe was, in the last resort, mental; that our logic
was participation in a cosmic *Logos*.

It is astonishing (at this time of day) that I could regard this
position as something quite distinct from Theism. I suspect
there was some willful blindness. But there were in those days
all sorts of blankets, insulators, and insurances which enabled
one to get all the conveniences of Theism, without believing in
God. The English Hegelians, writers like T. H. Green, Bradley, and Bosanquet (then mighty names), dealt in precisely such
wares. The Absolute Mind—better still, the Absolute—was
impersonal, or it knew itself (but not us?) only in us, and it was
so absolute that it wasn't really much more like a mind than
anything else. And anyway, the more muddled one got about
it and the more contradictions one committed, the more this
proved that our discursive thought moved only on the level
of "Appearance," and "Reality" must be somewhere else. And
where else but, of course, in the Absolute? There, not here, was
"the fuller splendor" behind the "sensuous curtain." The emotion that went with all this was certainly religious. But this was
a religion that cost nothing. We could talk religiously about the
Absolute: but there was no danger of Its doing anything about
us. It was "there"; safely and immovably "there." It would never
come "here," never (to be blunt) make a nuisance of Itself. This
quasi-religion was all a one-way street; all *eros* (as Dr. Nygren

would say) steaming up, but no *agape* darting down. There was nothing to fear; better still, nothing to obey.

Yet there was one really wholesome element in it. The Absolute was "there," and that "there" contained the reconciliation of all contraries, the transcendence of all finitude, the hidden glory which was the only perfectly real thing there is. In fact, it had much of the quality of Heaven. But it was a Heaven none of us could ever get to. For we are appearances. To be "there" is, by definition, not to be we. All who embrace such a philosophy live, like Dante's virtuous Pagans, "in desire without hope." Or like Spinoza they so love their God as to be unable even to wish that He should love them in return. I should be very sorry not to have passed through that experience. I think it is more religious than many experiences that have been called Christian. What I learned from the Idealists (and still most strongly hold) is this maxim: it is more important that Heaven should exist than that any of us should reach it.

And so the great Angler played His fish and I never dreamed that the hook was in my tongue. But two great advances had been made. Bergson had showed me necessary existence; and from Idealism I had come one step nearer to understanding the words, "We give thanks to thee for thy great glory." The Norse gods had given me the first hint of it; but then I didn't believe in them, and I did believe (so far as one can believe an *Unding*) in the Absolute.

XIV

Checkmate

The one principle of hell is—"I am my own."

GEORGE MACDONALD

I N THE summer of 1922 I finished Greats. As there were
no philosophical posts going, or none that I could get, my
long-suffering father offered me a fourth year at Oxford during which I read English so as to get a second string to my bow.
The Great War with Barfield had, I think, begun at this time.

No sooner had I entered the English School than I went
to George Gordon's discussion class. And there I made a new
friend. The very first words he spoke marked him out from the
ten or twelve others who were present; a man after my own
heart, and that too at an age when the instantaneous friendships of earlier youth were becoming rather rare events. His
name was Nevill Coghill. I soon had the shock of discovering
that he—clearly the most intelligent and best-informed man
in that class—was a Christian and a thoroughgoing supernat-
uralist. There were other traits that I liked but found (for I
was still very much a modern) oddly archaic; chivalry, honor,
courtesy, "freedom," and "gentillesse." One could imagine
him fighting a duel. He spoke much "ribaldry" but never "vil-
leinye." Barfield was beginning to overthrow my chronological

snobbery; Coghill gave it another blow. Had something really dropped out of our lives? Was the archaic simply the civilized, and the modern simply the barbaric? It will seem strange to many of my critics who regard me as a typical *laudator temporis acti* that this question should have arisen so comparatively late in my life. But then the key to my books is Donne's maxim, "The heresies that men leave are hated most." The things I assert most vigorously are those that I resisted long and accepted late.

These disturbing factors in Coghill ranged themselves with a wider disturbance which was now threatening my whole earlier outlook. All the books were beginning to turn against me. Indeed, I must have been as blind as a bat not to have seen, long before, the ludicrous contradiction between my theory of life and my actual experiences as a reader. George MacDonald had done more to me than any other writer; of course it was a pity he had that bee in his bonnet about Christianity. He was good *in spite of it*. Chesterton had more sense than all the other moderns put together; bating, of course, his Christianity. Johnson was one of the few authors whom I felt I could trust utterly; curiously enough, he had the same kink. Spenser and Milton by a strange coincidence had it too. Even among ancient authors the same paradox was to be found. The most religious (Plato, Aeschylus, Virgil) were clearly those on whom I could really feed. On the other hand, those writers who did not suffer from religion and with whom in theory my sympathy ought to have been complete—Shaw and Wells and Mill and Gibbon and Voltaire—all seemed a little thin; what as boys we called "tinny." It wasn't that I didn't like them. They were all (especially Gibbon) entertaining; but hardly more. There seemed to be no depth in them. They were too simple. The roughness and density of life did not appear in their books.

Now that I was reading more English, the paradox began to be aggravated. I was deeply moved by the *Dream of the Rood*; more deeply still by Langland: intoxicated (for a time) by Donne; deeply and lastingly satisfied by Thomas Browne. But the most alarming of all was George Herbert. Here was a man who seemed to me to excel all the authors I had ever read in conveying the very quality of life as we actually live it from moment to moment; but the wretched fellow, instead of doing it all directly, insisted on mediating it through what I would still have called "the Christian mythology." On the other hand most of the authors who might be claimed as precursors of modern enlightenment seemed to me very small beer and bored me cruelly. I thought Bacon (to speak frankly) a solemn, pretentious ass, yawned my way through Restoration Comedy, and, having manfully struggled on to the last line of *Don Juan*, wrote on the end leaf "Never again." The only non-Christians who seemed to me really to know anything were the Romantics; and a good many of them were dangerously tinged with something like religion, even at times with Christianity. The upshot of it all could nearly be expressed in a perversion of Roland's great line in the *Chanson*—

Christians are wrong, but all the rest are bores.

   The natural step would have been to inquire a little more closely whether the Christians were, after all, wrong. But I did not take it. I thought I could explain their superiority without that hypothesis. Absurdly (yet many Absolute Idealists have shared this absurdity) I thought that "the Christian myth" conveyed to unphilosophic minds as much of the truth, that is of Absolute Idealism, as they were capable of grasping, and that even that much put them above the irreligious. Those who could not rise to the notion of the Absolute would come nearer to the truth by belief in "a God" than by disbelief. Those who could not understand how, as Reasoners, we participated in a timeless and therefore deathless world, would get a symbolic shadow of the truth by believing in a life after death. The implication—that something which I and most other undergraduates could master without extraordinary pains would have been too hard for Plato, Dante, Hooker, and Pascal — did not yet strike me as absurd. I hope this is because I never looked it squarely in the face.

As the plot quickens and thickens toward its end, I leave out more and more of such matters as would go into a full autobiography. My father's death, with all the fortitude (even playfulness) which he displayed in his last illness, does not really come into the story I am telling. My brother was at that time in Shanghai. Nor would it be relevant to tell in detail how I became a temporary lecturer at Univ for a year and was elected a fellow of Magdalen in 1925. The worst is that I must leave undescribed many men whom I love and to whom I am deeply in debt; G. H. Stevenson and E. F. Carritt, my tutors, the Fark (but who could paint him anyway?), and five great Magdalen men who enlarged my very idea of what a learned life should be — P. V. M. Benecke, G. C. J. Webb, J. A. Smith, F. E. Brightman, and C. T. Onions. Except for Oldie, I have always been blessed both in my official and my unofficial teachers. In my earlier years at Magdalen I inhabited a world where hardly anything I wanted to know needed to be found out by my own unaided efforts. One or other of these could always give you a clue. ("You'll find something about it in Alanus. . . ." — "Macrobius would be the man to try. . . ." — "Doesn't Comparetti mention it?" . . . "Have you looked for it in Du Cange?") I found, as always, that the ripest are kindest to the raw and the most studious have most time to spare. When I began teaching for the English Faculty, I made two other friends, both Christians (these queer people seemed now to pop up on every side) who were later to give me much help in getting over the last stile. They were H. V. V. Dyson (then of Reading) and J. R. R. Tolkien. Friendship with the latter marked the breakdown of two old prejudices. At my first coming into the world I had been (implicitly) warned never to trust a Papist, and at my first coming into the English Faculty (explicitly) never to trust a philologist. Tolkien was both.

Realism had been abandoned; the New Look was somewhat damaged; and chronological snobbery was seriously shaken. All over the board my pieces were in the most disadvantageous positions. Soon I could no longer cherish even the illusion that the initiative lay with me. My Adversary began to make His final moves.

The first Move annihilated the last remains of the New Look. I was suddenly impelled to reread (which was certainly no business of mine at the moment) the *Hippolytus* of Euripides. In one chorus all that world's end imagery which I had rejected when I assumed my New Look rose before me. I liked, but did not yield; I tried to patronize it. But next day I was overwhelmed. There was a transitional moment of delicious uneasiness, and then—instantaneously—the long inhibition was over, the dry desert lay behind, I was off once more into the land of longing, my heart at once broken and exalted as it had never been since the old days at Bookham. There was nothing whatever to do about it; no question of returning to the desert. I had simply been ordered—or, rather, compelled—to "take that look off my face." And never to resume it either.

The next Move was intellectual, and consolidated the first Move. I read in Alexander's *Space Time and Deity* his theory of "Enjoyment" and "Contemplation." These are technical terms in Alexander's philosophy; "Enjoyment" has nothing to do with pleasure, nor "Contemplation" with the contemplative life. When you see a table you "enjoy" the act of seeing and "contemplate" the table. Later, if you took up Optics and thought about Seeing itself, you would be contemplating the seeing and enjoying the thought. In bereavement you contemplate the beloved and the beloved's death and, in Alexander's sense, "enjoy" the loneliness and grief; but a psychologist, if he were considering you as a case of melancholia, would be contemplating your grief and enjoying psychology. We do not "think a thought" in the same sense in which we "think that Herodotus is unreliable." When we think a thought, "thought" is a cognate accusative (like "blow" in "strike a blow"). We enjoy the thought (that Herodotus is unreliable) and, in so doing, contemplate the unreliability of Herodotus.

I accepted this distinction at once and have ever since regarded it as an indispensable tool of thought. A moment later its consequences—for me quite catastrophic—began to appear. It seemed to me self-evident that one essential property of love, hate, fear, hope, or desire was attention to their object. To cease thinking about or attending to the woman is, so far, to cease loving; to cease thinking about or attending to the dreaded thing is, so far, to cease being afraid. But to attend to your own love of fear is to cease attending to the loved or dreaded object. In other words the enjoyment and the contemplation of our inner activities are incompatible. You cannot hope and also think about hoping at the same moment; for in hope we look to hope's object and we interrupt this by (so to speak) turning round to look at the hope itself. Of course the two activities can and do alternate with great rapidity; but they are distinct and incompatible. This was not merely a logical result of Alexander's analysis, but could be verified in daily and hourly experience. The surest means of disarming an anger or a lust was to turn your attention from the girl or the insult and start examining the passion itself. The surest way of spoiling a pleasure was to start examining your satisfaction. But if so, it followed that all introspection is in one respect misleading. In introspection we try to look "inside ourselves" and see what is going on. But nearly everything that was going on a moment before is stopped by the very act of our turning to look at it. Unfortunately this does not mean that introspection finds nothing. On the contrary, it finds precisely what is left behind by the suspension of all our normal activities; and what is left behind is mainly mental images and physical sensations. The great error is to mistake this mere sediment or track or byproduct for the activities themselves. That is how men may come to believe that thought is only unspoken words, or the appreciation of poetry only a collection of mental pictures, when these in reality are what the thought or the appreciation, when interrupted, leave behind—like the swell at sea, working after the wind has dropped. Not, of course, that these activities, before we stopped them by introspection, were unconscious. We do not love, fear, or think without knowing it. Instead of the twofold division into Conscious and Unconscious, we need a threefold division: the Unconscious, the Enjoyed, and the Contemplated.

This discovery flashed a new light back on my whole life. I saw that all my waitings and watchings for Joy, all my vain hopes to find some mental content on which I could, so to speak, lay my finger and say, "This is it," had been a futile attempt to contemplate the enjoyed. All that such watching and waiting ever *could* find would be either an image (Asgard, the Western Garden, or what not) or a quiver in the diaphragm. I should never have to bother again about these images or sensations. I knew now that they were merely the mental track left by the passage of Joy—not the wave but the wave's imprint on the sand. The inherent dialectic of desire itself had in a way already shown me this; for all images and sensations, if idolatrously mistaken for Joy itself, soon honestly confessed themselves inadequate. All said, in the last resort, "It is not I. I am only a reminder. Look! Look! What do I remind you of?"

So far, so good. But it is at the next step that awe overtakes me. There was no doubt that Joy was a desire (and, in so far as it was also simultaneously a good, it was also a kind of love). But a desire is turned not to itself but to its object. Not only that, but it owes all its character to its object. Erotic love is not like desire for food, nay, a love for one woman differs from a love for another woman in the very same way and the very same degree as the two women differ from one another. Even our desire for one wine differs in tone from our desire for another. Our intellectual desire (curiosity) to know the true answer to a question is quite different from our desire to find that one answer, rather

than another, is true. The form of the desired is in the desire.
It is the object which makes the desire harsh or sweet, coarse
or choice, "high" or "low." It is the object that makes the desire
itself desirable or hateful. I perceived (and this was a wonder of
wonders) that just as I had been wrong in supposing that I really desired the Garden of the Hesperides, so also I had been
equally wrong in supposing that I desired Joy itself. Joy itself,
considered simply as an event in my own mind, turned out to
be of no value at all. All the value lay in that of which Joy was
the desiring. And that object, quite clearly, was no state of my
own mind or body at all. In a way, I had proved this by elimi-
nation. I had tried everything in my own mind and body; as it
were, asking myself, "Is it this you want? Is it this?" Last of all I
had asked if Joy itself was what I wanted; and, labelling it "aesthetic experience," had pretended I could answer Yes. But that
answer too had broken down. Inexorably Joy proclaimed, "You
want—I myself am your want of—something other, outside,
not you nor any state of you." I did *not* yet ask, Who is the desired? only What is it? But this brought me already into the
region of awe, for I thus understood that in deepest solitude
there is a road right out of the self, a commerce with something which, by refusing to identify itself with any object of the
senses, or anything whereof we have biological or social need,
or anything imagined, or any state of our own minds, proclaims
itself sheerly objective. Far more objective than bodies, for it is
not, like them, clothed in our senses; the naked Other, image-
less (though our imagination salutes it with a hundred images),
unknown, undefined, desired.

That was the second Move; equivalent, perhaps, to the loss
of one's last remaining bishop. The third Move did not seem
to me dangerous at the time. It consisted merely in linking up
this new *éclaircissement* about Joy with my idealistic philosophy.
I saw that Joy, as I now understood it, would fit in. We mortals, seen as the sciences see us and as we commonly see one
another, are mere "appearances." But appearances of the Abso-

lute. In so far as we really are at all (which isn't saying much) we have, so to speak, a root in the Absolute, which is the utter reality. And that is why we experience Joy: we yearn, rightly, for that unity which we can never reach except by ceasing to be the separate phenomenal beings called "we." Joy was not a deception. Its visitations were rather the moments of clearest consciousness we had, when we became aware of our fragmentary and phantasmal nature and ached for that impossible reunion which would annihilate us or that self-contradictory waking which would reveal, not that we had had, but that we *were*, a dream. This seemed quite satisfactory intellectually. Even emotionally too; for it matters more that Heaven should exist than that we should ever get there. What I did not notice was that I had passed an important milestone. Up till now my thoughts had been centrifugal; now the centripetal movement had begun. Considerations arising from quite different parts of my experience were beginning to come together with a click. This new dovetailing of my desire-life with my philosophy foreshadowed the day, now fast approaching, when I should be forced to take my "philosophy" more seriously than I ever intended. I did not foresee this. I was like a man who has lost "merely a pawn" and never dreams that this (in that state of the game) means mate in a few moves.

The fourth Move was more alarming. I was now teaching philosophy (I suspect very badly) as well as English. And my watered Hegelianism wouldn't serve for tutorial purposes.[1] A tutor must make things clear. Now the Absolute cannot be made clear. Do you mean Nobody-knows-what, or do you mean a superhuman mind and therefore (we may as well admit) a Person? After all, did Hegel and Bradley and all the rest of them ever do more than add mystifications to the simple, workable, theistic idealism of Berkeley? I thought not. And

---

1. Not, of course, that I thought it a tutor's business to make converts to his own philosophy. But I found I needed a position of my own as a basis from which to criticize my pupils' essays.

didn't Berkeley's "God" do all the same work as the Absolute, with the added advantage that we had at least some notion of what we meant by Him? I thought He did. So I was driven back into something like Berkeleyanism; but Berkeleyanism with a few top dressings of my own. I distinguished this philosophical "God" very sharply (or so I said) from "the God of popular religion." There was, I explained, no possibility of being in a personal relation with Him. For I thought He projected us as a dramatist projects his characters, and I could no more "meet" Him, than Hamlet could meet Shakespeare. I didn't call Him "God" either; I called Him "Spirit." One fights for one's remaining comforts.

Then I read Chesterton's *Everlasting Man* and for the first time saw the whole Christian outline of history set out in a form that seemed to me to make sense. Somehow I contrived not to be too badly shaken. You will remember that I already thought Chesterton the most sensible man alive "apart from his Christianity." Now, I veritably believe, I thought—I didn't of course *say;* words would have revealed the nonsense—that Christianity itself was very sensible "apart from its Christianity." But I hardly remember, for I had not long finished *The Everlasting Man* when something far more alarming happened to me. Early in 1926 the hardest boiled of all the atheists I ever knew sat in my room on the other side of the fire and remarked that the evidence for the historicity of the Gospels was really surprisingly good. "Rum thing," he went on. "All that stuff of Frazer's about the Dying God. Rum thing. It almost looks as if it had really happened once." To understand the shattering impact of it, you would need to know the man (who has certainly never since shown any interest in Christianity). If he, the cynic of cynics, the toughest of the toughs, were not—as I would still have put it—"safe," where could I turn? Was there then no escape?

The odd thing was that before God closed in on me, I was in fact offered what now appears a moment of wholly free choice.

In a sense. I was going up Headington Hill on the top of a bus. Without words and (I think) almost without images, a fact about myself was somehow presented to me. I became aware that I was holding something at bay, or shutting something out. Or, if you like, that I was wearing some stiff clothing, like corsets, or even a suit of armor, as if I were a lobster. I felt myself being, there and then, given a free choice. I could open the door or keep it shut; I could unbuckle the armor or keep it on. Neither choice was presented as a duty; no threat or promise was attached to either, though I knew that to open the door or to take off the corslet meant the incalculable. The choice appeared to be momentous but it was also strangely unemotional. I was moved by no desires or fears. In a sense I was not moved by anything. I chose to open, to unbuckle, to loosen the rein. I say, "I chose," yet it did not really seem possible to do the opposite. On the other hand, I was aware of no motives. You could argue that I was not a free agent, but I am more inclined to think that this came nearer to being a perfectly free act than most that I have ever done. Necessity may not be the opposite of freedom, and perhaps a man is most free when, instead of producing motives, he could only say, "I am what I do." Then came the repercussion on the imaginative level. I felt as if I were a man of snow at long last beginning to melt. The melting was starting in my back—drip-drip and presently trickle-trickle. I rather disliked the feeling.

The fox had been dislodged from Hegelian Wood and was now running in the open, "with all the wo in the world," bedraggled and weary, hounds barely a field behind. And nearly everyone was now (one way or another) in the pack; Plato, Dante, MacDonald, Herbert, Barfield, Tolkien, Dyson, Joy itself. Everyone and everything had joined the other side. Even my own pupil Griffiths—now Dom Bede Griffiths—though not yet himself a believer, did his share. Once, when he and Barfield were lunching in my room, I happened to refer to philosophy as "a subject." "It wasn't a *subject* to Plato," said Barfield, "it was a way." The quiet but fervent agreement of Griffiths, and the quick glance of understanding between these two, revealed to me my own frivolity. Enough had been thought, and said, and felt, and imagined. It was about time that something should be done.

For of course there had long been an ethic (theoretically) attached to my Idealism. I thought the business of us finite and half-unreal souls was to multiply the consciousness of Spirit by seeing the world from different positions while yet remaining qualitatively the same as Spirit; to be tied to a particular time and place and set of circumstances, yet there to will and think as Spirit itself does. This was hard; for the very act whereby Spirit projected souls and a world gave those souls different and competitive interests, so that there was a temptation to selfishness. But I thought each of us had it in his power to discount the emotional perspective produced by his own particular selfhood, just as we discount the optical perspective produced by our position in space. To prefer my own happiness to my neighbor's was like thinking that the nearest telegraph post was really the largest. The way to recover, and act upon, this universal and objective vision was daily and hourly to remember our true nature, to reascend or return into that Spirit which, in so far as we really were at all, we still were. Yes; but I now felt I had better try to do it. I faced at last (in MacDonald's words) "some thing to be neither more nor less nor other than *done*." An attempt at complete virtue must be made.

Really, a young Atheist cannot guard his faith too carefully. Dangers lie in wait for him on every side. You must not do, you must not even try to do, the will of the Father unless you are prepared to "know of the doctrine." All my acts, desires, and thoughts were to be brought into harmony with universal Spirit. For the first time I examined myself with a seriously practical purpose. And there I found what appalled me; a zoo of lusts, a bedlam of ambitions, a nursery of fears, a harem of fondled hatreds. My name was legion.

Of course I could do nothing—I could not last out one hour—without continual conscious recourse to what I called Spirit. But the fine, philosophical distinction between this and what ordinary people call "prayer to God" breaks down as soon as you start doing it in earnest. Idealism can be talked, and even felt; it cannot be lived. It became patently absurd to go on thinking of "Spirit" as either ignorant of, or passive to, my approaches. Even if my own philosophy were true, how could the initiative lie on my side? My own analogy, as I now first perceived, suggested the opposite: if Shakespeare and Hamlet could ever meet, it must be Shakespeare's doing.[2] Hamlet could initiate nothing. Perhaps, even now, my Absolute Spirit still differed in some way from the God of religion. The real issue was not, or not yet, there. The real terror was that if you seriously believed in even such a "God" or "Spirit" as I admitted, a wholly new situation developed. As the dry bones shook and came together in that dreadful valley of Ezekiel's, so now a philosophical theorem, cerebrally entertained, began to stir and heave and throw off its grave-cloths, and stood upright and became a living presence. I was to be allowed to play at philosophy no longer. It might, as I say, still be true that my "Spirit" differed in some way from "the God of popular religion." My Adversary waived the point. It sank into utter unimportance. He would not argue about it. He only said, "I am the Lord"; "I am that I am"; "I am."

People who are naturally religious find difficulty in understanding the horror of such a revelation. Amiable agnostics will talk cheerfully about "man's search for God." To me, as I then was, they might as well have talked about the mouse's search for the cat. The best image of my predicament is the meeting

---

2. *I.e.*, Shakespeare could, in principle, make himself appear as Author within the play, and write a dialogue between Hamlet and himself. The "Shakespeare" within the play would of course be at once Shakespeare and one of Shakespeare's creatures. It would bear some analogy to Incarnation.

of Mime and Wotan in the first act of *Siegfried; hier brauch' ich nicht Spärer noch Späher, Einsam will ich.* . . . (I've no use for spies and snoopers. I would be private. . . .)

Remember, I had always wanted, above all things, not to be "interfered with." I had wanted (mad wish) "to call my soul my own." I had been far more anxious to avoid suffering than to achieve delight. I had always aimed at limited liabilities. The supernatural itself had been to me, first, an illicit dram, and then, as by a drunkard's reaction, nauseous. Even my recent attempt to live my philosophy had secretly (I now knew) been hedged round by all sorts of reservations. I had pretty well known that my ideal of virtue would never be allowed to lead me into anything intolerably painful; I would be "reasonable." But now what had been an ideal became a command; and what might not be expected of one? Doubtless, by definition, God was Reason itself. But would He also be "reasonable" in that other, more comfortable, sense? Not the slightest assurance on that score was offered me. Total surrender, the absolute leap in the dark, were demanded. The reality with which no treaty can be made was upon me. The demand was not even "All or nothing." I think that stage had been passed, on the bus top when I unbuckled my armor and the snowman started to melt. Now, the demand was simply "All."

You must picture me alone in that room in Magdalen, night after night, feeling, whenever my mind lifted even for a second from my work, the steady, unrelenting approach of Him whom I so earnestly desired not to meet. That which I greatly feared had at last come upon me. In the Trinity Term of 1929 I gave in, and admitted that God was God, and knelt and prayed: perhaps, that night, the most dejected and reluctant convert in all England. I did not then see what is now the most shining and obvious thing; the Divine humility which will accept a convert even on such terms. The Prodigal Son at least walked home on his own feet. But who can duly adore that Love which will open the high gates to a prodigal who is brought in kicking, struggling, resentful, and darting his eyes in every direction for a chance of escape? The words *compelle intrare*, compel them to come in, have been so abused by wicked men that we shudder at them; but, properly understood, they plumb the depth of the Divine mercy. The hardness of God is kinder than the softness of men, and His compulsion is our liberation.

XV

The Beginning

Aliud est de silvestri cacumine videre patriam pacis
. . . et aliud tenere viam illuc ducentem.

ST. AUGUSTINE, *Confessions*, VII, XXI

For it is one thing to see the land of peace from a wooded
ridge . . . and another to tread the road that leads to it.

I T MUST be understood that the conversion recorded in
the last chapter was only to Theism, pure and simple, not
to Christianity. I knew nothing yet about the Incarnation. The
God to whom I surrendered was sheerly nonhuman.

It may be asked whether my terror was at all relieved by the
thought that I was now approaching the source from which
those arrows of Joy had been shot at me ever since childhood.
Not in the least. No slightest hint was vouchsafed me that
there ever had been or ever would be any connection between
God and Joy. If anything, it was the reverse. I had hoped that
the heart of reality might be of such a kind that we can best
symbolize it as a place; instead, I found it to be a Person. For
all I knew, the total rejection of what I called Joy might be
one of the demands, might be the very first demand, He would
make upon me. There was no strain of music from within, no

smell of eternal orchards at the threshold, when I was dragged through the doorway. No kind of desire was present at all.

My conversion involved as yet no belief in a future life. I now number it among my greatest mercies that I was permitted for several months, perhaps for a year, to know God and to attempt obedience without even raising that question. My training was like that of the Jews, to whom He revealed Himself centuries before there was a whisper of anything better (or worse) beyond the grave than shadowy and featureless *Sheol.* And I did not dream even of that. There are men, far better men than I, who have made immortality almost the central doctrine of their religion; but for my own part I have never seen how a preoccupation with that subject at the outset could fail to corrupt the whole thing. I had been brought up to believe that goodness was goodness only if it were disinterested, and that any hope of reward or fear of punishment contaminated the will. If I was wrong in this (the question is really much more complicated than I then perceived) my error was most tenderly allowed for. I was afraid that threats or promises would demoralize me; no threats or promises were made. The commands were inexorable, but they were backed by no "sanctions." God was to be obeyed simply because he was God. Long since, through the gods of Asgard, and later through the notion of the Absolute, He had taught me how a thing can be revered not for what it can do to us but for what it is in itself. That is why, though it was a terror, it was no surprise to learn that God is to be obeyed because of what He is in Himself. If you ask why we should obey God, in the last resort the answer is, "I am." To know God is to know that our obedience is due to Him. In His nature His sovereignty *de jure* is revealed.

Of course, as I have said, the matter is more complicated than that. The primal and necessary Being, the Creator, has sovereignty *de facto* as well as *de jure.* He has the power as well as the kingdom and the glory. But the *de jure* sovereignty was made known to me before the power, the right before the might. And for this I am thankful. I think it is well, even now, sometimes to say to ourselves, "God is such that if *(per impossibile)* his power could vanish and His other attributes remain, so that the supreme right were forever robbed of the supreme might, we should still owe Him precisely the same kind and degree of allegiance as we now do." On the other hand, while it is true to say that God's own nature is the real sanction of His commands, yet to understand this must, in the end, lead us to the conclusion that union with that Nature is bliss and separation from it horror. Thus Heaven and Hell come in. But it may well be that to think much of either except in this context of thought, to hypostatize them as if they had a substantial meaning apart from the presence or absence of God, corrupts the doctrine of both and corrupts us while we so think of them.

The last stage in my story, the transition from mere Theism to Christianity, is the one on which I am now least informed. Since it is also the most recent, this ignorance may seem strange. I think there are two reasons. One is that as we grow older we remember the more distant past better than what is nearer. But the other is, I believe, that one of the first results of my Theistic conversion was a marked decrease (and high time, as all readers of this book will agree) in the fussy attentiveness which I had so long paid to the progress of my own opinions and the states of my own mind. For many healthy extroverts self-examination first begins with conversion. For me it was almost the other way round. Self-examination did of course continue. But it was (I suppose, for I cannot quite remember) at stated intervals, and for a practical purpose; a duty, a discipline, an uncomfortable thing, no longer a hobby or a habit. To believe and to pray were the beginning of extroversion. I had been, as they say, "taken out of myself." If Theism had done nothing else for me, I should still be thankful that it cured me of the time-wasting and foolish practice of keeping a diary. (Even for autobiographical purposes a diary is nothing like so useful as I had hoped. You put down each day what you think important; but of course you cannot each day see what will prove to have been important in the long run.[1])

As soon as I became a Theist I started attending my parish church on Sundays and my college chapel on weekdays; not because I believed in Christianity, nor because I thought the difference between it and simple Theism a small one, but because I thought one ought to "fly one's flag" by some unmistakable overt sign. I was acting in obedience to a (perhaps mistaken) sense of honor. The idea of churchmanship was to me wholly unattractive. I was not in the least anticlerical, but I was deeply antiecclesiastical. That curates and archdeacons and churchwardens should exist was admirable. They gratified my Jenkinian love of everything which has its own strong flavor. And (apart from Oldie) I had been fortunate in my clerical acquaintances; especially in Adam Fox, the Dean of Divinity at Magdalen, and in Arthur Barton (later Archbishop of Dublin) who had been our Rector at home in Ireland. (He, by the by, had once suffered under Oldie at Belsen. Speaking of Oldie's death, I had said to him, "Well, we shan't see *him* again." "You mean," he answered with a grim smile, "we *hope* we shan't.") But though I liked clergymen as I liked bears, I had as little wish to be in the Church as in the zoo. It was, to begin with, a kind of collective; a wearisome "get-together" affair. I couldn't yet see how a concern of that sort should have anything to do with one's spiritual life. To me, religion ought to have been a matter of good men praying alone and meeting by twos and threes to talk of spiritual matters. And then the fussy, time-wasting botheration of it all! the bells, the crowds, the umbrellas, the notices, the bustle, the perpetual arranging and orga-

---

1. The only real good I got from keeping a diary was that it taught me a just appreciation of Boswell's amazing genius. I tried very hard to reproduce conversations, in some of which very amusing and striking people had taken part. But none of these people came to life in the diary at all. Obviously something quite different from mere accurate reporting went to the presentation of Boswell's Langton, Beauclerk, Wilkes, and the rest.

nizing. Hymns were (and are) extremely disagreeable to me. Of all musical instruments I liked (and like) the organ least. I have, too, a sort of spiritual *gaucherie* which makes me unapt to participate in any rite.

Thus my churchgoing was a merely symbolical and provisional practice. If it in fact helped to move me in the Christian direction, I was and am unaware of this. My chief companion on this stage of the road was Griffiths, with whom I kept up a copious correspondence. Both now believed in God, and were ready to Hear more of Him from any source, Pagan or Christian. In my mind (I cannot now answer for his, and he has told his own story admirably in *The Golden String*) the perplexing multiplicity of "religions" began to sort itself out. The real clue had been put into my hand by that hard-boiled Atheist when he said, "Rum thing, all that about the Dying God. Seems to have really happened once"; by him and by Barfield's encouragement of a more respectful, if not more delighted, attitude to Pagan myth. The question was no longer to find the one simply true religion among a thousand religions simply false. It was rather, "Where has religion reached its true maturity? Where, if anywhere, have the hints of all Paganism been fulfilled?" With the irreligious I was no longer concerned; their view of life was henceforth out of court. As against them, the whole mass of those who had worshiped—all who had danced and sung and sacrificed and trembled and adored—were clearly right. But the intellect and the conscience, as well as the orgy and the ritual, must be our guide. There could be no question of going back to primitive, untheologized and unmoralized, Paganism. The God whom I had at last acknowledged was one, and was righteous. Paganism had been only the childhood of religion, or only a prophetic dream. Where was the thing full grown? or where was the awakening? (*The Everlasting Man* was helping me here.) There were really only two answers possible: either in Hinduism or in Christianity. Everything else was either a preparation for, or else (in the French sense) a *vulgarization* of, these. Whatever you could find elsewhere you could find better in one of these. But Hinduism seemed to have two disqualifications. For one thing, it appeared to be not so much a moralized and philosophical maturity of Paganism as a mere oil-and-water coexistence of philosophy side by side with Paganism unpurged; the Brahmin meditating in the forest, and, in the village a few miles away, temple prostitution, *sati*, cruelty, monstrosity. And secondly, there was no such historical claim as in Christianity. I was by now too experienced in literary criticism to regard the Gospels as myths. They had not the mythical taste. And yet the very matter which they set down in their artless, historical fashion—those narrow, unattractive Jews, too blind to the mythical wealth of the Pagan world around them—was precisely the matter of the great myths. If ever a myth had become fact, had been incarnated, it would be just like this. And nothing else in all literature was just like this. Myths were like it in one way. Histories were like it in another. But nothing was simply like it. And no person was like the Person it depicted; as real, as recognizable, through all that depth of time, as Plato's Socrates or Boswell's Johnson (ten times more so than Eckermann's Goethe or Lockhart's Scott), yet also numinous, lit by a light from beyond the world, a god. But if a god—we are no longer polytheists—then not a god, but God. Here and here only in all time the myth must have become fact; the Word, flesh; God, Man. This is not "a religion," nor "a philosophy." It is the summing up and actuality of them all.

As I have said, I speak of this last transition less certainly than of any which went before it, and it may be that in the preceding paragraph I have mixed thoughts that came later. But I can hardly be wrong about the main lines. Of one thing I am sure. As I drew near the conclusion, I felt a resistance almost as strong as my previous resistance to Theism. As strong, but shorter-lived, for I understood it better. Every step I had taken, from the Absolute to "Spirit" and from "Spirit" to "God," had been a step toward the more concrete, the more imminent, the more compulsive. At each step one had less chance "to call one's soul one's own." To accept the Incarnation was a further step in the same direction. It brings God nearer, or near in a new way. And this, I found, was something I had not wanted. But to recognize the ground for my evasion was of course to recognize both its shame and its futility. I know very well when, but hardly how, the final step was taken. I was driven to Whipsnade one sunny morning. When we set out I did not believe that Jesus Christ is the Son of God, and when we reached the zoo I did. Yet I had not exactly spent the journey in thought. Nor in great emotion. "Emotional" is perhaps the last word we can apply to some of the most important events. It was more like when a man, after long sleep, still lying motionless in bed, becomes aware that he is now awake. And it was, like that moment on top of the bus, ambiguous. Freedom, or necessity? Or do they differ at their maximum? At that maximum a man is what he does; there is nothing of him left over or outside the act. As for what we commonly call Will, and what we commonly call Emotion, I fancy these usually talk too loud, protest too much, to be quite believed, and we have a secret suspicion that the great passion or the iron resolution is partly a put-up job.

They have spoiled Whipsnade since then. Wallaby Wood, with the birds singing overhead and the bluebells underfoot and the Wallabies hopping all round one, was almost Eden come again.

But what, in conclusion, of Joy? for that, after all, is what the story has mainly been about. To tell you the truth, the subject has lost nearly all interest for me since I became a Christian. I cannot, indeed, complain, like Wordsworth, that the visionary gleam has passed away. I believe (if the thing were at all worth recording) that the old stab, the old bittersweet, has come to me as often and as sharply since my conversion as at any time of my life whatever. But I now know that the experience, considered as a state of my own mind, had never had the kind of importance I once gave it. It was valuable only as a pointer to something other and outer. While that other was in doubt, the pointer naturally loomed large in my thoughts. When we are lost in the woods the sight of a signpost is a great matter. He who first sees it cries, "Look!" The whole party gathers round and stares. But when we have found the road and are passing signposts every few miles, we shall not stop and stare. They will encourage us and we shall be grateful to the authority that set them up. But we shall not stop and stare, or not much; not on this road, though their pillars are of silver and their lettering of gold. "We would be at Jerusalem."

Not, of course, that I don't often catch myself stopping to stare at roadside objects of even less importance.

The Four Loves

To Chad Walsh

That our affection kills us not, nor dye.

— DONNE

Contents

Introduction

G OD is love," says St. John. When I first tried to write this book I thought that his maxim would provide me with a very plain highroad through the whole subject. I thought I should be able to say that human loves deserved to be called loves at all just in so far as they resembled that Love which is God. The first distinction I made was therefore between what I called Gift-love and Need-love. The typical example of Gift-love would be that love which moves a man to work and plan and save for the future well-being of his family which he will die without sharing or seeing; of the second, that which sends a lonely or frightened child to its mother's arms.

There was no doubt which was more like Love Himself. Divine Love is Gift-love. The Father gives all He is and has to the Son. The Son gives Himself back to the Father, and gives Himself to the world, and for the world to the Father, and thus gives the world (in Himself) back to the Father too.

And what, on the other hand, can be less like anything we believe of God's life than Need-love? He lacks nothing, but our Need-love, as Plato saw, is "the son of Poverty." It is the accurate reflection in consciousness of our actual nature. We are born helpless. As soon as we are fully conscious we discover loneliness. We need others physically, emotionally, intellectually; we need them if we are to know anything, even ourselves.

I was looking forward to writing some fairly easy panegyrics
on the first sort of love and disparagements of the second. And
much of what I was going to say still seems to me to be true.
I still think that if all we mean by our love is a craving to be
loved, we are in a very deplorable state. But I would not now
say (with my master, MacDonald) that if we mean only this
craving we are mistaking for love something that is not love at
all. I cannot now deny the name *love* to Need-love. Every time I
have tried to think the thing out along those lines I have ended
in puzzles and contradictions. The reality is more complicated
than I supposed.

First of all, we do violence to most languages, including our
own, if we do not call Need-love "love." Of course language
is not an infallible guide, but it contains, with all its defects,
a good deal of stored insight and experience. If you begin by
flouting it, it has a way of avenging itself later on. We had better not follow Humpty Dumpty in making words mean whatever we please.

Secondly, we must be cautious about calling Need-love
"mere selfishness." *Mere* is always a dangerous word. No doubt
Need-love, like all our impulses, can be selfishly indulged. A
tyrannous and gluttonous demand for affection can be a horrible thing. But in ordinary life no one calls a child selfish because it turns for comfort to its mother; nor an adult who turns
to his fellow "for company." Those, whether children or adults,
who do so least are not usually the most selfless. Where Need-
love is felt there may be reasons for denying or totally mortify-
ing it; but not to feel it is in general the mark of the cold egoist.
Since we do in reality need one another ("it is not good for man
to be alone"), then the failure of this need to appear as Need-
love in consciousness—in other words, the illusory feeling that
it *is* good for us to be alone—is a bad spiritual symptom; just as
lack of appetite is a bad medical symptom because men do really need food.

But thirdly, we come to something far more important. Every Christian would agree that a man's spiritual health is exactly proportional to his love for God. But man's love for God, from the very nature of the case, must always be very largely, and must often be entirely, a Need-love. This is obvious when we implore forgiveness for our sins or support in our tribulations. But in the long run it is perhaps even more apparent in our growing—for it ought to be growing—awareness that our whole being by its very nature is one vast need; incomplete, preparatory, empty yet cluttered, crying out for Him who can untie things that are now knotted together and tie up things that are still dangling loose. I do not say that man can never bring to God anything at all but sheer Need-love. Exalted souls may tell us of a reach beyond that. But they would also, I think, be the first to tell us that those heights would cease to be true Graces, would become Neo-Platonic or finally diabolical illusions, the moment a man dared to think that he could live on them and henceforth drop out the element of need. "The highest," says the *Imitation*, "does not stand without the lowest." It would be a bold and silly creature that came before its Creator with the boast "I'm no beggar. I love you disinterestedly." Those who come nearest to a Gift-love for God will next moment, even at the very same moment, be beating their breasts with the publican and laying their indigence before the only real Giver. And God will have it so. He addresses our Need-love: "Come unto me all ye that travail and are heavy-laden," or, in the Old Testament, "Open your mouth wide and I will fill it."

Thus one Need-love, the greatest of all, either coincides with or at least makes a main ingredient in man's highest, healthiest, and most realistic spiritual condition. A very strange corollary follows. Man approaches God most nearly when he is in one sense least like God. For what can be more unlike than fullness and need, sovereignty and humility, righteousness and penitence, limitless power and a cry for help? This paradox staggered me when I first ran into it; it also wrecked all my previous attempts to write about love. When we face it, something like this seems to result.

We must distinguish two things which might both possibly be called "nearness to God." One is likeness to God. God has impressed some sort of likeness to Himself, I suppose, in all that He has made. Space and time, in their own fashion, mirror His greatness; all life, His fecundity; animal life, His activity. Man has a more important likeness than these by being rational. Angels, we believe, have likenesses which Man lacks: immortality and intuitive knowledge. In that way all men, whether good or bad, all angels including those that fell, are more like God than the animals are. Their natures are in this sense "nearer" to the Divine Nature. But, secondly, there is what we may call nearness of approach. If this is what we mean, the states in which a man is "nearest" to God are those in which he is most surely and swiftly approaching his final union with God, vision of God and enjoyment of God. And as soon as we distinguish nearness-by-likeness and nearness-of-approach, we see that they do not necessarily coincide. They may or may not.

Perhaps an analogy may help. Let us suppose that we are doing a mountain walk to the village which is our home. At midday we come to the top of a cliff where we are, in space, very near it because it is just below us. We could drop a stone into it. But as we are no cragsmen we can't get down. We must go a long way round; five miles, maybe. At many points during that *détour* we shall, statically, be farther from the village than we were when we sat above the cliff. But only statically. In terms of progress we shall be far "nearer" our baths and teas.

Since God is blessed, omnipotent, sovereign and creative, there is obviously a sense in which happiness, strength, freedom and fertility (whether of mind or body), wherever they appear in human life, constitute likenesses, and in that way proximities, to God. But no one supposes that the possession of

these gifts has any necessary connection with our sanctification. No kind of riches is a passport to the Kingdom of Heaven.

At the cliff's top we are near the village, but however long
we sit there we shall never be any nearer to our bath and our
tea. So here; the likeness, and in that sense nearness, to Himself which God has conferred upon certain creatures and certain states of those creatures is something finished, built in.
What is near Him by likeness is never, by that fact alone, going to be any nearer. But nearness of approach is, by definition, increasing nearness. And whereas the likeness is given to
us—and can be received with or without thanks, can be used
or abused—the approach, however initiated and supported by
Grace, is something we must do. Creatures are made in their
varying ways images of God without their own collaboration
or even consent. It is not so that they become sons of God.
And the likeness they receive by sonship is not that of images
or portraits. It is in one way more than likeness, for it is union
or unity with God in will; but this is consistent with all the dif-
ferences we have been considering. Hence, as a better writer
has said, our imitation of God in this life—that is, our willed
imitation as distinct from any of the likenesses which He has
impressed upon our natures or states—must be an imitation
of God incarnate: our model is the Jesus, not only of Calvary,
but of the workshop, the roads, the crowds, the clamorous demands and surly oppositions, the lack of all peace and privacy,
the interruptions. For this, so strangely unlike anything we can
attribute to the Divine life in itself, is apparently not only like,
but is, the Divine life operating under human conditions.

I must now explain why I have found this distinction necessary to any treatment of our loves. St. John's saying that God is
love has long been balanced in my mind against the remark of
a modern author (M. Denis de Rougemont) that "love ceases to
be a demon only when he ceases to be a god"; which of course
can be re-stated in the form "begins to be a demon the moment

he begins to be a god." This balance seems to me an indispensable safeguard. If we ignore it the truth that God is love may slyly come to mean for us the converse, that love is God.

I suppose that everyone who has thought about the matter will see what M. de Rougemont meant. Every human love, at its height, has a tendency to claim for itself a divine authority. Its voice tends to sound as if it were the will of God Himself. It tells us not to count the cost, it demands of us a total commitment, it attempts to over-ride all other claims and insinuates that any action which is sincerely done "for love's sake" is thereby lawful and even meritorious. That erotic love and love of one's country may thus attempt to "become gods" is generally recognised. But family affection may do the same. So, in a different way, may friendship. I shall not here elaborate the point, for it will meet us again and again in later chapters.

Now it must be noticed that the natural loves make this blasphemous claim not when they are in their worst, but when they are in their best, natural condition; when they are what our grandfathers called "pure" or "noble." This is especially obvious in the erotic sphere. A faithful and genuinely self-sacrificing passion will speak to us with what seems the voice of God. Merely animal or frivolous lust will not. It will corrupt its addict in a dozen ways, but not in that way; a man may act upon such feelings but he cannot revere them any more than a man who scratches reveres the itch. A silly woman's temporary indulgence, which is really self-indulgence, to a spoiled child—her living doll while the fit lasts—is much less likely to "become a god" than the deep, narrow devotion of a woman who (quite really) "lives for her son." And I am inclined to think that the sort of love for a man's country which is worked up by beer and brass bands will not lead him to do much harm (or much good) for her sake. It will probably be fully discharged by ordering another drink and joining in the chorus.

And this of course is what we ought to expect. Our loves do not make their claim to divinity until the claim becomes plausible. It does not become plausible until there is in them a real resemblance to God, to Love Himself. Let us here make no mistake. Our Gift-loves are really God-like; and among our Gift-loves those are most God-like which are most boundless and unwearied in giving. All the things the poets say about them are true. Their joy, their energy, their patience, their readiness to forgive, their desire for the good of the beloved—all this is a real and all but adorable image of the Divine life. In its presence we are right to thank God "who has given such power to men." We may say, quite truly and in an intelligible sense, that those who love greatly are "near" to God. But of course it is "nearness by likeness." It will not of itself produce "nearness of approach." The likeness has been given us. It has no necessary connection with that slow and painful approach which must be our own (though by no means our unaided) task. Meanwhile, however, the likeness is a splendour. That is why we may mistake Like for Same. We may give our human loves the unconditional allegiance which we owe only to God. Then they become gods: then they become demons. Then they will destroy us, and also destroy themselves. For natural loves that are allowed to become gods do not remain loves. They are still called so, but can become in fact complicated forms of hatred.

Our Need-loves may be greedy and exacting but they do not set up to be gods. They are not near enough (by likeness) to God to attempt that.

It follows from what has been said that we must join neither the idolaters nor the "debunkers" of human love. Idolatry both of erotic love and of "the domestic affections" was the great error of nineteenth-century literature. Browning, Kingsley, and Patmore sometimes talk as if they thought that falling in love was the same thing as sanctification; the novelists habitually oppose to "the World" not the Kingdom of Heaven but the home. We live in the reaction against this. The debunkers stigmatise as slush and sentimentality a very great deal of what their fathers said in praise of love. They are always pulling up and exposing the grubby roots of our natural loves. But I take it we must listen neither "to the over-wise nor to the over-foolish giant." The highest does not stand without the lowest. A plant must have roots below as well as sunlight above and roots must be grubby. Much of the grubbiness is clean dirt if only you will leave it in the garden and not keep on sprinkling it over the library table. The human loves can be glorious images of Divine love. No less than that: but also no more—proximities of likeness which in one instance may help, and in another may hinder, proximity of approach. Sometimes perhaps they have not very much to do with it either way.

Likings and Loves for
the Sub-Human

MOST of my generation were reproved as children for saying that we "loved" strawberries, and some people take a pride in the fact that English has the two verbs *love* and *like* while French has to get on with *aimer* for both. But French has a good many other languages on its side. Indeed it very often has actual English usage on its side too. Nearly all speakers, however pedantic or however pious, talk every day about "loving" a food, a game, or a pursuit. And in fact there is a continuity between our elementary likings for things and our loves for people. Since "the highest does not stand without the lowest" we had better begin at the bottom, with mere likings; and since to "like" anything means to take some sort of pleasure in it, we must begin with pleasure.

Now it is a very old discovery that pleasures can be divided into two classes; those which would not be pleasures at all unless they were preceded by desire, and those which are pleasures in their own right and need no such preparation. An example of the first would be a drink of water. This is a pleasure if you are thirsty and a great one if you are very thirsty. But probably no one in the world, except in obedience to thirst or to a doctor's orders, ever poured himself out a glass of water and drank it just for the fun of the thing. An example of the other class would be the unsought and unexpected pleasures of smell—the breath from a bean-field or a row of sweet-peas meeting you on your morning walk. You were in want of nothing, completely contented, before it; the pleasure, which may be very great, is an unsolicited, super-added gift. I am taking very simple instances for clarity's sake, and of course there are many complications. If you are given coffee or beer where you expected (and would have been satisfied with) water, then of course you get a pleasure of the first kind (allaying of thirst) and one of the second (a nice taste) at the same time. Again, an addiction may turn what was once a pleasure of the second kind into one of the first. For the temperate man an occasional glass of wine is a treat—like the smell of the bean-field. But to the alcoholic, whose palate and digestion have long since been destroyed, no liquor gives any pleasure except that of relief from an unbearable craving. So far as he can still discern tastes at all, he rather dislikes it; but it is better than the misery of remaining sober. Yet through all their permutations and combinations the distinction between the two classes remains tolerably clear. We may call them Need-pleasures and Pleasures of Appreciation.

The resemblance between these Need-pleasures and the "Need-loves" in my first chapter will occur to everyone. But there, you remember, I confessed that I had had to resist a tendency to disparage the Need-loves or even to say they were not loves at all. Here, for most people, there may be an opposite inclination. It would be very easy to spread ourselves in laudation of the Need-pleasures and to frown upon those that are Appreciative: the one so natural (a word to conjure with), so necessary, so shielded from excess by its very naturalness, the other unnecessary and opening the door to every kind of luxury and vice. If we were short of matter on this theme we could turn on the tap by opening the works of the Stoics and it would run till we had a bathful. But throughout this inquiry we must be careful never to adopt prematurely a moral or evaluating attitude. The human mind is generally far more eager to praise and dispraise than to describe and define. It wants to make every distinction a distinction of value; hence those fatal critics who can never point out the differing quality of two poets without putting them in an order of preference as if they were candidates for a prize. We must do nothing of the sort about the pleasures. The reality is too complicated. We are already warned of this by the fact that Need-pleasure is the state in which Appreciative pleasures end up when they go bad (by addiction).

For us at any rate the importance of the two sorts of pleasure lies in the extent to which they foreshadow characteristics in our "loves" (properly so called).

The thirsty man who has just drunk off a tumbler of water may say, "By Jove, I *wanted* that." So may the alcoholic who has just had his "nip." The man who passes the sweet-peas in his morning walk is more likely to say, "How lovely the smell *is*." The connoisseur after his first sip of the famous claret, may similarly say, "This *is* a great wine." When Need-pleasures are in question we tend to make statements about ourselves in the past tense; when Appreciative pleasures are in question we tend to make statements about the object in the present tense. It is easy to see why.

Shakespeare has described the satisfaction of a tyrannous lust as something

> *Past reason hunted and, no sooner had,*
> *Past reason hated.*

But the most innocent and necessary of Need-pleasures have about them something of the same character—only something, of course. They are not hated once we have had them, but they certainly "die on us" with extraordinary abruptness, and completely. The scullery tap and the tumbler are very attractive indeed when we come in parched from mowing the grass; six seconds later they are emptied of all interest. The smell of frying food is very different before and after breakfast. And, if you will forgive me for citing the most extreme instance of all, have there not for most of us been moments (in a strange town) when the sight of the word GENTLEMEN over a door has roused a joy almost worthy of celebration in verse?

Pleasures of Appreciation are very different. They make us feel that something has not merely gratified our senses in fact but claimed our appreciation by right. The connoisseur does not merely enjoy his claret as he might enjoy warming his feet when they were cold. He feels that here is a wine that deserves his full attention; that justifies all the tradition and skill that have gone to its making and all the years of training that have made his own palate fit to judge it. There is even a glimmering of unselfishness in his attitude. He wants the wine to be preserved and kept in good condition, not entirely for his own sake. Even if he were on his death-bed and was never going to drink wine again, he would be horrified at the thought of this vintage being spilled or spoiled or even drunk by clods (like myself) who can't tell a good claret from a bad. And so with the man who passes the sweet-peas. He does not simply enjoy, he feels that this fragrance somehow deserves to be enjoyed. He would blame himself if he went past inattentive and undelighted. It would be blockish, insensitive. It would be a shame that so fine a thing should have been wasted on him. He will remember the delicious moment years hence. He will be sorry when he hears that the garden past which his walk led him that day has now been swallowed up by cinemas, garages, and the new by-pass.

Scientifically both sorts of pleasure are, no doubt, relative to our organisms. But the Need-pleasures loudly proclaim their relativity not only to the human frame but to its momentary condition, and outside that relation have no meaning or interest for us at all. The objects which afford pleasures of appreciation give us the feeling—whether irrational or not—that we somehow owe it to them to savour, to attend to and praise them. "It would be a sin to set a wine like that before Lewis," says the expert in claret. "How can you walk past this garden taking no notice of the smell?" we ask. But we should never feel this about a Need-pleasure: never blame ourselves or others for not having been thirsty and therefore walking past a well without taking a drink of water.

How the Need-pleasures foreshadow our Need-loves is obvious enough. In the latter the beloved is seen in relation to our own needs, just as the scullery tap is seen by the thirsty man or the glass of gin by the alcoholic. And the Need-love, like the Need-pleasure, will not last longer than the need. This does not, fortunately, mean that all affections which begin in Need-love are transitory. The need itself may be permanent or recurrent. Another kind of love may be grafted on the Need-love. Moral principles (conjugal fidelity, filial piety, gratitude, and the like) may preserve the relationship for a lifetime. But where Need-love is left unaided we can hardly expect it not to "die on us" once the need is no more. That is why the world rings with the complaints of mothers whose grown-up children neglect them and of forsaken mistresses whose lovers' love was pure need—which they have satisfied. Our Need-love for God is in a different position because our need of Him can never end either in this world or in any other. But our awareness of it can, and then the Need-love dies too. "The Devil was sick, the Devil a monk would be." There seems no reason for describing as hypocritical the short-lived piety of those whose religion fades away once they have emerged from "danger, necessity, or tribulation." Why should they not have been sincere? They were desperate and they howled for help. Who wouldn't?

What Appreciative pleasure foreshadows is not so quickly described.

First of all, it is the starting point for our whole experience of beauty. It is impossible to draw a line below which such pleasures are "sensual" and above which they are "aesthetic." The experiences of the expert in claret already contain elements of concentration, judgment, and disciplined perceptiveness, which are not sensual; those of the musician still contain elements which are. There is no frontier—there is seamless continuity—between the sensuous pleasure of garden smells and an enjoyment of the countryside (or "beauty") as a whole, or even our enjoyment of the painters and poets who treat it.

And, as we have seen, there is in these pleasures from the very beginning a shadow or dawn of, or an invitation to, disinterestedness. Of course in one way we can be disinterested or unselfish, and far more heroically so, about the Need-pleasures: it is a cup of water that the wounded Sidney sacrifices to the dying soldier. But that is not the sort of disinterestedness I now mean. Sidney loves his neighbour. But in the Appreciative pleasures, even at their lowest, and more and more as they grow up into the full appreciation of all beauty, we get something that we can hardly help calling *love* and hardly help calling *disinterested*, towards the object itself. It is the feeling which would make a man unwilling to deface a great picture even if he were the last man left alive and himself about to die; which makes us glad of unspoiled forests that we shall never see; which makes us anxious that the garden or bean-field should continue to exist. We do not merely like the things; we pronounce them, in a momentarily God-like sense, "very good."

And now our principle of starting at the lowest—without which "the highest does not stand"—begins to pay a dividend. It has revealed to me a deficiency in our previous classification of the loves into those of Need and those of Gift. There is a third element in love, no less important than these, which is foreshadowed by our Appreciative pleasures. This judgment that the object is very good, this attention (almost homage) offered to it as a kind of debt, this wish that it should be and should continue being what it is even if we were never to enjoy it, can go out not only to things but to persons. When it is offered to a woman we call it admiration; when to a man, hero-worship; when to God, worship simply.

Need-love cries to God from our poverty; Gift-love longs to serve, or even to suffer for, God; Appreciative love says: "We give thanks to thee for thy great glory." Need-love says of a woman "I cannot live without her"; Gift-love longs to give her happiness, comfort, protection—if possible, wealth; Appreciative love gazes and holds its breath and is silent, rejoices that such a wonder should exist even if not for him, will not be wholly dejected by losing her, would rather have it so than never to have seen her at all.

We murder to dissect. In actual life, thank God, the three elements of love mix and succeed one another, moment by moment. Perhaps none of them except Need-love ever exists alone, in "chemical" purity, for more than a few seconds. And perhaps that is because nothing about us except our neediness is, in this life, permanent.

Two forms of love for what is not personal demand special treatment.

For some people, perhaps especially for Englishmen and Russians, what we call "the love of nature" is a permanent and serious sentiment. I mean here that love of nature which cannot be adequately classified simply as an instance of our love for beauty. Of course many natural objects—trees, flowers and animals—are beautiful. But the nature-lovers whom I have in mind are not very much concerned with individual beautiful objects of that sort. The man who is distracts them. An enthusiastic botanist is for them a dreadful companion on a ramble. He is always stopping to draw their attention to particulars. Nor are they looking for "views" or landscapes. Wordsworth, their spokesman, strongly deprecates this. It leads to "a comparison of scene with scene," makes you "pamper" yourself with "meagre novelties of colour and proportion." While you are busying yourself with this critical and discriminating activity you lose what really matters—the "moods of time and season," the "spirit" of the place. And of course Wordsworth is right. That is why, if you love nature in his fashion, a landscape painter is (out of doors) an even worse companion than a botanist.

It is the "moods" or the "spirit" that matter. Nature-lovers want to receive as fully as possible whatever nature, at each particular time and place, is, so to speak, saying. The obvious richness, grace, and harmony of some scenes are no more precious to them than the grimness, bleakness, terror, monotony, or "visionary dreariness" of others. The featureless itself gets from them a willing response. It is one more word uttered by nature. They lay themselves bare to the sheer quality of every countryside, every hour of the day. They want to absorb it into themselves, to be coloured through and through by it.

This experience, like so many others, after being lauded to the skies in the nineteenth century, has been debunked by the moderns. And one must certainly concede to the debunkers that Wordsworth, not when he was communicating it as a poet, but when he was merely talking about it as a philosopher (or philosophaster), said some very silly things. It is silly, unless you have found any evidence, to believe that flowers enjoy the air they breathe, and sillier not to add that, if this were true, flowers would undoubtedly have pains as well as pleasures. Nor have many people been taught moral philosophy by an "impulse from a vernal wood."

If they were, it would not necessarily be the sort of moral philosophy Wordsworth would have approved. It might be that of ruthless competition. For some moderns I think it is. They love nature in so far as, for them, she calls to "the dark gods in the blood"; not although, but because, sex and hunger and sheer power there operate without pity or shame.

If you take nature as a teacher she will teach you exactly the lessons you had already decided to learn; this is only another way of saying that nature does not teach. The tendency to take her as a teacher is obviously very easily grafted on to the experience we call "love of nature." But it is only a graft. While we are actually subjected to them, the "moods" and "spirits" of nature point no morals. Overwhelming gaiety, insupportable grandeur, sombre desolation are flung at you. Make what you can of them, if you must make at all. The only imperative that nature utters is, "Look. Listen. Attend."

The fact that this imperative is so often misinterpreted and sets people making theologies and pantheologies and antitheologies—all of which can be debunked—does not really touch the central experience itself. What nature-lovers—whether they are Wordsworthians or people with "dark gods in their blood"—get from nature is an iconography, a language of images. I do not mean simply visual images; it is the "moods" or "spirits" themselves—the powerful expositions of terror, gloom, jocundity, cruelty, lust, innocence, purity—that are the images. In them each man can clothe his own belief. We must learn our theology or philosophy elsewhere (not surprisingly, we often learn them from theologians and philosophers).

But when I speak of "clothing" our belief in such images I do not mean anything like using nature for similes or metaphors in the manner of the poets. Indeed I might have said "filling" or "incarnating" rather than clothing. Many people—I am one myself—would never, but for what nature does to us, have had any content to put into the words we must use in confessing our faith. Nature never taught me that there exists a God of glory and of infinite majesty. I had to learn that in other ways. But nature gave the word *glory* a meaning for me. I still do not know where else I could have found one. I do not see how the "fear" of God could have ever meant to me anything but the lowest prudential efforts to be safe, if I had never seen certain ominous ravines and unapproachable crags. And if nature had never awakened certain longings in me, huge areas of what I can now mean by the "love" of God would never, so far as I can see, have existed.

Of course the fact that a Christian can so use nature is not even the beginning of a proof that Christianity is true. Those suffering from Dark Gods can equally use her (I suppose) for their creed. That is precisely the point. Nature does not teach. A true philosophy may sometimes validate an experience of nature; an experience of nature cannot validate a philosophy. Nature will not verify any theological or metaphysical proposition (or not in the manner we are now considering); she will help to show what it means.

And not, on the Christian premises, by accident. The created glory may be expected to give us hints of the uncreated; for the one is derived from the other and in some fashion reflects it.

In some fashion. But not perhaps in so direct and simple a fashion as we at first might suppose. For of course all the facts stressed by nature-lovers of the other school are facts too; there are worms in the belly as well as primroses in the wood. Try to reconcile them, or to show that they don't really need reconciliation, and you are turning from direct experience of nature—our present subject—to metaphysics or theodicy or something of that sort. That may be a sensible thing to do; but I think it should be kept distinct from the love of nature. While we are on that level, while we are still claiming to speak of what nature has directly "said" to us, we must stick to it. We have seen an image of glory. We must not try to find a direct path through it and beyond it to an increasing knowledge of God. The path peters out almost at once. Terrors and mysteries, the whole depth of God's counsels and the whole tangle of the history of the universe, choke it. We can't get through; not that way. We must make a *détour*—leave the hills and woods and go back to our studies, to church, to our Bibles, to our knees. Otherwise the love of nature is beginning to turn into a nature religion. And then, even if it does not lead us to the Dark Gods, it will lead us to a great deal of nonsense.

But we need not surrender the love of nature—chastened and limited as I have suggested—to the debunkers. Nature cannot satisfy the desires she arouses nor answer theological questions nor sanctify us. Our real journey to God involves constantly turning our backs on her; passing from the dawn-lit fields into some poky little church, or (it might be) going to work in an East End parish. But the love of her has been a valuable and, for some people, an indispensable initiation.

I need not say "has been." For in fact those who allow no more than this to the love of nature seem to be those who retain it. This is what one should expect. This love, when it sets up as a religion, is beginning to be a god—therefore to be a demon. And demons never keep their promises. Nature "dies" on those who try to live for a love of nature. Coleridge ended by being insensible to her; Wordsworth, by lamenting that the glory had passed away. Say your prayers in a garden early, ignoring steadfastly the dew, the birds and the flowers, and you will come away overwhelmed by its freshness and joy; go there in order to be overwhelmed and, after a certain age, nine times out of ten nothing will happen to you.

I turn now to the love of one's country. Here there is no need to labour M. de Rougemont's maxim; we all know now that this love becomes a demon when it becomes a god. Some begin to suspect that it is never anything but a demon. But then they have to reject half the high poetry and half the heroic action our race has achieved. We cannot keep even Christ's lament over Jerusalem. He too exhibits love for His country.

Let us limit our field. There is no need here for an essay on international ethics. When this love becomes demoniac it will of course produce wicked acts. But others, more skilled, may say what acts between nations are wicked. We are only considering the sentiment itself in the hope of being able to distinguish its innocent from its demoniac condition. Neither of these is the efficient cause of national behaviour. For strictly speaking it is rulers, not nations, who behave internationally. Demoniac patriotism in their subjects—I write only for subjects—will make it easier for them to act wickedly; healthy patriotism may make it harder: when they are wicked they may by propaganda encourage a demoniac condition of our sentiments in order to secure our acquiescence in their wickedness. If they are good, they could do the opposite. That is one reason why we private persons should keep a wary eye on the health or disease of our own love for our country. And that is what I am writing about.

How ambivalent patriotism is may be gauged by the fact that no two writers have expressed it more vigorously than Kipling and Chesterton. If it were one element two such men could not both have praised it. In reality it contains many ingredients, of which many different blends are possible.

First, there is love of home, of the place we grew up in or the places, perhaps many, which have been our homes; and of all places fairly near these and fairly like them; love of old acquaintances, of familiar sights, sounds and smells. Note that at its largest this is, for us, a love of England, Wales, Scotland, or Ulster. Only foreigners and politicians talk about "Britain." Kipling's "I do not love my empire's foes" strikes a ludicrously false note. *My* empire! With this love for the place there goes a love for the way of life; for beer and tea and open fires, trains with compartments in them and an unarmed police force and all the rest of it; for the local dialect and (a shade less) for our native language. As Chesterton says, a man's reasons for not wanting his country to be ruled by foreigners are very like his reasons for not wanting his house to be burned down; because he "could not even begin" to enumerate all the things he would miss.

It would be hard to find any legitimate point of view from which this feeling could be condemned. As the family offers us

the first step beyond self-love, so this offers us the first step beyond family selfishness. Of course it is not pure charity; it involves love of our neighbours in the local, not of our Neighbour, in the Dominical, sense. But those who do not love the
fellow-villagers or fellow-townsmen whom they *have* seen are
not likely to have got very far towards loving "Man" whom
they have not. All natural affections, including this, can become
rivals to spiritual love: but they can also be preparatory imita-
tions of it, training (so to speak) of the spiritual muscles which
Grace may later put to a higher service; as women nurse dolls in
childhood and later nurse children. There may come an occasion for renouncing this love; pluck out your right eye. But you
need to have an eye first: a creature which had none—which
had only got so far as a "photo-sensitive" spot—would be very
ill employed in meditation on that severe text.

Of course patriotism of this kind is not in the least aggres-
sive. It asks only to be let alone. It becomes militant only to
protect what it loves. In any mind which has a pennyworth
of imagination it produces a good attitude towards foreigners. How can I love my home without coming to realise that
other men, no less rightly, love theirs? Once you have realised
that the Frenchmen like *café complet* just as we like bacon and
eggs—why, good luck to them and let them have it. The last
thing we want is to make everywhere else just like our own
home. It would not be home unless it were different.

The second ingredient is a particular attitude to our country's past. I mean to that past as it lives in popular imagination; the great deeds of our ancestors. Remember Marathon.
Remember Waterloo. "We must be free or die who speak the
tongue that Shakespeare spoke." This past is felt both to impose an obligation and to hold out an assurance; we must not
fall below the standard our fathers set us, and because we are
their sons there is good hope we shall not.

This feeling has not quite such good credentials as the sheer
love of home. The actual history of every country is full of

shabby and even shameful doings. The heroic stories, if taken
to be typical, give a false impression of it and are often themselves open to serious historical criticism. Hence a patriotism
based on our glorious past is fair game for the debunker. As
knowledge increases it may snap and be converted into disillu-
sioned cynicism, or may be maintained by a voluntary shutting
of the eyes. But who can condemn what clearly makes many
people, at many important moments, behave so much better
than they could have done without its help?

I think it is possible to be strengthened by the image of the
past without being either deceived or puffed up. The image becomes dangerous in the precise degree to which it is mistaken,
or substituted, for serious and systematic historical study. The
stories are best when they are handed on and accepted as stories. I do not mean by this that they should be handed on as
mere fictions (some of them are after all true). But the emphasis should be on the tale as such, on the picture which fires the
imagination, the example that strengthens the will. The schoolboy who hears them should dimly feel—though of course he
cannot put it into words—that he is hearing *saga*. Let him be
thrilled—preferably "out of school"—by the "Deeds that won
the Empire"; but the less we mix this up with his "history lessons" or mistake it for a serious analysis—worse still, a justification—of imperial policy, the better. When I was a child I
had a book full of coloured pictures called *Our Island Story*.
That title has always seemed to me to strike exactly the right
note. The book did not look at all like a text-book either. What
does seem to me poisonous, what breeds a type of patriotism
that is pernicious if it lasts but not likely to last long in an educated adult, is the perfectly serious indoctrination of the young
in knowably false or biased history—the heroic legend drably
disguised as text-book fact. With this creeps in the tacit assumption that other nations have not equally their heroes; perhaps even the belief—surely it is very bad biology—that we

can literally "inherit" a tradition. And these almost inevitably lead on to a third thing that is sometimes called patriotism.

This third thing is not a sentiment but a belief: a firm, even prosaic belief that our own nation, in sober fact, has long been, and still is markedly superior to all others. I once ventured to say to an old clergyman who was voicing this sort of patriotism, "But, sir, aren't we told that *every* people thinks its own men the bravest and its own women the fairest in the world?" He replied with total gravity—he could not have been graver if he had been saying the Creed at the altar—"Yes, but in England it's true." To be sure, this conviction had not made my friend (God rest his soul) a villain; only an extremely lovable old ass. It can however produce asses that kick and bite. On the lunatic fringe it may shade off into that popular Racialism which Christianity and science equally forbid.

This brings us to the fourth ingredient. If our nation is really so much better than others it may be held to have either the duties or the rights of a superior being towards them. In the nineteenth century the English became very conscious of such duties: the "white man's burden." What we called *natives* were our wards and we their self-appointed guardians. This was not all hypocrisy. We did do them some good. But our habit of talking as if England's motives for acquiring an empire (or any youngster's motives for seeking a job in the Indian Civil Service) had been mainly altruistic nauseated the world. And yet this showed the sense of superiority working at its best. Some nations who have also felt it have stressed the rights not the duties. To them, some foreigners were so bad that one had the right to exterminate them. Others, fitted only to be hewers of wood and drawers of water to the chosen people, had better be made to get on with their hewing and drawing. Dogs, know your betters! I am far from suggesting that the two attitudes are on the same level. But both are fatal. Both demand that the area in which they operate should grow "wider still and wider."

And both have about them this sure mark of evil: only by being terrible do they avoid being comic. If there were no broken treaties with Redskins, no extermination of the Tasmanians, no gas-chambers and no Belsen, no Amritsar, Black and Tans or Apartheid, the pomposity of both would be roaring farce.

Finally we reach the stage where patriotism in its demoniac form unconsciously denies itself. Chesterton picked on two lines from Kipling as the perfect example. It was unfair to Kipling, who knew—wonderfully, for so homeless a man—what the love of home can mean. But the lines, in isolation, can be taken to sum up the thing. They run:

> *If England was what England seems*
> *'Ow quick we'd drop 'er. But she ain't!*

Love never spoke that way. It is like loving your children only "if they're good," your wife only while she keeps her looks, your husband only so long as he is famous and successful. "No man," said one of the Greeks, "loves his city because it is great, but because it is his." A man who really loves his country will love her in her ruin and degeneration—"England, with all thy faults, I love thee still." She will be to him "a poor thing but mine own." He may think her good and great, when she is not, because he loves her; the delusion is up to a point pardonable. But Kipling's soldier reverses it; he loves her because he thinks her good and great—loves her on her merits. She is a fine going concern and it gratifies his pride to be in it. How if she ceased to be such? The answer is plainly given: "'Ow quick we'd drop 'er." When the ship begins to sink he will leave her. Thus that kind of patriotism which sets off with the greatest swagger of drums and banners actually sets off on the road that can lead to Vichy. And this is a phenomenon which will meet us again. When the natural loves become lawless they do not merely do harm to other loves; they themselves cease to be the loves they were—to be loves at all.

Patriotism has, then, many faces. Those who would reject

it entirely do not seem to have considered what will certainly step—has already begun to step—into its place. For a long time yet, or perhaps forever, nations will live in danger. Rulers must somehow nerve their subjects to defend them or at least to prepare for their defence. Where the sentiment of patriotism has been destroyed this can be done only by presenting every international conflict in a purely ethical light. If people will spend neither sweat nor blood for "their country" they must be made to feel that they are spending them for justice, or civilisation, or humanity. This is a step down, not up. Patriotic sentiment did not of course need to disregard ethics. Good men needed to be convinced that their country's cause was just; but it was still their country's cause, not the cause of justice as such. The difference seems to me important. I may without self-righteousness or hypocrisy think it just to defend my house by force against a burglar; but if I start pretending that I blacked his eye purely on moral grounds—wholly indifferent to the fact that the house in question was mine—I become insufferable. The pretence that when England's cause is just we are on England's side—as some neutral Don Quixote might be—for that reason alone, is equally spurious. And nonsense draws evil after it. If our country's cause is the cause of God, wars must be wars of annihilation. A false transcendence is given to things which are very much of this world.

The glory of the old sentiment was that while it could steel men to the utmost endeavour, it still knew itself to be a sentiment. Wars could be heroic without pretending to be Holy Wars. The hero's death was not confused with the martyr's. And (delightfully) the same sentiment which could be so serious in a rear-guard action could also in peacetime take itself as lightly as all happy loves often do. It could laugh at itself. Our older patriotic songs cannot be sung without a twinkle in the eye; later ones sound more like hymns. Give me "The British Grenadiers" *(with a tow-row-row-row)* any day rather than "Land of Hope and Glory."

It will be noticed that the sort of love I have been describing, and all its ingredients, can be for something other than a country: for a school, a regiment, a great family, or a class. All the same criticisms will still apply. It can also be felt for bodies that claim more than a natural affection: for a Church or (alas) a party in a Church, or for a religious order. This terrible subject would require a book to itself. Here it will be enough to say that the Heavenly Society is also an earthly society. Our (merely natural) patriotism towards the latter can very easily borrow the transcendent claims of the former and use them to justify the most abominable actions. If ever the book which I am not going to write is written it must be the full confession by Christendom of Christendom's specific contribution to the sum of human cruelty and treachery. Large areas of "the World" will not hear us till we have publicly disowned much of our past. Why should they? We have shouted the name of Christ and enacted the service of Moloch.

It may be thought that I should not end this chapter without a word about our love for animals. But that will fit in better in the next. Whether animals are in fact sub-personal or not, they are never loved as if they were. The fact or the illusion of personality is always present, so that love for them is really an instance of that Affection which is the subject of the following chapter.

Affection

I BEGIN with the humblest and most widely diffused of loves, the love in which our experience seems to differ least from that of the animals. Let me add at once that I do not on that account give it a lower value. Nothing in Man is either worse or better for being shared with the beasts. When we blame a man for being "a mere animal," we mean not that he displays animal characteristics (we all do) but that he displays these, and only these, on occasions where the specifically human was demanded. (When we call him "brutal" we usually mean that he commits cruelties impossible to most real brutes; they're not clever enough.)

The Greeks called this love *storge* (two syllables and the g is "hard"). I shall here call it simply Affection. My Greek Lexicon defines *storge* as "affection, especially of parents to offspring"; but also of offspring to parents. And that, I have no doubt, is the original form of the thing as well as the central meaning of the word. The image we must start with is that of a mother nursing a baby; a bitch or a cat with a basketful of puppies or kittens; all in a squeaking, nuzzling heap together; purrings, lickings, baby-talk, milk, warmth, the smell of young life.

The importance of this image is that it presents us at the very outset with a certain paradox. The Need and Need-love of the young is obvious; so is the Gift-love of the mother. She gives birth, gives suck, gives protection. On the other hand, she must give birth or die. She must give suck or suffer. That way, her Affection too is a Need-love. There is the paradox. It is a Need-love but what it needs is to give. It is a Gift-love but it needs to be needed. We shall have to return to this point.

But even in animal life, and still more in our own, Affection extends far beyond the relation of mother and young. This warm comfortableness, this satisfaction in being together, takes in all sorts of objects. It is indeed the least discriminating of loves. There are women for whom we can predict few wooers and men who are likely to have few friends. They have nothing to offer. But almost anyone can become an object of Affection; the ugly, the stupid, even the exasperating. There need be no apparent fitness between those whom it unites. I have seen it felt for an imbecile not only by his parents but by his brothers. It ignores the barriers of age, sex, class and education. It can exist between a clever young man from the university and an old nurse, though their minds inhabit different worlds. It ignores even the barriers of species. We see it not only between dog and man but, more surprisingly, between dog and cat. Gilbert White claims to have discovered it between a horse and a hen.

Some of the novelists have seized this well. In *Tristram Shandy* "My Father" and Uncle Toby are so far from being united by any community of interests or ideas that they cannot converse for ten minutes without cross-purposes; but we are made to feel their deep mutual affection. So with Don Quixote and Sancho Panza, Pickwick and Sam Weller, Dick Swiveller and the Marchioness. So too, though probably without the author's conscious intention, in *The Wind in the Willows*; the quaternion of Mole, Rat, Badger, and Toad suggests the amazing heterogeneity possible between those who are bound by Affection.

But Affection has its own criteria. Its objects have to be familiar. We can sometimes point to the very day and hour when we fell in love or began a new friendship. I doubt if we ever catch Affection beginning. To become aware of it is to become aware that it has already been going on for some time. The use of "old" or *vieux* as a term of Affection is significant. The dog barks at strangers who have never done it any harm and wags its tail for old acquaintances even if they never did it a good turn. The child will love a crusty old gardener who has hardly ever taken any notice of it and shrink from the visitor who is making every attempt to win its regard. But it must be an *old* gardener, one who has "always" been there—the short but seemingly immemorial "always" of childhood.

Affection, as I have said, is the humblest love. It gives itself no airs. People can be proud of being "in love," or of friendship. Affection is modest—even furtive and shame-faced. Once when I had remarked on the affection quite often found between cat and dog, my friend replied, "Yes. But I bet no dog would ever confess it to the other dogs." That is at least a good caricature of much human Affection. "Let homely faces stay at home," says Comus. Now Affection has a very homely face. So have many of those for whom we feel it. It is no proof of our refinement or perceptiveness that we love them; nor that they love us. What I have called Appreciative love is no basic element in Affection. It usually needs absence or bereavement to set us praising those to whom only Affection binds us. We take them for granted: and this taking for granted, which is an outrage in erotic love, is here right and proper up to a point. It fits the comfortable, quiet nature of the feeling. Affection would not be affection if it was loudly and frequently expressed; to produce it in public is like getting your household furniture out for a move. It did very well in its place, but it looks shabby or tawdry or grotesque in the sunshine. Affection almost slinks or seeps through our lives. It lives with humble un-dress, private things; soft slippers, old clothes, old jokes, the thump of a sleepy dog's tail on the kitchen floor, the sound of a sewing-machine, a gollywog left on the lawn.

But I must at once correct myself. I am talking of Affection as it is when it exists apart from the other loves. It often does so exist; often not. As gin is not only a drink in itself but also a base for many mixed drinks, so Affection, besides being a love itself, can enter into the other loves and colour them all through and become the very medium in which from day to day they operate. They would not perhaps wear very well without it. To make a friend is not the same as to become affectionate. But when your friend has become an old friend, all those things about him which had originally nothing to do with the friendship become familiar and dear with familiarity. As for erotic love, I can imagine nothing more disagreeable than to experience it for more than a very short time without this homespun clothing of affection. That would be a most uneasy condition, either too angelic or too animal or each by turn; never quite great enough or little enough for man. There is indeed a peculiar charm, both in friendship and in Eros, about those moments when Appreciative love lies, as it were, curled up asleep, and the mere ease and ordinariness of the relationship (free as solitude, yet neither is alone) wraps us round. No need to talk. No need to make love. No needs at all except perhaps to stir the fire.

This blending and overlapping of the loves is well kept before us by the fact that at most times and places all three of them had in common, as their expression, the kiss. In modern England friendship no longer uses it, but Affection and Eros do. It belongs so fully to both that we cannot now tell which borrowed it from the other or whether there were borrowing at all. To be sure, you may say that the kiss of Affection differs from the kiss of Eros. Yes; but not all kisses between lovers are lovers' kisses. Again, both these loves tend—and it embarrasses many moderns—to use a "little language" or "baby talk." And this is not peculiar to the human species. Professor Lorenz has told us that when jackdaws are amorous their calls "consist chiefly of infantile sounds reserved by adult jackdaws for these occasions" (*King Solomon's Ring*, p. 158). We and the birds have the same excuse. Different sorts of tenderness are both tenderness and the language of the earliest tenderness we have ever known is recalled to do duty for the new sort.

One of the most remarkable by-products of Affection has not yet been mentioned. I have said that is not primarily an Appreciative love. It is not discriminating. It can "rub along" with the most unpromising people. Yet oddly enough this very fact means that it can in the end make appreciations possible which, but for it, might never have existed. We may say, and not quite untruly, that we have chosen our friends and the woman we love for their various excellences—for beauty, frankness, goodness of heart, wit, intelligence, or what not. But it had to be the particular kind of wit, the particular kind of beauty, the particular kind of goodness that we like, and we have our personal tastes in these matters. That is why friends and lovers feel that they were "made for one another." The especial glory of Affection is that it can unite those who most emphatically, even comically, are not; people who, if they had not found themselves put down by fate in the same household or community, would have had nothing to do with each other. If Affection grows out of this—of course it often does not—their eyes begin to open. Growing fond of "old so-and-so," at first simply because he happens to be there, I presently begin to see that there is "something in him" after all. The moment when one first says, really meaning it, that though he is not "my sort of man" he is a very good man "in his own way" is one of liberation. It does not feel like that; we may feel only tolerant and indulgent. But really we have crossed a frontier. That "in his own way" means that we are getting beyond our own idiosyncrasies, that we are learning to appreciate goodness or intelligence in themselves, not merely goodness or intelligence flavoured and served to suit our own palate.

"Dogs and cats should always be brought up together," said someone, "it broadens their minds so." Affection broadens

ours; of all natural loves it is the most catholic, the least fini-
cal, the broadest. The people with whom you are thrown together in the family, the college, the mess, the ship, the religious house, are from this point of view a wider circle than the
friends, however numerous, whom you have made for yourself
in the outer world. By having a great many friends I do not
prove that I have a wide appreciation of human excellence. You
might as well say I prove the width of my literary taste by being able to enjoy all the books in my own study. The answer is
the same in both cases—"You chose those books. You chose
those friends. Of course they suit you." The truly wide taste in
reading is that which enables a man to find something for his
needs on the sixpenny tray outside any secondhand bookshop.
The truly wide taste in humanity will similarly find something
to appreciate in the cross-section of humanity whom one has
to meet every day. In my experience it is Affection that creates this taste, teaching us first to notice, then to endure, then
to smile at, then to enjoy, and finally to appreciate, the people
who "happen to be there." Made for us? Thank God, no. They
are themselves, odder than you could have believed and worth
far more than we guessed.

And now we are drawing near the point of danger. Affection, I have said, gives itself no airs; charity, said St. Paul, is
not puffed up. Affection can love the unattractive: God and
His saints love the unlovable. Affection "does not expect too
much," turns a blind eye to faults, revives easily after quarrels;
just so charity suffers long and is kind and forgives. Affection
opens our eyes to goodness we could not have seen, or should
not have appreciated without it. So does humble sanctity. If we
dwelled exclusively on these resemblances we might be led on
to believe that this Affection is not simply one of the natural
loves but is Love Himself working in our human hearts and
fulfilling the law. Were the Victorian novelists right after all? Is
love (of this sort) really enough? Are the "domestic affections,"
when in their best and fullest development, the same thing as

the Christian life? The answer to all these questions, I submit, is certainly No.

I do not mean simply that those novelists sometimes wrote as if they had never heard the text about "hating" wife and mother and one's own life also. That of course is true. The rivalry between all natural loves and the love of God is something a Christian dare not forget. God is the great Rival, the ultimate object of human jealousy; that beauty, terrible as the Gorgon's, which may at any moment steal from me — or it seems like stealing to me — my wife's or husband's or daughter's heart. The bitterness of some unbelief, though disguised even from those who feel it as anti-clericalism or hatred of superstition, is really due to this. But I am not at present thinking of that rivalry; we shall have to face it in a later chapter. For the moment our business is more down to earth.

How many of these "happy homes" really exist? Worse still; are all the unhappy ones unhappy because Affection is absent? I believe not. It can be present, causing the unhappiness. Nearly all the characteristics of this love are ambivalent. They may work for ill as well as for good. By itself, left simply to follow its own bent, it can darken and degrade human life. The debunkers and anti-sentimentalists have not said all the truth about it, but all they have said is true.

Symptomatic of this, perhaps, is the odiousness of nearly all those treacly tunes and saccharine poems in which popular art expresses Affection. They are odious because of their falsity. They represent as a ready-made recipe for bliss (and even for goodness) what is in fact only an opportunity. There is no hint that we shall have to do anything: only let Affection pour over us like a warm shower-bath and all, it is implied, will be well.

Affection, we have seen, includes both Need-love and Gift-love. I begin with the Need — our craving for the Affection of others.

Now there is a clear reason why this craving, of all love-cravings, easily becomes the most unreasonable. I have said that almost anyone may be the object of Affection. Yes; and almost everyone expects to be. The egregious Mr. Pontifex in *The Way of All Flesh* is outraged to discover that his son does not love him; it is "unnatural" for a boy not to love his own father. It never occurs to him to ask whether, since the first day the boy can remember, he has ever done or said anything that could excite love. Similarly, at the beginning of *King Lear* the hero is shown as a very unlovable old man devoured with a ravenous appetite for Affection. I am driven to literary examples because you, the reader, and I do not live in the same neighbourhood; if we did, there would unfortunately be no difficulty about replacing them with examples from real life. The thing happens every day. And we can see why. We all know that we must do something, if not to merit, at least to attract, erotic love or friendship. But Affection is often assumed to be provided, ready made, by nature; "built-in," "laid-on," "on the house." We have a right to expect it. If the others do not give it, they are "unnatural."

This assumption is no doubt the distortion of a truth. Much has been "built-in." Because we are a mammalian species, instinct will provide at least some degree, often a high one, of maternal love. Because we are a social species familiar association provides a *milieu* in which, if all goes well, Affection will arise and grow strong without demanding any very shining qualities in its objects. If it is given us it will not necessarily be given us on our merits; we may get it with very little trouble. From a dim perception of the truth (many are loved with Affection far beyond their deserts) Mr. Pontifex draws the ludicrous conclusion, "Therefore I, without desert, have a right to it." It is as if, on a far higher plane, we argued that because no man by merit has a right to the Grace of God, I, having no merit, am entitled to it. There is no question of rights in either case. What we have is not "a right to expect" but a "reasonable expectation" of being loved by our intimates if we, and they, are more or less ordinary people. But we may not be. We may be intolerable. If we are, "nature" will work against us. For the very same conditions of intimacy which make Affection possible also—and no less naturally—make possible a peculiarly incurable distaste; a hatred as immemorial, constant, unemphatic, almost at times unconscious, as the corresponding form of love. Siegfried, in the opera, could not remember a time before every shuffle, mutter, and fidget of his dwarfish foster-father had become odious. We never catch this kind of hatred, any more than Affection, at the moment of its beginning. It was always there before. Notice that *old* is a term of wearied loathing as well as of endearment: "at his old tricks," "in his old way," "the same old thing."

It would be absurd to say that Lear is lacking in Affection. In so far as Affection is Need-love he is half-crazy with it. Unless, in his own way, he loved his daughters he would not so desperately desire their love. The most unlovable parent (or child) may be full of such ravenous love. But it works to their own misery and everyone else's. The situation becomes suffocating. If people are already unlovable a continual demand on their part (as of right) to be loved—their manifest sense of injury, their reproaches, whether loud and clamorous or merely implicit in every look and gesture of resentful self-pity—produce in us a sense of guilt (they are intended to do so) for a fault we could not have avoided and cannot cease to commit. They seal up the very fountain for which they are thirsty. If ever, at some favoured moment, any germ of Affection for them stirs in us, their demand for more and still more petrifies us again. And of course such people always desire the same proof of our love; we are to join their side, to hear and share their grievance against someone else. If my boy really loved me he would see how selfish his father is . . . if my brother loved me he would make a party with me against my sister . . . if you loved me you wouldn't let me be treated like this . . .

And all the while they remain unaware of the real road. "If you would be loved, be lovable," said Ovid. That cheery old reprobate only meant, "If you want to attract the girls you must be attractive," but his maxim has a wider application. The amorist was wiser in his generation than Mr. Pontifex and King Lear.

The really surprising thing is not that these insatiable demands made by the unlovable are sometimes made in vain, but that they are so often met. Sometimes one sees a woman's girlhood, youth and long years of her maturity up to the verge of old age all spent in tending, obeying, caressing, and perhaps supporting, a maternal vampire who can never be caressed and obeyed enough. The sacrifice—but there are two opinions about that—may be beautiful; the old woman who exacts it is not.

The "built-in" or unmerited character of Affection thus invites a hideous misinterpretation. So does its ease and informality.

We hear a great deal about the rudeness of the rising generation. I am an oldster myself and might be expected to take the oldsters' side, but in fact I have been far more impressed by the bad manners of parents to children than by those of children to parents. Who has not been the embarrassed guest at family meals where the father or mother treated their grown-up offspring with an incivility which, offered to any other young people, would simply have terminated the acquaintance? Dogmatic assertions on matters which the children understand and their elders don't, ruthless interruptions, flat contradictions, ridicule of things the young take seriously—sometimes of their religion—insulting references to their friends, all provide an easy answer to the question "Why are they always out? Why do they like every house better than their home?" Who does not prefer civility to barbarism?

If you asked any of these insufferable people—they are not all parents of course—why they behaved that way at home, they would reply, "Oh, hang it all, one comes home to relax. A chap can't be always on his best behaviour. If a man can't be himself in his own house, where can he? Of course we don't want Company Manners at home. We're a happy family. We can say *anything* to one another here. No one minds. We all understand."

Once again it is so nearly true yet so fatally wrong. Affection is an affair of old clothes, and ease, of the unguarded moment, of liberties which would be ill-bred if we took them with strangers. But old clothes are one thing; to wear the same shirt till it stank would be another. There are proper clothes for a garden party; but the clothes for home must be proper too, in their own different way. Similarly there is a distinction between public and domestic courtesy. The root principle of both is the same: "that no one give any kind of preference to himself." But the more public the occasion, the more our obedience to this principle has been "taped" or formalised. There are "rules" of good manners. The more intimate the occasion, the less the formalisation; but not therefore the less need of courtesy. On the contrary, Affection at its best practises a courtesy which is incomparably more subtle, sensitive, and deep than the public kind. In public a ritual would do. At home you must have the reality which that ritual represented, or else the deafening triumphs of the greatest egoist present. You must really give no kind of preference to yourself; at a party it is enough to conceal the preference. Hence the old proverb "come live with me and you'll know me." Hence a man's familiar manners first reveal the true value of his (significantly odious phrase!) "Company" or "Party" manners. Those who leave their manners behind them when they come home from the dance or the sherry party have no real courtesy even there. They were merely aping those who had.

"We can say *anything* to one another." The truth behind this is that Affection at its best can say whatever Affection at its best wishes to say, regardless of the rules that govern public courtesy; for Affection at its best wishes neither to wound nor to humiliate nor to domineer. You may address the wife of your

bosom as "Pig!" when she has inadvertently drunk your cock-
tail as well as her own. You may roar down the story which
your father is telling once too often. You may tease and hoax
and banter. You can say "Shut up. I want to read." You can do
anything in the right tone and at the right moment—the tone
and moment which are not intended to, and will not, hurt. The
better the Affection the more unerringly it knows which these
are (every love has its *art of love*). But the domestic Rudesby
means something quite different when he claims liberty to say
"anything." Having a very imperfect sort of Affection himself,
or perhaps at that moment none, he arrogates to himself the
beautiful liberties which only the fullest Affection has a right
to or knows how to manage. He then uses them spitefully in
obedience to his resentments; or ruthlessly in obedience to his
egoism; or at best stupidly, lacking the art. And all the time he
may have a clear conscience. He knows that Affection takes liberties. He is taking liberties. Therefore (he concludes) he is being affectionate. Resent anything and he will say that the defect
of love is on your side. He is hurt. He has been misunderstood.

He then sometimes avenges himself by getting on his high
horse and becoming elaborately "polite." The implication is of
course, "Oh! So we are not to be intimate? We are to behave
like mere acquaintances? I had hoped—but no matter. Have it
your own way." This illustrates prettily the difference between
intimate and formal courtesy. Precisely what suits the one may
be a breach of the other. To be free and easy when you are
presented to some eminent stranger is bad manners; to practise formal and ceremonial courtesies at home ("public faces in
private places") is—and is always intended to be—bad manners. There is a delicious illustration of really good domestic
manners in *Tristram Shandy*. At a singularly unsuitable moment
Uncle Toby has been holding forth on his favourite theme of
fortification. "My Father," driven for once beyond endurance,
violently interrupts. Then he sees his brother's face; the utterly
unretaliating face of Toby, deeply wounded, not by the slight

to himself—he would never think of that—but by the slight to the noble art. "My Father" at once repents. There is an apology, a total reconciliation. Uncle Toby, to show how complete is his forgiveness, to show that he is not on his dignity, resumes the lecture on fortification.

But we have not yet touched on jealousy. I suppose no one now believes that jealousy is especially connected with erotic love. If anyone does, the behaviour of children, employees, and domestic animals ought soon to undeceive him. Every kind of love, almost every kind of association, is liable to it. The jealousy of Affection is closely connected with its reliance on what is old and familiar. So also with the total, or relative, unimportance for Affection of what I call Appreciative love. We don't want the "old, familiar faces" to become brighter or more beautiful, the old ways to be changed even for the better, the old jokes and interests to be replaced by exciting novelties. Change is a threat to Affection.

A brother and sister, or two brothers—for sex here is not at work—grow to a certain age sharing everything. They have read the same comics, climbed the same trees, been pirates or spacemen together, taken up and abandoned stamp-collecting at the same moment. Then a dreadful thing happens. One of them flashes ahead—discovers poetry or science or serious music or perhaps undergoes a religious conversion. His life is flooded with the new interest. The other cannot share it; he is left behind. I doubt whether even the infidelity of a wife or husband raises a more miserable sense of desertion or a fiercer jealousy than this can sometimes do. It is not yet jealousy of the new friends whom the deserter will soon be making. That will come; at first it is jealousy of the thing itself—of this science, this music, of God (always called "religion" or "all this religion" in such contexts). The jealousy will probably be expressed by ridicule. The new interest is "all silly nonsense," contemptibly childish (or contemptibly grown-up), or else the deserter is not really interested in it at all—he's showing off, swanking; it's all affectation. Presently the books will be hidden, the scientific specimens destroyed, the radio forcibly switched off the classical programmes. For Affection is the most instinctive, in that sense the most animal, of the loves; its jealousy is proportionately fierce. It snarls and bares its teeth like a dog whose food has been snatched away. And why would it not? Something or someone has snatched away from the child I am picturing his life-long food, his second self. His world is in ruins.

But it is not only children who react thus. Few things in the ordinary peacetime life of a civilised country are more nearly fiendish than the rancour with which a whole unbelieving family will turn on the one member of it who has become a Christian, or a whole low-brow family on the one who shows signs of becoming an intellectual. This is not, as I once thought, simply the innate and, as it were, disinterested hatred of darkness for light. A church-going family in which one has gone atheist will not always behave any better. It is the reaction to a desertion, even to robbery. Someone or something has stolen "our" boy (or girl). He who was one of Us has become one of Them. What right had anybody to do it? He is *ours*. But once change has thus begun, who knows where it will end? (And we all so happy and comfortable before and doing no harm to no one!)

Sometimes a curious double jealousy is felt, or rather two inconsistent jealousies which chase each other round in the sufferer's mind. On the one hand "This" is "All nonsense, all bloody high-brow nonsense, all canting humbug." But on the other, "Supposing—it can't be, it mustn't be, but just supposing—there were something in it?" Supposing there really were anything in literature, or in Christianity? How if the deserter has really entered a new world which the rest of us never suspected? But, if so, how unfair! Why him? Why was it never opened to us? "A chit of a girl—a whipper-snapper of a boy—being shown things that are hidden from their elders?" And since that is clearly incredible and unendurable, jealousy returns to the hypothesis "All nonsense."

Parents in this state are much more comfortably placed than brothers and sisters. Their past is unknown to their children. Whatever the deserter's new world is, they can always claim that they have been through it themselves and come out the other end. "It's a phase," they say. "It'll blow over." Nothing could be more satisfactory. It cannot be there and then refuted, for it is a statement about the future. It stings, yet—so indulgently said—is hard to resent. Better still, the elders may really believe it. Best of all, it may finally turn out to have been true. It won't be their fault if it doesn't.

"Boy, boy, these wild courses of yours will break your mother's heart." That eminently Victorian appeal may often have been true. Affection was bitterly wounded when one member of the family fell from the homely *ethos* into something worse—gambling, drink, keeping an opera girl. Unfortunately it is almost equally possible to break your mother's heart by rising above the homely *ethos*. The conservative tenacity of Affection works both ways. It can be a domestic counterpart to that nationally suicidal type of education which keeps back the promising child because the idlers and dunces might be "hurt" if it were undemocratically moved into a higher class than themselves.

All these perversions of Affection are mainly connected with Affection as a Need-love. But Affection as a Gift-love has its perversions too.

I am thinking of Mrs. Fidget, who died a few months ago. It is really astonishing how her family have brightened up. The drawn look has gone from her husband's face; he begins to be able to laugh. The younger boy, whom I had always thought an embittered, peevish little creature, turns out to be quite human. The elder, who was hardly ever at home except when he was in bed, is nearly always there now and has begun to reorganise the garden. The girl, who was always supposed to be "delicate" (though I never found out what exactly the trouble was), now has the riding lessons which were once out of the question, dances all night, and plays any amount of tennis. Even the dog who was never allowed out except on a lead is now a well-known member of the Lamp-post Club in their road.

Mrs. Fidget very often said that she lived for her family. And it was not untrue. Everyone in the neighbourhood knew it. "She lives for her family," they said; "what a wife and mother!" She did all the washing; true, she did it badly, and they could have afforded to send it out to a laundry, and they frequently begged her not to do it. But she did. There was always a hot lunch for anyone who was at home and always a hot meal at night (even in midsummer). They implored her not to provide this. They protested almost with tears in their eyes (and with truth) that they liked cold meals. It made no difference. She was living for her family. She always sat up to "welcome" you home if you were out late at night; two or three in the morning, it made no odds; you would always find the frail, pale, weary face awaiting you, like a silent accusation. Which meant of course that you couldn't with any decency go out very often. She was always making things too; being in her own estimation (I'm no judge myself) an excellent amateur dressmaker and a great knitter. And of course, unless you were a heartless brute, you had to wear the things. (The Vicar tells me that, since her death, the contributions of that family alone to "sales of work" outweigh those of all his other parishioners put together.) And then her care for their health! She bore the whole burden of that daughter's "delicacy" alone. The Doctor—an old friend, and it was not being done on National Health—was never allowed to discuss matters with his patient. After the briefest examination of her, he was taken into another room by the mother. The girl was to have no worries, no responsibility for her own health. Only loving care; caresses, special foods, horrible tonic wines, and breakfast in bed. For Mrs. Fidget, as she so often said, would "work her fingers to the bone" for her family. They couldn't stop her. Nor could they—being decent people—quite sit still and watch her do it. They had to help. Indeed they were always having to help. That is, they did things for her to help her to do things for them which they didn't want done. As for the dear dog, it was to her, she said, "Just like one of the children." It was in fact, as like one of them as she could make it. But since it had no scruples it got on rather better than they, and though vetted, dieted and guarded within an inch of its life, contrived sometimes to reach the dustbin or the dog next door.

The Vicar says Mrs. Fidget is now at rest. Let us hope she is. What's quite certain is that her family are.

It is easy to see how liability to this state is, so to speak, congenital in the maternal instinct. This, as we saw, is a Gift-love, but one that needs to give; therefore needs to be needed. But the proper aim of giving is to put the recipient in a state where he no longer needs our gift. We feed children in order that they may soon be able to feed themselves; we teach them in order that they may soon not need our teaching. Thus a heavy task is laid upon this Gift-love. It must work towards its own abdication. We must aim at making ourselves superfluous. The hour when we can say "They need me no longer" should be our reward. But the instinct, simply in its own nature, has no power to fulfil this law. The instinct desires the good of its object, but not simply; only the good it can itself give. A much higher love—a love which desires the good of the object as such, from whatever source that good comes—must step in and help or tame the instinct before it can make the abdication. And of course it often does. But where it does not, the ravenous need to be needed will gratify itself either by keeping its objects needy or by inventing for them imaginary needs. It will do this all the more ruthlessly because it thinks (in one sense truly) that it is a Gift-love and therefore regards itself as "unselfish."

It is not only mothers who can do this. All those other Affections which, whether by derivation from parental instinct or by similarity of function, need to be needed may fall into the same pit. The Affection of patron for *protégé* is one. In Jane

Austen's novel, Emma intends that Harriet Smith should have a happy life; but only the sort of happy life which Emma herself has planned for her. My own profession—that of a university teacher—is in this way dangerous. If we are any good we must always be working towards the moment at which our pupils are fit to become our critics and rivals. We should be delighted when it arrives, as the fencing master is delighted when his pupil can pink and disarm him. And many are.

But not all. I am old enough to remember the sad case of Dr. Quartz. No university boasted a more effective or devoted teacher. He spent the whole of himself on his pupils. He made an indelible impression on nearly all of them. He was the object of much well-merited hero-worship. Naturally, and delightfully, they continued to visit him after the tutorial relation had ended—went round to his house of an evening and had famous discussions. But the curious thing is that this never lasted. Sooner or later—it might be within a few months or even a few weeks—came the fatal evening when they knocked on his door and were told that the Doctor was engaged. After that he would always be engaged. They were banished from him forever. This was because, at their last meeting, they had rebelled. They had asserted their independence—differed from the master and supported their own view, perhaps not without success. Faced with that very independence which he had laboured to produce and which it was his duty to produce if he could, Dr. Quartz could not bear it. Wotan had toiled to create the free Siegfried; presented with the free Siegfried, he was enraged. Dr. Quartz was an unhappy man.

This terrible need to be needed often finds its outlet in pampering an animal. To learn that someone is "fond of animals" tells us very little until we know in what way. For there are two ways. On the one hand the higher and domesticated animal is, so to speak, a "bridge" between us and the rest of nature. We all at times feel somewhat painfully our human isolation from the subhuman world—the atrophy of instinct which our intelligence entails, our excessive self-consciousness, the innumerable complexities of our situation, our inability to live in the present. If only we could shuffle it all off! We must not—and incidentally we can't—become beasts. But we can be *with* a beast. It is personal enough to give the word *with* a real meaning; yet it remains very largely an unconscious little bundle of biological impulses. It has three legs in nature's world and one in ours. It is a link, an ambassador. Who would not wish, as Bosanquet put it, "to have a representative at the court of Pan"? Man with dog closes a gap in the universe. But of course animals are often used in a worse fashion. If you need to be needed and if your family, very properly, decline to need you, a pet is the obvious substitute. You can keep it all its life in need of you. You can keep it permanently infantile, reduce it to permanent invalidism, cut it off from all genuine animal well-being, and compensate for this by creating needs for countless little indulgences which only you can grant. The unfortunate creature thus becomes very useful to the rest of the household; it acts as a sump or drain—you are too busy spoiling a dog's life to spoil theirs. Dogs are better for this purpose than cats: a monkey, I am told, is best of all. Also it is more like the real thing. To be sure, it's all very bad luck for the animal. But probably it cannot fully realise the wrong you have done it. Better still, you would never know if it did. The most down-trodden human, driven too far, may one day turn and blurt out a terrible truth. Animals can't speak.

Those who say "The more I see of men the better I like dogs"—those who find in animals a *relief* from the demands of human companionship—will be well advised to examine their real reasons.

I hope I am not being misunderstood. If this chapter leads anyone to doubt that the lack of "natural affection" is an extreme depravity I shall have failed. Nor do I question for a moment that Affection is responsible for nine-tenths of whatever solid and durable happiness there is in our natural lives. I shall therefore have some sympathy with those whose comment on the last few pages takes the form "Of course. Of course. These things do happen. Selfish or neurotic people can twist anything, even love, into some sort of misery or exploitation. But why stress these marginal cases? A little common sense, a little give and take, prevents their occurrence among decent people." But I think this comment itself needs a commentary.

Firstly, as to *neurotic*. I do not think we shall see things more clearly by classifying all these malefical states of Affection as pathological. No doubt there are really pathological conditions which make the temptation to these states abnormally hard or even impossible to resist for particular people. Send those people to the doctors by all means. But I believe that everyone who is honest with himself will admit that he has felt these temptations. Their occurrence is not a disease; or if it is, the name of that disease is Being a Fallen Man. In ordinary people the yielding to them—and who does not sometimes yield?—is not disease, but sin. Spiritual direction will here help us more than medical treatment. Medicine labours to restore "natural" structure or "normal" function. But greed, egoism, self-deception and self-pity are not unnatural or abnormal in the same sense as astigmatism or a floating kidney. For who, in Heaven's name, would describe as natural or normal the man from whom these failings were wholly absent? "Natural," if you like, in a quite different sense; archnatural, unfallen. We have seen only one such Man. And He was not at all like the psychologist's picture of the integrated, balanced, adjusted, happily married, employed, popular citizen. You can't really be very well "adjusted" to your world if it says you "have a devil" and ends by nailing you up naked to a stake of wood.

But secondly, the comment in its own language admits the very thing I am trying to say. Affection produces happiness if—and only if—there is common sense and give and take and "decency." In other words, only if something more, and other, than Affection is added. The mere feeling is not enough. You need "common sense," that is, reason. You need "give and take"; that is, you need justice, continually stimulating mere Affection when it fades and restraining it when it forgets or would defy the *art* of love. You need "decency." There is no disguising the fact that this means goodness; patience, self-denial, humility, and the continual intervention of a far higher sort of love than Affection, in itself, can ever be. That is the whole point. If we try to live by Affection alone, Affection will "go bad on us."

How bad, I believe we seldom recognise. Can Mrs. Fidget really have been quite unaware of the countless frustrations and miseries she inflicted on her family? It passes belief. She knew—of course she knew—that it spoiled your whole evening to know that when you came home you would find her uselessly, accusingly, "sitting up for you." She continued all these practices because if she had dropped them she would have been faced with the fact she was determined not to see; would have known that she was not necessary. That is the first motive. Then too, the very laboriousness of her life silenced her secret doubts as to the quality of her love. The more her feet burned and her back ached, the better, for this pain whispered in her ear "How much I must love them if I do all this!" That is the second motive. But I think there is a lower depth. The unappreciativeness of the others, those terrible, wounding words—anything will "wound" a Mrs. Fidget—in which they begged her to send the washing out, enabled her to feel ill-used, therefore, to have a continual grievance, to enjoy the pleasures of resentment. If anyone says he does not know those pleasures, he is a liar or a saint. It is true that they are pleasures only to those who hate. But then a love like Mrs. Fidget's contains a good deal of hatred. It was of erotic love that the Roman poet said, "I love and hate," but other kinds of love admit the same mixture. They carry in them the seeds of hatred. If Affection is made the absolute sovereign of a human life the seeds will germinate. Love, having become a god, becomes a demon.

Friendship

WHEN either Affection or Eros is one's theme, one finds a prepared audience. The importance and beauty of both have been stressed and almost exaggerated again and again. Even those who would debunk them are in conscious reaction against this laudatory tradition and, to that extent, influenced by it. But very few modern people think Friendship a love of comparable value or even a love at all. I cannot remember that any poem since *In Memoriam*, or any novel, has celebrated it. Tristan and Isolde, Antony and Cleopatra, Romeo and Juliet, have innumerable counterparts in modern literature: David and Jonathan, Pylades and Orestes, Roland and Oliver, Amis and Amile, have not. To the Ancients, Friendship seemed the happiest and most fully human of all loves; the crown of life and the school of virtue. The modern world, in comparison, ignores it. We admit of course that besides a wife and family a man needs a few "friends." But the very tone of the admission, and the sort of acquaintanceships which those who make it would describe as "friendships," show clearly that what they are talking about has very little to do with that *Philia* which Aristotle classified among the virtues or that *Amicitia* on which Cicero wrote a book. It is something quite marginal; not a main course in life's banquet; a diversion; something that fills up the chinks of one's time. How has this come about?

The first and most obvious answer is that few value it because few experience it. And the possibility of going through life without the experience is rooted in that fact which separates Friendship so sharply from both the other loves. Friendship is—in a sense not at all derogatory to it—the least *natural* of loves; the least instinctive, organic, biological, gregarious and necessary. It has least commerce with our nerves; there is nothing throaty about it; nothing that quickens the pulse or turns you red and pale. It is essentially between individuals; the moment two men are friends they have in some degree drawn apart together from the herd. Without Eros none of us would have been begotten and without Affection none of us would have been reared; but we can live and breed without Friendship. The species, biologically considered, has no need of it. The pack or herd—the community—may even dislike and distrust it. Its leaders very often do. Headmasters and Headmistresses and Heads of religious communities, colonels and ships' captains, can feel uneasy when close and strong friendships arise between little knots of their subjects.

This (so to call it) "non-natural" quality in Friendship goes far to explain why it was exalted in ancient and medieval times and has come to be made light of in our own. The deepest and most permanent thought of those ages was ascetic and world-renouncing. Nature and emotion and the body were feared as dangers to our souls, or despised as degradations of our human status. Inevitably that sort of love was most prized which seemed most independent, or even defiant, of mere nature. Affection and Eros were too obviously connected with our nerves, too obviously shared with the brutes. You could feel these tugging at your guts and fluttering in your diaphragm. But in Friendship—in that luminous, tranquil, rational world of relationships freely chosen—you got away from all that.

This alone, of all the loves, seemed to raise you to the level of gods or angels.

But then came Romanticism and "tearful comedy" and the "return to nature" and the exaltation of Sentiment; and in their train all that great wallow of emotion which, though often criticised, has lasted ever since. Finally, the exaltation of instinct, the dark gods in the blood; whose hierophants may be incapable of male friendship. Under this new dispensation all that had once commended this love now began to work against it. It had not tearful smiles and keepsakes and baby-talk enough to please the sentimentalists. There was not blood and guts enough about it to attract the primitivists. It looked thin and etiolated; a sort of vegetarian substitute for the more organic loves.

Other causes have contributed. To those—and they are now the majority—who see human life merely as a development and complication of animal life all forms of behaviour which cannot produce certificates of an animal origin and of survival value are suspect. Friendship's certificates are not very satisfactory. Again, that outlook which values the collective above the individual necessarily disparages Friendship; it is a relation between men at their highest level of individuality. It withdraws men from collective "togetherness" as surely as solitude itself could do; and more dangerously, for it withdraws them by two's and three's. Some forms of democratic sentiment are naturally hostile to it because it is selective and an affair of the few. To say "These are my friends" implies "Those are not." For all these reasons if a man believes (as I do) that the old estimate of Friendship was the correct one, he can hardly write a chapter on it except as a rehabilitation.

This imposes on me at the outset a very tiresome bit of demolition. It has actually become necessary in our time to rebut the theory that every firm and serious friendship is really homosexual.

The dangerous word *really* is here important. To say that every Friendship is consciously and explicitly homosexual would be too obviously false; the wiseacres take refuge in the less palpable charge that it is *really* — unconsciously, cryptically, in some Pickwickian sense — homosexual. And this, though it cannot be proved, can never of course be refuted. The fact that no positive evidence of homosexuality can be discovered in the behaviour of two Friends does not disconcert the wiseacres at all: "That," they say gravely, "is just what we should expect." The very lack of evidence is thus treated as evidence; the absence of smoke proves that the fire is very carefully hidden. Yes — if it exists at all. But we must first prove its existence. Otherwise we are arguing like a man who should say "If there were an invisible cat in that chair, the chair would look empty; but the chair does look empty; therefore there is an invisible cat in it."

A belief in invisible cats cannot perhaps be logically disproved, but it tells us a good deal about those who hold it. Those who cannot conceive Friendship as a substantive love but only as a disguise or elaboration of Eros betray the fact that they have never had a Friend. The rest of us know that though we can have erotic love and friendship for the same person yet in some ways nothing is less like a Friendship than a love-affair. Lovers are always talking to one another about their love; Friends hardly ever about their Friendship. Lovers are normally face to face, absorbed in each other; Friends, side by side, absorbed in some common interest. Above all, Eros (while it lasts) is necessarily between two only. But two, far from being the necessary number for Friendship, is not even the best. And the reason for this is important.

Lamb says somewhere that if, of three friends (A, B, and C), A should die, then B loses not only A but "A's part in C," while C loses not only A but "A's part in B." In each of my friends there is something that only some other friend can fully bring out. By myself I am not large enough to call the whole man into activity; I want other lights than my own to show all his facets. Now that Charles is dead, I shall never again see Ronald's reaction to a specifically Caroline joke. Far from having more of Ronald, having him "to myself" now that Charles is away, I have less of Ronald. Hence true Friendship is the least jealous of loves. Two friends delight to be joined by a third, and three by a fourth, if only the newcomer is qualified to become a real friend. They can then say, as the blessed souls say in Dante, "Here comes one who will augment our loves." For in this love "to divide is not to take away." Of course the scarcity of kindred souls—not to mention practical considerations about the size of rooms and the audibility of voices—set limits to the enlargement of the circle; but within those limits we possess each friend not less but more as the number of those with whom we share him increases. In this, Friendship exhibits a glorious "nearness by resemblance" to Heaven itself where the very multitude of the blessed (which no man can number) increases the fruition which each has of God. For every soul, seeing Him in her own way, doubtless communicates that unique vision to all the rest. That, says an old author, is why the Seraphim in Isaiah's vision are crying "Holy, Holy, Holy" *to one another* (Isaiah VI, 3). The more we thus share the Heavenly Bread between us, the more we shall all have.

The homosexual theory therefore seems to me not even plausible. This is not to say that Friendship and abnormal Eros have never been combined. Certain cultures at certain periods seem to have tended to the contamination. In war-like societies it was, I think, especially likely to creep into the relation between the mature Brave and his young armour-bearer or squire. The absence of the women while you were on the warpath had no doubt something to do with it. In deciding, if we think we need or can decide, where it crept in and where it did not, we must surely be guided by the evidence (when there is any) and not by an *a priori* theory. Kisses, tears and embraces are not in themselves evidence of homosexuality. The implications would be, if nothing else, too comic. Hrothgar embracing Beowulf, Johnson embracing Boswell (a pretty flagrantly heterosexual couple) and all those hairy old toughs of centurions in Tacitus, clinging to one another and begging for last kisses when the legion was broken up . . . all pansies? If you can believe that you can believe anything. On a broad historical view it is, of course, not the demonstrative gestures of Friendship among our ancestors but the absence of such gestures in our own society that calls for some special explanation. We, not they, are out of step.

I have said that Friendship is the least biological of our loves. Both the individual and the community can survive without it. But there is something else, often confused with Friendship, which the community does need; something which, though not Friendship, is the matrix of Friendship.

In early communities the co-operation of the males as hunters or fighters was no less necessary than the begetting and rearing of children. A tribe where there was no taste for the one would die no less surely than a tribe where there was no taste for the other. Long before history began we men have got together apart from the women and done things. We had to. And to like doing what must be done is a characteristic that has survival value. We not only had to do the things, we had to talk about them. We had to plan the hunt and the battle. When they were over we had to hold a *post mortem* and draw conclusions for future use. We liked this even better. We ridiculed or punished the cowards and bunglers, we praised the star-performers. We revelled in technicalities. ("He might have known he'd never get near the brute, not with the wind that way" . . . "You see, I had a lighter arrowhead; that's what did it" . . . "What I always say is—— " . . . "stuck him just like that, see? Just the way I'm holding this stick" . . .) In fact, we talked shop. We enjoyed one another-'s society greatly: we Braves, we hunters, all bound together by shared skill, shared dangers and hardships, esoteric jokes—away from the women and children. As some wag has said, palaeolithic man may or may not have had a club on his shoulder but he certainly had a club of the other sort. It was probably part of his religion; like that sacred smoking-club where the savages in Melville's *Typee* were "famously snug" every evening of their lives.

What were the women doing meanwhile? How should I know? I am a man and never spied on the mysteries of the Bona Dea. They certainly often had rituals from which men were excluded. When, as sometimes happened, agriculture was in their hands, they must, like the men, have had common skills, toils and triumphs. Yet perhaps their world was never as emphatically feminine as that of their menfolk was masculine. The children were with them; perhaps the old men were there too. But I am only guessing. I can trace the pre-history of Friendship only in the male line.

This pleasure in co-operation, in talking shop, in the mutual respect and understanding of men who daily see one another tested, is biologically valuable. You may, if you like, regard it as a product of the "gregarious instinct." To me that seems a round-about way of getting at something which we all understand far better already than anyone has ever understood the word *instinct*—something which is going on at this moment in dozens of ward-rooms, bar-rooms, common-rooms, messes and golf-clubs. I prefer to call it Companionship—or Club-bableness.

This Companionship is, however, only the matrix of Friendship. It is often called Friendship, and many people when they speak of their "friends" mean only their companions. But it is not Friendship in the sense I give to the word. By saying this I do not at all intend to disparage the merely Clubbable relation. We do not disparage silver by distinguishing it from gold.

Friendship arises out of mere Companionship when two or more of the companions discover that they have in common some insight or interest or even taste which the others do not share and which, till that moment, each believed to be his own unique treasure (or burden). The typical expression of opening Friendship would be something like, "What? You too? I thought I was the only one." We can imagine that among those early hunters and warriors single individuals—one in a century? one in a thousand years?—saw what others did not; saw that the deer was beautiful as well as edible, that hunting was fun as well as necessary, dreamed that his gods might be not only powerful but holy. But as long as each of these percipient persons dies without finding a kindred soul, nothing (I suspect) will come of it; art or sport or spiritual religion will not be born. It is when two such persons discover one another, when, whether with immense difficulties and semi-articulate fumblings or with what would seem to us amazing and elliptical speed, they share their vision—it is then that Friendship is born. And instantly they stand together in an immense solitude.

Lovers seek for privacy. Friends find this solitude about them, this barrier between them and the herd, whether they want it or not. They would be glad to reduce it. The first two would be glad to find a third.

In our own time Friendship arises in the same way. For us of course the shared activity and therefore the companionship on which Friendship supervenes will not often be a bodily one like hunting or fighting. It may be a common religion, common studies, a common profession, even a common recreation. All who share it will be our companions; but one or two or three who share something more will be our Friends. In this kind of love, as Emerson said, *Do you love me?* means *Do you see the same truth?*—Or at least, "Do you *care about* the same truth?" The man who agrees with us that some question, little regarded by others, is of great importance can be our Friend. He need not agree with us about the answer.

Notice that Friendship thus repeats on a more individual and less socially necessary level the character of the Companionship which was its matrix. The Companionship was between people who were doing something together — hunting, study-ing, painting or what you will. The Friends will still be doing something together, but something more inward, less widely shared and less easily defined; still hunters, but of some imma-terial quarry; still collaborating, but in some work the world does not, or not yet, take account of; still travelling compan-ions, but on a different kind of journey. Hence we picture lov-ers face to face but Friends side by side; their eyes look ahead.

That is why those pathetic people who simply "want friends" can never make any. The very condition of having Friends is that we should want something else besides Friends. Where the truthful answer to the question *Do you see the same truth?* would be "I see nothing and I don't care about the truth; I only want a Friend," no Friendship can arise — though Affection of course may. There would be nothing for the Friendship to be *about*; and Friendship must be about something, even if it were only an enthusiasm for dominoes or white mice. Those who have nothing can share nothing; those who are going nowhere can have no fellow-travellers.

When the two people who thus discover that they are on the same secret road are of different sexes, the friendship which arises between them will very easily pass — may pass in the first half-hour — into erotic love. Indeed, unless they are physically repulsive to each other or unless one or both already loves else-where, it is almost certain to do so sooner or later. And con-versely, erotic love may lead to Friendship between the lov-ers. But this, so far from obliterating the distinction between the two loves, puts it in a clearer light. If one who was first, in the deep and full sense, your Friend, is then gradually or sud-denly revealed as also your lover you will certainly not want to share the Beloved's erotic love with any third. But you will have no jealousy at all about sharing the Friendship. Nothing so enriches an erotic love as the discovery that the Beloved can deeply, truly and spontaneously enter into Friendship with the Friends you already had: to feel that not only are we two united by erotic love but we three or four or five are all travellers on the same quest, have all a common vision.

The co-existence of Friendship and Eros may also help some moderns to realise that Friendship is in reality a love, and even as great a love as Eros. Suppose you are fortunate enough to have "fallen in love with" and married your Friend. And now suppose it possible that you were offered the choice of two futures: "*Either* you two will cease to be lovers but remain forever joint seekers of the same God, the same beauty, the same truth, *or else*, losing all that, you will retain as long as you live the raptures and ardours, all the wonder and the wild desire of Eros. Choose which you please." Which should we choose? Which choice should we not regret after we had made it?

I have stressed the "unnecessary" character of Friendship, and this of course requires more justification than I have yet given it.

It could be argued that Friendships are of practical value to the Community. Every civilised religion began in a small group of friends. Mathematics effectively began when a few Greek friends got together to talk about numbers and lines and angles. What is now the Royal Society was originally a few gentlemen meeting in their spare time to discuss things which they (and not many others) had a fancy for. What we now call "the Romantic Movement" once *was* Mr. Wordsworth and Mr. Coleridge talking incessantly (at least Mr. Coleridge was) about a secret vision of their own. Communism, Tractarianism, Methodism, the movement against slavery, the Reformation, the Renaissance, might perhaps be said, without much exaggeration, to have begun in the same way.

There is something in this. But nearly every reader would probably think some of these movements good for society and some bad. The whole list, if accepted, would tend to show, at best, that Friendship is both a possible benefactor and a possible danger to the community. And even as a benefactor it would have, not so much survival value, as what we may call "civilisation-value"; would be something (in Aristotelian phrase) which helps the community not to live but to live well. Survival value and civilisation value coincide at some periods and in some circumstances, but not in all. What at any rate seems certain is that when Friendship bears fruit which the community can use it has to do so accidentally, as a by-product. Religions devised for a social purpose, like Roman emperor-worship or modern attempts to "sell" Christianity as a means of "saving civilisation," do not come to much. The little knots of Friends who turn their backs on the "World" are those who really transform it. Egyptian and Babylonian Mathematics were practical and social, pursued in the service of Agriculture and Magic. But the free Greek Mathematics, pursued by Friends as a leisure occupation, have mattered to us more.

Others again would say that Friendship is extremely useful, perhaps necessary for survival, to the individual. They could produce plenty of authority: "bare is back without brother behind it" and "there is a friend that sticketh closer than a brother." But when we speak thus we are using *friend* to mean "ally." In ordinary usage *friend* means, or should mean, more than that. A Friend will, to be sure, prove himself to be also an ally when alliance becomes necessary; will lend or give when we are in need, nurse us in sickness, stand up for us among our enemies, do what he can for our widows and orphans. But such good offices are not the stuff of Friendship. The occasions for them are almost interruptions. They are in one way relevant to it, in another not. Relevant, because you would be a false friend if you would not do them when the need arose; irrelevant, because the role of benefactor always remains accidental, even a little alien, to that of Friend. It is almost embarrassing. For Friendship is utterly free from Affection's need to be needed. We are sorry that any gift or loan or night-watching should have been necessary—and now, for heaven's sake, let us forget all about it and go back to the things we really want to do or talk of together. Even gratitude is no enrichment to this love.

The stereotyped "Don't mention it" here expresses what we really feel. The mark of perfect Friendship is not that help will be given when the pinch comes (of course it will) but that, having been given, it makes no difference at all. It was a distraction, an anomaly. It was a horrible waste of the time, always too short, that we had together. Perhaps we had only a couple of hours in which to talk and, God bless us, twenty minutes of it has had to be devoted to *affairs!*

For of course we do not want to know our Friend's affairs at all. Friendship, unlike Eros, is uninquisitive. You become a man's Friend without knowing or caring whether he is married or single or how he earns his living. What have all these "unconcerning things, matters of fact" to do with the real question, *Do you see the same truth?* In a circle of true Friends each man is simply what he is: stands for nothing but himself. No one cares twopence about anyone else's family, profession, class, income, race, or previous history. Of course you will get to know about most of these in the end. But casually. They will come out bit by bit, to furnish an illustration or an analogy, to serve as pegs for an anecdote; never for their own sake. That is the kingliness of Friendship. We meet like sovereign princes of independent states, abroad, on neutral ground, freed from our contexts. This love (essentially) ignores not only our physical bodies but that whole embodiment which consists of our family, job, past and connections. At home, besides being Peter or Jane, we also bear a general character; husband or wife, brother or sister, chief, colleague or subordinate. Not among our Friends. It is an affair of disentangled, or stripped, minds. Eros will have naked bodies; Friendship naked personalities.

Hence (if you will not misunderstand me) the exquisite arbitrariness and irresponsibility of this love. I have no duty to be anyone's Friend and no man in the world has a duty to be mine. No claims, no shadow of necessity. Friendship is unnecessary, like philosophy, like art, like the universe itself (for God did not need to create). It has no survival value; rather it is one of those things which give value to survival.

When I spoke of Friends as side by side or shoulder to shoulder I was pointing a necessary contrast between their posture and that of the lovers whom we picture face to face. Beyond that contrast I do not want the image pressed. The common quest or vision which unites Friends does not absorb them in such a way that they remain ignorant or oblivious of one another. On the contrary it is the very medium in which their mutual love and knowledge exist. One knows nobody so well as one's "fellow." Every step of the common journey tests his metal; and the tests are tests we fully understand because we are undergoing them ourselves. Hence, as he rings true time after time, our reliance, our respect and our admiration blossom into an Appreciative love of a singularly robust and well-informed kind. If, at the outset, we had attended more to him and less to the thing our Friendship is "about," we should not have come to know or love him so well. You will not find the warrior, the poet, the philosopher or the Christian by staring in his eyes as if he were your mistress: better fight beside him, read with him, argue with him, pray with him.

In a perfect Friendship this Appreciative love is, I think, often so great and so firmly based that each member of the circle feels, in his secret heart, humbled before all the rest. Sometimes he wonders what he is doing there among his betters. He is lucky beyond desert to be in such company. Especially when the whole group is together, each bringing out all that is best, wisest, or funniest in all the others. Those are the golden sessions; when four or five of us after a hard day's walking have come to our inn; when our slippers are on, our feet spread out towards the blaze and our drinks at our elbows; when the whole world, and something beyond the world, opens itself to our minds as we talk; and no one has any claim on or any responsibility for another, but all are freemen and equals as if we had first met an hour ago, while at the same time an Affection mellowed by the years enfolds us. Life—natural life—has no better gift to give. Who could have deserved it?

From what has been said it will be clear that in most societies at most periods Friendships will be between men and men or between women and women. The sexes will have met one another in Affection and in Eros but not in this love. For they will seldom have had with each other the companionship in common activities which is the matrix of Friendship. Where men are educated and women not, where one sex works and the other is idle, or where they do totally different work, they will usually have nothing to be Friends about. But we can easily see that it is this lack, rather than anything in their natures, which excludes Friendship; for where they can be companions they can also become Friends. Hence in a profession (like my own) where men and women work side by side, or in the mission field, or among authors and artists, such Friendship is common. To be sure, what is offered as Friendship on one side may be mistaken for Eros on the other, with painful and embarrassing results. Or what begins as Friendship in both may become also Eros. But to say that something can be mistaken for, or turn into, something else is not to deny the difference between them. Rather it implies it; we should not otherwise speak of "turning into" or being "mistaken for."

In one respect our own society is unfortunate. A world where men and women never have common work or a common education can probably get along comfortably enough. In it men turn to each other, and only to each other, for Friendship, and they enjoy it very much. I hope the women enjoy their feminine Friends equally. Again, a world where all men and women had sufficient common ground for this relationship could also be comfortable. At present, however, we fall between two stools. The necessary common ground, the matrix, exists between the sexes in some groups but not in others. It is notably lacking in many residential suburbs. In a plutocratic neighbourhood where the men have spent their whole lives in acquiring money some at least of the women have used their leisure to develop an intellectual life—have become musical or literary. In such places the men appear among the women as barbarians among civilised people. In another neighbourhood you will find the situation reversed. Both sexes have, indeed, "been to school." But since then the men have had a much more serious education; they have become doctors, lawyers, clergymen, architects, engineers, or men of letters. The women are to them as children to adults. In neither neighbourhood is real Friendship between the sexes at all probable. But this, though an impoverishment, would be tolerable if it were admitted and accepted. The peculiar trouble of our own age is that men and women in this situation, haunted by rumours and glimpses of happier groups where no such chasm between the sexes exists, and bedevilled by the egalitarian idea that what is possible for some ought to be (and therefore is) possible to all, refuse to acquiesce in it. Hence, on the one hand, we get the wife as schoolmarm, the "cultivated" woman who is always trying to bring her husband "up to her level." She drags him to concerts and would like him to learn morris-dancing and invites "cultivated" people to the house. It often does surprisingly little harm. The middle-aged male has great powers of passive resistance and (if she but knew) of indulgence; "women will have their fads." Something much more painful happens when it is the men who are civilised and the women not, and when all the women, and many of the men too, simply refuse to recognise the fact.

When this happens we get a kind, polite, laborious and pitiful pretence. The women are "deemed" (as lawyers say) to be full members of the male circle. The fact—in itself not important—that they now smoke and drink like the men seems to simple-minded people a proof that they really are. No stagparties are allowed. Wherever the men meet, the women must come too. The men have learned to live among ideas. They know what discussion, proof and illustration mean. A woman who has had merely school lessons and has abandoned soon after marriage whatever tinge of "culture" they gave her—whose reading is the Women's Magazines and whose general conversation is almost wholly narrative—cannot really enter such a circle. She can be locally and physically present with it in the same room. What of that? If the men are ruthless, she sits bored and silent through a conversation which means nothing to her. If they are better bred, of course, they try to bring her in. Things are explained to her: people try to sublimate her irrelevant and blundering observations into some kind of sense. But the efforts soon fail and, for manners' sake, what might have been a real discussion is deliberately diluted and peters out in gossip, anecdotes, and jokes. Her presence has thus destroyed the very thing she was brought to share. She can never really enter the circle because the circle ceases to be itself when she enters it—as the horizon ceases to be the horizon when you get there. By learning to drink and smoke and perhaps to tell *risqué* stories, she has not, for this purpose, drawn an inch nearer to the men than her grandmother. But her grandmother was far happier and more realistic. She was at home talking real women's talk to other women and perhaps doing so with great charm, sense and even wit. She herself might be able to do the same. She may be quite as clever as the men whose evening she has spoiled, or cleverer. But she is not really interested in the same things, nor mistress of the same methods. (We all appear as dunces when feigning an interest in things we care nothing about.)

The presence of such women, thousands strong, helps to account for the modern disparagement of Friendship. They are often completely victorious. They banish male companionship, and therefore male Friendship, from whole neighbourhoods. In the only world they know, an endless prattling "Jolly" replaces the intercourse of minds. All the men they meet talk like women while women are present.

This victory over Friendship is often unconscious. There is, however, a more militant type of woman who plans it. I have heard one say "Never let two men sit together or they'll get talking about some *subject* and then there'll be no fun." Her point could not have been more accurately made. Talk, by all means; the more of it the better; unceasing cascades of the human voice; but not, please, a subject. The talk must not be about anything.

This gay lady—this lively, accomplished, "charming," unendurable bore—was seeking only each evening's amusement, making the meeting "go." But the conscious war against Friendship may be fought on a deeper level. There are women who regard it with hatred, envy and fear as the enemy of Eros and, perhaps even more, of Affection. A woman of that sort has a hundred arts to break up her husband's Friendships. She will quarrel with his Friends herself or, better still, with their wives. She will sneer, obstruct and lie. She does not realise that the husband whom she succeeds in isolating from his own kind will not be very well worth having; she has emasculated him. She will grow to be ashamed of him herself. Nor does she remember how much of his life lies in places where she cannot watch him. New Friendships will break out, but this time they will be secret. Lucky for her, and lucky beyond her deserts, if there are not soon other secrets as well.

All these, of course, are silly women. The sensible women who, if they wanted, would certainly be able to qualify themselves for the world of discussion and ideas, are precisely those who, if they are not qualified, never try to enter it or to destroy it. They have other fish to fry. At a mixed party they gravitate to one end of the room and talk women's talk to one another. They don't want us, for this sort of purpose, any more than we want them. It is only the riff-raff of each sex that wants to be incessantly hanging on the other. Live and let live. They laugh at us a good deal. That is just as it should be. Where the sexes, having no real shared activities, can meet only in Affection and Eros—cannot be Friends—it is healthy that each should have a lively sense of the other's absurdity. Indeed it is always healthy. No one ever really appreciated the other sex—just as no one really appreciates children or animals—without at times feeling them to be funny. For both sexes are. Humanity is tragi-comical; but the division into sexes enables each to see in the other the joke that often escapes it in itself—and the pathos too.

I gave warning that this chapter would be largely a rehabilitation. The preceding pages have, I hope, made clear why to me at least it seems no wonder if our ancestors regarded Friendship as something that raised us almost above humanity. This love, free from instinct, free from all duties but those which love has freely assumed, almost wholly free from jealousy, and free without qualification from the need to be needed, is eminently spiritual. It is the sort of love one can imagine between angels. Have we here found a natural love which is Love itself?

Before we rush to any such conclusion let us beware of the ambiguity in the word *spiritual*. There are many New Testament contexts in which it means "pertaining to the (Holy) Spirit," and in such contexts the spiritual is, by definition, good. But when *spiritual* is used simply as the opposite of corporeal, or instinctive, or animal, this is not so. There is spiritual evil as well as spiritual good. There are unholy, as well as holy, angels. The worst sins of men are spiritual. We must not think that in finding Friendship to be *spiritual* we have found it to be in itself holy or inerrant. Three significant facts remain to be taken into account.

The first, already mentioned, is the distrust which Authorities tend to have of close Friendships among their subjects. It may be unjustified; or there may be some basis for it.

Secondly, there is the attitude of the majority towards all circles of close Friends. Every name they give such a circle is more or less derogatory. It is at best a "set"; lucky if not a *coterie*, a "gang," a "little senate," or a "mutual admiration society." Those who in their own lives know only Affection, Companionship and Eros, suspect Friends to be "stuck-up prigs who think themselves too good for us." Of course this is the voice of Envy. But Envy always brings the truest charge, or the charge nearest to the truth, that she can think up; it hurts more. This charge, therefore, will have to be considered.

Finally, we must notice that Friendship is very rarely the image under which Scripture represents the love between God and Man. It is not entirely neglected; but far more often, seeking a symbol for the highest love of all, Scripture ignores this seemingly almost angelic relation and plunges into the depth of what is most natural and instinctive. Affection is taken as the image when God is represented as our Father; Eros, when Christ is represented as the Bridegroom of the Church.

Let us begin with the suspicions of those in Authority. I think there is a ground for them and that a consideration of this ground brings something important to light. Friendship, I have said, is born at the moment when one man says to another "What! You too? I thought that no one but myself . . ." But the common taste or vision or point of view which is thus discovered need not always be a nice one. From such a moment art, or philosophy, or an advance in religion or morals might well take their rise; but why not also torture, cannibalism, or human sacrifice? Surely most of us have experienced the ambivalent nature of such moments in our own youth? It was wonderful when we first met someone who cared for our favourite poet. What we had hardly understood before now took clear shape. What we had been half ashamed of we now freely acknowledged. But it was no less delightful when we first met someone who shared with us a secret evil. This too became far more palpable and explicit; of this too, we ceased to be ashamed. Even now, at whatever age, we all know the perilous charm of a shared hatred or grievance. (It is difficult not to hail as a Friend the only other man in College who really sees the faults of the Sub-Warden.)

Alone among unsympathetic companions, I hold certain

views and standards timidly, half ashamed to avow them and half doubtful if they can after all be right. Put me back among my Friends and in half an hour—in ten minutes—these same views and standards become once more indisputable. The opinion of this little circle, while I am in it, outweighs that of a thousand outsiders: as Friendship strengthens, it will do this even when my Friends are far away. For we all wish to be judged by our peers, by the men "after our own heart." Only they really know our mind and only they judge it by standards we fully acknowledge. Theirs is the praise we really covet and the blame we really dread. The little pockets of early Christians survived because they cared exclusively for the love of "the brethren" and stopped their ears to the opinion of the Pagan society all round them. But a circle of criminals, cranks, or perverts survives in just the same way; by becoming deaf to the opinion of the outer world, by discounting it as the chatter of outsiders who "don't understand," of the "conventional," "the bourgeois," the "Establishment," of prigs, prudes and humbugs.

It is therefore easy to see why Authority frowns on Friendship. Every real Friendship is a sort of secession, even a rebellion. It may be a rebellion of serious thinkers against accepted clap-trap or of faddists against accepted good sense; of real artists against popular ugliness or of charlatans against civilised taste; of good men against the badness of society or of bad men against its goodness. Whichever it is, it will be unwelcome to Top People. In each knot of Friends there is a sectional "public opinion" which fortifies its members against the public opinion of the community in general. Each therefore is a pocket of potential resistance. Men who have real Friends are less easy to manage or "get at"; harder for good Authorities to correct or for bad Authorities to corrupt. Hence if our masters, by force or by propaganda about "Togetherness" or by unobtrusively making privacy and unplanned leisure impossible, ever succeed in producing a world where all are Companions and none are Friends, they will have removed certain dangers, and will also have taken from us what is almost our strongest safeguard against complete servitude.

But the dangers are perfectly real. Friendship (as the ancients saw) can be a school of virtue; but also (as they did not see) a school of vice. It is ambivalent. It makes good men better and bad men worse. It would be a waste of time to elaborate the point. What concerns us is not to expatiate on the badness of bad Friendships but to become aware of the possible danger in good ones. This love, like the other natural loves, has its congenital liability to a particular disease.

It will be obvious that the element of secession, of indifference or deafness (at least on some matters) to the voices of the outer world, is common to all Friendships, whether good, bad, or merely innocuous. Even if the common ground of the Friendship is nothing more momentous than stamp-collecting, the circle rightly and inevitably ignores the views of the millions who think it a silly occupation and of the thousands who have merely dabbled in it. The founders of meteorology rightly and inevitably ignored the views of the millions who still attributed storms to witchcraft. There is no offence in this. As I know that I should be an Outsider to a circle of golfers, mathematicians, or motorists, so I claim the equal right of regarding them as Outsiders to mine. People who bore one another should meet seldom; people who interest one another, often.

The danger is that this partial indifference or deafness to outside opinion, justified and necessary though it is, may lead to a wholesale indifference or deafness. The most spectacular instances of this can be seen not in a circle of Friends but in a Theocratic or aristocratic class. We know what the Priests in Our Lord's time thought of the common people. The Knights in Froissart's chronicles had neither sympathy nor mercy for the "outsiders," the churls or peasantry. But this deplorable indifference was very closely intertwined with a good quality. They really had, among themselves, a very high standard of valour, generosity, courtesy and honour. This standard the cautious, close-fisted churl would have thought merely silly. The Knights, in maintaining it, were, and had to be, wholly indifferent to his views. They "didn't give a damn" what he thought. If they had, our own standard today would be the poorer and the coarser for it. But the habit of "not giving a damn" grows on a class. To discount the voice of the peasant where it really ought to be discounted makes it easier to discount his voice when he cries for justice or mercy. The partial deafness which is noble and necessary encourages the wholesale deafness which is arrogant and inhuman.

A circle of Friends cannot of course oppress the outer world as a powerful social class can. But it is subject, on its own scale, to the same danger. It can come to treat as "outsiders" in a general (and derogatory) sense those who were quite properly outsiders for a particular purpose. Thus, like an aristocracy, it can create around it a vacuum across which no voice will carry. The literary or artistic circle which began by discounting, perhaps rightly, the plain man's ideas about literature or art may come to discount equally his idea that they should pay their bills, cut their nails and behave civilly. Whatever faults the circle has—and no circle is without them—thus become incurable. But that is not all. The partial and defensible deafness was based on some kind of superiority—even if it were only a superior knowledge about stamps. The sense of superiority will then get itself attached to the total deafness. The group will disdain as well as ignore those outside it. It will, in effect, have turned itself into something very like a class. A *coterie* is a self-appointed aristocracy.

I said above that in a good Friendship each member often feels humility towards the rest. He sees that they are splendid and counts himself lucky to be among them. But unfortunately the *they* and *them* are also, from another point of view *we* and *us*. Thus the transition from individual humility to corporate pride is very easy.

I am not thinking of what we should call a social or snobbish pride: a delight in knowing, and being known to know, distinguished people. That is quite a different thing. The snob wishes to attach himself to some group because it is already regarded as an *élite;* friends are in danger of coming to regard themselves as an *élite* because they are already attached. We seek men after our own heart for their own sake and are then alarmingly or delightfully surprised by the feeling that we have become an aristocracy. Not that we'd call it that. Every reader who has known Friendship will probably feel inclined to deny with some heat that his own circle was ever guilty of such an absurdity. I feel the same. But in such matters it is best not to begin with ourselves. However it may be with us, I think we have all recognised some such tendency in those other circles to which we are the Outsiders.

I was once at some kind of conference where two clergymen, obviously close friends, began talking about "uncreated energies" other than God. I asked how there could be any uncreated things except God if the Creed was right in calling Him the "maker of all things visible and invisible." Their reply was to glance at one another and laugh. I had no objection to their laughter, but I wanted an answer in words as well. It was not at all a sneering or unpleasant laugh. It expressed very much what Americans would express by saying "Isn't he cute?" It was like the laughter of jolly grown-ups when an *enfant terrible* asks the sort of question that is never asked. You can hardly imagine how inoffensively it was done, nor how clearly it conveyed the impression that they were fully aware of living habitually on a higher plane than the rest of us, of coming among us as Knights among churls or as grown-ups among children. Very possibly they had an answer to my question and knew that I was too ignorant to follow it. If they had said in so many words "I'm afraid it would take too long to explain," I would not be attributing to them the pride of Friendship. The glance and the laugh are the real point—the audible and visible embodiment of a corporate superiority taken for granted and unconcealed. The almost complete inoffensiveness, the absence of any apparent wish to wound or exult (they were very nice young men) really underline the Olympian attitude. Here was a sense of superiority so secure that it could afford to be tolerant, urbane, unemphatic.

This sense of corporate superiority is not always Olympian; that is, tranquil and tolerant. It may be Titanic; restive, militant and embittered. Another time, when I had been addressing an undergraduate society and some discussion (very properly) followed my paper, a young man with an expression as tense as that of a rodent so dealt with me that I had to say, "Look, sir. Twice in the last five minutes you have as good as called me a liar. If you cannot discuss a question of criticism without that kind of thing I must leave." I expected he would do one of two things; lose his temper and redouble his insults, or else blush and apologise. The startling thing is that he did neither. No new perturbation was added to the habitual *malaise* of his expression. He did not repeat the Lie Direct; but apart from that he went on just as before. One had come up against an iron curtain. He was forearmed against the risk of any strictly personal relation, either friendly or hostile, with such as me. Behind this, almost certainly, there lies a circle of the Titanic sort—self-dubbed Knights Templars perpetually in arms to defend a critical Baphomet. We—who are *they* to them—do not exist as persons at all. We are specimens; specimens of various Age Groups, Types, Climates of Opinion, or Interests, to be exterminated. Deprived of one weapon, they cooly take up another. They are not, in the ordinary human sense, meeting us at all; they are merely doing a job of work—spraying (I have heard one use that image) insecticide.

My two nice young clergymen and my not so nice Rodent were on a high intellectual level. So were that famous set who in Edwardian times reached the sublime fatuity of calling themselves "the Souls." But the same feeling of corporate superior-

ity can possess a group of much more commonplace friends.
It will then be flaunted in a cruder way. We have all seen this
done by the "old hands" at school talking in the presence of a
new boy, or two Regulars in the Army talking before a "Temporary"; sometimes by very loud and vulgar friends to impress
mere strangers in a bar or a railway carriage. Such people talk
very intimately and esoterically in order to be overheard. Everyone who is not in the circle must be shown that he is not in
it. Indeed the Friendship may be "about" almost nothing except the fact that it excludes. In speaking to an Outsider each
member of it delights to mention the others by their Christian
names or nicknames; not although, but because, the Outsider
won't know who he means. A man I once knew was even subtler. He simply referred to his friends as if we all knew, certainly ought to know, who they were. "As Richard Button once
said to me . . . ," he would begin. We were all very young. We
never dared to admit that we hadn't heard of Richard Button.
It seemed so obvious that to everyone who was anyone he must
be a household word; "not to know him argued ourselves unknown." Only much later did we come to realise that no one
else had heard of him either. (Indeed I now have a suspicion
that some of these Richard Buttons, Hezekiah Cromwells, and
Eleanor Forsyths had no more existence than Mrs. Harris. But
for a year or so we were completely overawed.)

   We can thus detect the pride of Friendship—whether Olympian, Titanic, or merely vulgar—in many circles of Friends. It
would be rash to assume that our own is safe from its danger; for of course it is in our own that we should be slowest to
recognise it. The danger of such pride is indeed almost insepa-
rable from Friendly love. Friendship must exclude. From the
innocent and necessary act of excluding to the spirit of exclusiveness is an easy step; and thence to the degrading pleasure of
exclusiveness. If that is once admitted the downward slope will
grow rapidly steeper. We may never perhaps become Titans or
plain cads; we might—which is in some ways worse—become

"Souls." The common vision which first brought us together may fade quite away. We shall be a *coterie* that exists for the sake of being a *coterie;* a little self-elected (and therefore absurd) aristocracy, basking in the moonshine of our collective self-approval.

Sometimes a circle in this condition begins to dabble in the world of practice. Judiciously enlarging itself to admit recruits whose share in the original common interest is negligible but who are felt to be (in some undefined sense) "sound men," it becomes a power in the land. Membership of it comes to have a sort of political importance, though the politics involved may be only those of a regiment, a college, or a cathedral close. The manipulation of committees, the capture of jobs (for sound men) and the united front against the Have-nots now become its principal occupation, and those who once met to talk about God or poetry now meet to talk about lectureships or livings. Notice the justice of their doom. "Dust thou art and unto dust shalt thou return," said God to Adam. In a circle which has thus dwindled into a coven of wanglers Friendship has sunk back again into the mere practical Companionship which was its matrix. They are now the same sort of body as the primitive horde of hunters. Hunters, indeed, is precisely what they are; and not the kind of hunters I most respect.

The mass of the people, who are never quite right, are never quite wrong. They are hopelessly mistaken in their belief that every knot of friends came into existence for the sake of the pleasures of conceit and superiority. They are, I trust, mistaken in their belief that every Friendship actually indulges in these pleasures. But they would seem to be right in diagnosing pride as the danger to which Friendships are naturally liable. Just because this is the most spiritual of loves the danger which besets it is spiritual too. Friendship is even, if you like, angelic. But man needs to be triply protected by humility if he is to eat the bread of angels without risk.

Perhaps we may now hazard a guess why Scripture uses

Friendship so rarely as an image of the highest love. It is already, in actual fact, too spiritual to be a good symbol of Spiritual things. The highest does not stand without the lowest. God can safely represent Himself to us as Father and Husband because only a lunatic would think that He is physically our sire or that His marriage with the Church is other than mystical. But if Friendship were used for this purpose we might mistake the symbol for the thing symbolised. The danger inherent in it would be aggravated. We might be further encouraged to mistake that nearness (by resemblance) to the heavenly life which Friendship certainly displays for a nearness of approach.

Friendship, then, like the other natural loves, is unable to save itself. In reality, because it is spiritual and therefore faces a subtler enemy, it must, even more wholeheartedly than they, invoke the divine protection if it hopes to remain sweet. For consider how narrow its true path is. It must not become what the people call a "mutual admiration society"; yet if it is not full of mutual admiration, of Appreciative love, it is not Friendship at all. For unless our lives are to be miserably impoverished it must be for us in our Friendships as it was for Christiana and her party in *The Pilgrim's Progress:*

> They seemed to be a terror one to the other, for that they could not see that glory each one on herself which they could see in each other. Now therefore they began to esteem each other better than themselves. For you are fairer than I am, said one; and you are more comely than I am, said another.

There is in the long run only one way in which we can taste this illustrious experience with safety. And Bunyan has indicated it in the same passage. It was in the House of the Interpreter, after they had been bathed, sealed and freshly clothed in "White Raiment" that the women saw one another in this light. If we remember the bathing, sealing and robing, we shall be safe. And the higher the common ground of the Friendship is, the more necessary the remembrance. In an explicitly religious Friendship, above all, to forget it would be fatal.

For then it will seem to us that we—we four or five—have chosen one another, the insight of each finding the intrinsic beauty of the rest, like to like, a voluntary nobility; that we have ascended above the rest of mankind by our native powers. The other loves do not invite the same illusion. Affection obviously requires kinships or at least proximities which never depended on our own choice. And as for Eros, half the love songs and half the love poems in the world will tell you that the Beloved is your fate or destiny, no more your choice than a thunderbolt, for "it is not in our power to love or hate." Cupid's archery, genes—anything but ourselves. But in Friendship, being free of all that, we think we have chosen our peers. In reality, a few years' difference in the dates of our births, a few more miles between certain houses, the choice of one university instead of another, posting to different regiments, the accident of a topic being raised or not raised at a first meeting—any of these chances might have kept us apart. But, for a Christian, there are, strictly speaking, no chances. A secret Master of the Ceremonies has been at work. Christ, who said to the disciples "Ye have not chosen me, but I have chosen you," can truly say to every group of Christian friends "You have not chosen one another but I have chosen you for one another." The Friendship is not a reward for our discrimination and good taste in finding one another out. It is the instrument by which God reveals to each the beauties of all the others. They are no greater than the beauties of a thousand other men; by Friendship God opens our eyes to them. They are, like all beauties, derived from Him, and then, in a good Friendship, increased by Him through the Friendship itself, so that it is His instrument for creating as well as for revealing. At this feast it is He who has spread the board and it is He who has chosen the guests. It is He, we may dare to hope, who sometimes does, and always should, preside. Let us not reckon without our Host.

Not that we must always partake of it solemnly. "God who
made good laughter" forbid. It is one of the difficult and delightful subtleties of life that we must deeply acknowledge certain things to be serious and yet retain the power and will to
treat them often as lightly as a game. But there will be a time
for saying more about this in the next chapter. For the moment
I will only quote Dunbar's beautifully balanced advice:

> *Man, please thy Maker, and be merry,*
> *And give not for this world a cherry.*

Eros

BY EROS I mean of course that state which we call "being in love"; or, if you prefer, that kind of love which lovers are "in." Some readers may have been surprised when, in an earlier chapter, I described Affection as the love in which our experience seems to come closest to that of the animals. Surely, it might be asked, our sexual functions bring us equally close? This is quite true as regards human sexuality in general. But I am not going to be concerned with human sexuality simply as such. Sexuality makes part of our subject only when it becomes an ingredient in the complex state of "being in love." That sexual experience can occur without Eros, without being "in love," and that Eros includes other things besides sexual activity, I take for granted. If you prefer to put it that way, I am inquiring not into the sexuality which is common to us and the beasts or even common to all men but into one uniquely human variation of it which develops within "love"—what I call Eros. The carnal or animally sexual element within Eros, I intend (following an old usage) to call Venus. And I mean by Venus what is sexual not in some cryptic or rarefied sense—such as a depth-psychologist might explore—but in a perfectly obvious sense; what is known to be sexual by those who experience it; what could be proved to be sexual by the simplest observations.

Sexuality may operate without Eros or as part of Eros. Let me hasten to add that I make the distinction simply in order to limit our inquiry and without any moral implications. I am not at all subscribing to the popular idea that it is the absence or presence of Eros which makes the sexual act "impure" or "pure," degraded or fine, unlawful or lawful. If all who lay together without being in the state of Eros were abominable, we all come of tainted stock. The times and places in which marriage depends on Eros are in a small minority. Most of our ancestors were married off in early youth to partners chosen by their parents on grounds that had nothing to do with Eros. They went to the act with no other "fuel," so to speak, than plain animal desire. And they did right; honest Christian husbands and wives, obeying their fathers and mothers, discharging to one another their "marriage debt," and bringing up families in the fear of the Lord. Conversely, this act, done under the influence of a soaring and iridescent Eros which reduces the role of the senses to a minor consideration, may yet be plain adultery, may involve breaking a wife's heart, deceiving a husband, betraying a friend, polluting hospitality and deserting your children. It has not pleased God that the distinction between a sin and a duty should turn on fine feelings. This act, like any other, is justified (or not) by far more prosaic and definable criteria; by the keeping or breaking of promises, by justice or injustice, by charity or selfishness, by obedience or disobedience. My treatment rules out mere sexuality—sexuality without Eros—on grounds that have nothing to do with morals; because it is irrelevant to our purpose.

To the evolutionist Eros (the human variation) will be something that grows out of Venus, a late complication and development of the immemorial biological impulse. We must not assume, however, that this is necessarily what happens within the consciousness of the individual. There may be those who have first felt mere sexual appetite for a woman and then gone on at a later stage to "fall in love with her." But I doubt if this is at all common. Very often what comes first is simply a de-lighted pre-occupation with the Beloved—a general, unspeci-fied pre-occupation with her in her totality. A man in this state really hasn't leisure to think of sex. He is too busy thinking of a person. The fact that she is a woman is far less important than the fact that she is herself. He is full of desire, but the desire may not be sexually toned. If you asked him what he wanted, the true reply would often be, "To go on thinking of her." He is love's contemplative. And when at a later stage the explicitly sexual element awakes, he will not feel (unless scientific theo-ries are influencing him) that this had all along been the root of the whole matter. He is more likely to feel that the incoming tide of Eros, having demolished many sand-castles and made islands of many rocks, has now at last with a triumphant sev-enth wave flooded this part of his nature also—the little pool of ordinary sexuality which was there on his beach before the tide came in. Eros enters him like an invader, taking over and reorganising, one by one, the institutions of a conquered coun-try. It may have taken over many others before it reaches the sex in him; and it will reorganise that too.

No one has indicated the nature of that reorganisation more briefly and accurately than George Orwell, who disliked it and preferred sexuality in its native condition, uncontaminated by Eros. In *Nineteen Eighty-Four* his dreadful hero (how much less human than the four-footed heroes of his excellent *Animal Farm!*), before towsing the heroine, demands a reassurance, "You like doing this?" he asks, "I don't mean simply me; I mean the thing in itself." He is not satisfied till he gets the answer, "I adore it." This little dialogue defines the reorganisation. Sexual desire, without Eros, wants *it*, the *thing in itself*; Eros wants the Beloved.

The *thing* is a sensory pleasure; that is, an event occuring within one's own body. We use a most unfortunate idiom when we say, of a lustful man prowling the streets, that he "wants a woman." Strictly speaking, a woman is just what he does not

want. He wants a pleasure for which a woman happens to be
the necessary piece of apparatus. How much he cares about the
woman as such may be gauged by his attitude to her five minutes after fruition (one does not keep the carton after one has
smoked the cigarettes). Now Eros makes a man really want,
not a woman, but one particular woman. In some mysterious
but quite indisputable fashion the lover desires the Beloved
herself, not the pleasure she can give. No lover in the world
ever sought the embraces of the woman he loved as the result of a calculation, however unconscious, that they would be
more pleasurable than those of any other woman. If he raised
the question he would, no doubt, expect that this would be so.
But to raise it would be to step outside the world of Eros altogether. The only man I know of who ever did raise it was Lucretius, and he was certainly not in love when he did. It is interesting to note his answer. That austere voluptuary gave it as his
opinion that love actually impairs sexual pleasure. The emotion was a distraction. It spoiled the cool and critical receptivity of his palate. (A great poet; but "Lord, what beastly fellows
these Romans were!")

The reader will notice that Eros thus wonderfully transforms what is *par excellence* a Need-pleasure into the most Appreciative of all pleasures. It is the nature of a Need-pleasure to
show us the object solely in relation to our need, even our momentary need. But in Eros, a Need, at its most intense, sees the
object most intensely as a thing admirable in herself, important
far beyond her relation to the lover's need.

If we had not all experienced this, if we were mere logicians,
we might boggle at the conception of desiring a human being,
as distinct from desiring any pleasure, comfort, or service that
human being can give. And it is certainly hard to explain. Lovers themselves are trying to express part of it (not much) when
they say they would like to "eat" one another. Milton has expressed more when he fancies angelic creatures with bodies
made of light who can achieve total interpenetration instead of

our mere embraces. Charles Williams has said something of it in the words, "Love you? I *am* you."

Without Eros sexual desire, like every other desire, is a fact about ourselves. Within Eros it is rather about the Beloved. It becomes almost a mode of perception, entirely a mode of expression. It feels objective; something outside us, in the real world. That is why Eros, though the king of pleasures, always (at his height) has the air of regarding pleasure as a by-product. To think about it would plunge us back in ourselves, in our own nervous system. It would kill Eros, as you can "kill" the finest mountain prospect by locating it all in your own retina and optic nerves. Anyway, whose pleasure? For one of the first things Eros does is to obliterate the distinction between giving and receiving.

Hitherto I have been trying merely to describe, not to evaluate. But certain moral questions now inevitably arise, and I must not conceal my own view of them. It is submitted rather than asserted, and of course open to correction by better men, better lovers and better Christians.

It has been widely held in the past, and is perhaps held by many unsophisticated people to-day, that the spiritual danger of Eros arises almost entirely from the carnal element within it; that Eros is "noblest" or "purest" when Venus is reduced to the minimum. The older moral theologians certainly seem to have thought that the danger we chiefly had to guard against in marriage was that of a soul-destroying surrender to the senses. It will be noticed, however, that this is not the Scriptural approach. St. Paul, dissuading his converts from marriage, says nothing about that side of the matter except to discourage prolonged abstinence from Venus (I *Cor.* VII, 5). What he fears is pre-occupation, the need of constantly "pleasing"—that is, considering—one's partner, the multiple distractions of domesticity. It is marriage itself, not the marriage bed, that will be likely to hinder us from waiting uninterruptedly on God. And surely St. Paul is right? If I may trust my own experience, it is (within marriage as without) the practical and prudential cares of this world, and even the smallest and most prosaic of those cares, that are the great distraction. The gnat-like cloud of petty anxieties and decisions about the conduct of the next hour have interfered with my prayers more often than any passion or appetite whatever. The great, permanent temptation of marriage is not to sensuality but (quite bluntly) to avarice. With all proper respect to the medieval guides, I cannot help remembering that they were all celibates, and probably did not know what Eros does to our sexuality; how, far from aggravating, he reduces the nagging and addictive character of mere appetite. And that not simply by satisfying it. Eros, without diminishing desire, makes abstinence easier. He tends, no doubt, to a pre-occupation with the Beloved which can indeed be an obstacle to the spiritual life; but not chiefly a sensual pre-occupation.

The real spiritual danger in Eros as a whole lies, I believe, elsewhere. I will return to the point. For the moment, I want to speak of the danger which at present, in my opinion, especially haunts the act of love. This is a subject on which I disagree, not with the human race (far from it), but with many of its gravest spokesmen. I believe we are all being encouraged to take Venus too seriously; at any rate, with a wrong kind of seriousness. All my life a ludicrous and portentous solemnisation of sex has been going on.

One author tells us that Venus should recur through the married life in "a solemn, sacramental rhythm." A young man to whom I had described as "pornographic" a novel that he much admired, replied with genuine bewilderment, "Pornographic? But how can it be? It treats the whole thing so seriously"—as if a long face were a sort of moral disinfectant. Our friends who harbour Dark Gods, the "pillar of blood" school, attempt seriously to restore something like the Phallic religion. Our advertisements, at their sexiest, paint the whole business in terms of the rapt, the intense, the swoony-devout; seldom a hint of gaiety. And the psychologists have so bedevilled us with the infinite importance of complete sexual adjustment and the all but impossibility of achieving it, that I could believe some young couples now go to it with the complete works of Freud, Kraft-Ebbing, Havelock Ellis and Dr. Stopes spread out on bed-tables all round them. Cheery old Ovid, who never either ignored a mole-hill or made a mountain of it, would be more to the point. We have reached the stage at which nothing is more needed than a roar of old-fashioned laughter.

But, it will be replied, the thing *is* serious. Yes; quadruply so. First, theologically, because this is the body's share in marriage which, by God's choice, is the mystical image of the union between God and Man. Secondly, as what I will venture to call a sub-Christian, or Pagan or natural sacrament, our human participation in, and exposition of, the natural forces of life and fertility—the marriage of Sky-Father and Earth-Mother. Thirdly, on the moral level, in view of the obligations involved and the incalculable momentousness of being a parent and ancestor. Finally it has (sometimes, not always) a great emotional seriousness in the minds of the participants.

But eating is also serious; theologically, as the vehicle of the Blessed Sacrament; ethically in view of our duty to feed the hungry; socially, because the table is from time immemorial the place for talk; medically, as all dyspeptics know. Yet we do not bring bluebooks to dinner nor behave there as if we were in church. And it is *gourmets*, not saints, who come nearest to doing so. Animals are always serious about food.

We must not be totally serious about Venus. Indeed we can't be totally serious without doing violence to our humanity. It is not for nothing that every language and literature in the world is full of jokes about sex. Many of them may be dull or disgusting and nearly all of them are old. But we must insist that they embody an attitude to Venus which in the long run endangers the Christian life far less than a reverential gravity. We must not attempt to find an absolute in the flesh. Banish play and

laughter from the bed of love and you may let in a false goddess. She will be even falser than the Aphrodite of the Greeks;
for they, even while they worshipped her, knew that she was
"laughter-loving." The mass of the people are perfectly right in
their conviction that Venus is a partly comic spirit. We are under no obligation at all to sing all our love-duets in the throb-
bing, world-without-end, heart-breaking manner of Tristan
and Isolde; let us often sing like Papageno and Papagena instead.

Venus herself will have a terrible revenge if we take her
(occasional) seriousness at its face value. And that in two ways.
One is most comically—though with no comic intention—illustrated by Sir Thomas Browne when he says that her service
is "the foolishest act a wise man commits in all his life, nor is
there anything that will more deject his cool'd imagination,
when he shall consider what an odd and unworthy piece of
folly he hath committed." But if he had gone about that act
with less solemnity in the first place he would not have suffered this "dejection." If his imagination had not been misled,
its cooling would have brought no such revulsion. But Venus
has another and worse revenge.

She herself is a mocking, mischievous spirit, far more elf
than deity, and makes game of us. When all external circumstances are fittest for her service she will leave one or both the
lovers totally indisposed for it. When every overt act is impossible and even glances cannot be exchanged—in trains, in
shops, and at interminable parties—she will assail them with
all her force. An hour later, when time and place agree, she will
have mysteriously withdrawn; perhaps from only one of them.
What a pother this must raise—what resentments, self-pities,
suspicions, wounded vanities and all the current chatter about
"frustration"—in those who have deified her! But sensible lovers laugh. It is all part of the game; a game of catch-as-catch-
can, and the escapes and tumbles and head-on collisions are to
be treated as a romp.

For I can hardly help regarding it as one of God's jokes that a passion so soaring, so apparently transcendent, as Eros, should thus be linked in incongruous symbiosis with a bodily appetite which, like any other appetite, tactlessly reveals its connections with such mundane factors as weather, health, diet, circulation, and digestion. In Eros at times we seem to be flying; Venus gives us the sudden twitch that reminds us we are really captive balloons. It is a continual demonstration of the truth that we are composite creatures, rational animals, akin on one side to the angels, on the other to tom-cats. It is a bad thing not to be able to take a joke. Worse, not to take a divine joke; made, I grant you, at our expense, but also (who doubts it?) for our endless benefit.

Man has held three views of his body. First there is that of those ascetic Pagans who called it the prison or the "tomb" of the soul, and of Christians like Fisher to whom it was a "sack of dung," food for worms, filthy, shameful, a source of nothing but temptation to bad men and humiliation to good ones. Then there are the Neo-Pagans (they seldom know Greek), the nudists and the sufferers from Dark Gods, to whom the body is glorious. But thirdly we have the view which St. Francis expressed by calling his body "Brother Ass." All three may be—I am not sure—defensible; but give me St. Francis for my money.

Ass is exquisitely right because no one in his senses can either revere or hate a donkey. It is a useful, sturdy, lazy, obstinate, patient, lovable and infuriating beast; deserving now the stick and now a carrot; both pathetically and absurdly beautiful. So the body. There's no living with it till we recognise that one of its functions in our lives is to play the part of buffoon. Until some theory has sophisticated them, every man, woman and child in the world knows this. The fact that we have bodies is the oldest joke there is. Eros (like death, figure-drawing, and the study of medicine) may at moments cause us to take it with total seriousness. The error consists in concluding that Eros should always do so and permanently abolish the joke. But this is not what happens. The very faces of all the happy lovers we know make it clear. Lovers, unless their love is very shortlived, again and again feel an element not only of comedy, not only of play, but even of buffoonery, in the body's expression of Eros. And the body would frustrate us if this were not so. It Would be too clumsy an instrument to render love's music unless its very clumsiness could be felt as adding to the total experience its own grotesque charm—a sub-plot or antimasque miming with its own hearty rough-and-tumble what the soul enacts in statelier fashion. (Thus in old comedies the lyric loves of the hero and heroine are at once parodied and corroborated by some much more earthy affair between a Touchstone and an Audrey or a valet and a chambermaid.) The highest does not stand without the lowest. There is indeed at certain moments a high poetry in the flesh itself; but also, by your leave, an irreducible element of obstinate and ludicrous unpoetry. If it does not make itself felt on one occasion, it will on another. Far better plant it foursquare within the drama of Eros as comic relief than pretend you haven't noticed it.

For indeed we require this relief. The poetry is there as well as the un-poetry; the gravity of Venus as well as her levity, the *gravis ardor* or burning weight of desire. Pleasure, pushed to its extreme, shatters us like pain. The longing for a union which only the flesh can mediate while the flesh, our mutually excluding bodies, renders it forever unattainable can have the grandeur of a metaphysical pursuit. Amorousness as well as grief can bring tears to the eyes. But Venus does not always come thus "entire, fastened to her prey," and the fact that she sometimes does so is the very reason for preserving always a hint of playfulness in our attitude to her. When natural things look most divine, the demoniac is just round the corner.

This refusal to be quite immersed—this recollection of the levity even when, for the moment, only the gravity is displayed—is especially relevant to a certain attitude which Venus, in her intensity, evokes from most (I believe, not all) pairs of lovers. This act can invite the man to an extreme, though short-lived, masterfulness, to the dominance of a conqueror or a captor, and the woman to a correspondingly extreme subjection and surrender. Hence the roughness, even fierceness, of some erotic play; the "lover's pinch which hurts and is desired." How should a sane couple think of this? or a Christian couple permit it?

I think it is harmless and wholesome on one condition. We must recognise that we have here to do with what I called "the Pagan sacrament" in sex. In Friendship, as we noticed, each participant stands for precisely himself—the contingent individual he is. But in the act of love we are not merely ourselves. We are also representatives. It is here no impoverishment but an enrichment to be aware that forces older and less personal than we work through us. In us all the masculinity and femininity of the world, all that is assailant and responsive, are momentarily focused. The man does play the Sky-Father and the woman the Earth-Mother; he does play Form, and she Matter. But we must give full value to the word *play*. Of course neither "plays a part" in the sense of being a hypocrite. But each plays a part or role in—well, in something which is comparable to a mystery-play or ritual (at one extreme) and to a masque or even a charade (at the other).

A woman who accepted as literally her own this extreme self-surrender would be an idolatress offering to a man what belongs only to God. And a man would have to be the coxcomb of all coxcombs, and indeed a blasphemer, if he arrogated to himself, as the mere person he is, the sort of sovereignty to which Venus for a moment exalts him. But what cannot lawfully be yielded or claimed can be lawfully enacted. Outside this ritual or drama he and she are two immortal souls, two free-born adults, two citizens. We should be much mistaken if we supposed that those marriages where this mastery is most asserted and acknowledged in the act of Venus were those where the husband is most likely to be dominant in the married life as a whole; the reverse is perhaps more probable. But within the rite or drama they become a god and goddess between whom there is no equality—whose relations are asymmetrical.

Some will think it strange I should find an element of ritual or masquerade in that action which is often regarded as the most real, the most unmasked and sheerly genuine, we ever do. Are we not our true selves when naked? In a sense, no. The word *naked* was originally a past participle; the naked man was the man who had undergone a process of *naking*, that is, of stripping or peeling (you used the verb of nuts and fruit). Time out of mind the naked man has seemed to our ancestors not the natural but the abnormal man; not the man who has abstained from dressing but the man who has been for some reason undressed. And it is a simple fact—anyone can observe it at a men's bathing place—that nudity emphasises common humanity and soft-pedals what is individual. In that way we are "more ourselves" when clothed. By nudity the lovers cease to be solely John and Mary; the universal He and She are emphasised. You could almost say they *put* on nakedness as a ceremonial robe—or as the costume for a charade. For we must still be aware—and never more than when we thus partake of the Pagan sacrament in our love-passages—of being serious in the wrong way. The Sky-Father himself is only a Pagan dream of One far greater than Zeus and far more masculine than the male. And a mortal man is not even the Sky-Father, and cannot really wear his crown. Only a copy of it, done in tinselled paper. I do not call it this in contempt. I like ritual; I like private theatricals; I even like charades. Paper crowns have their legitimate, and (in the proper context) their serious, uses. They are not in the last resort much flimsier ("if imagination mend them") then all earthly dignities.

But I dare not mention this Pagan sacrament without turning aside to guard against any danger of confusing it with an incomparably higher mystery. As nature crowns man in that brief action, so the Christian law has crowned him in the permanent relationship of marriage, bestowing—or should I say, inflicting?—a certain "headship" on him. This is a very different coronation. And as we could easily take the natural mystery too seriously, so we might take the Christian mystery not seriously enough. Christian writers (notably Milton) have sometimes spoken of the husband's headship with a complacency to make the blood run cold. We must go back to our Bibles. The husband is the head of the wife just in so far as he is to her what Christ is to the Church. He is to love her as Christ loved the Church—read on—*and give his life for her* (*Eph.* V, 25). This headship, then, is most fully embodied not in the husband we should all wish to be but in him whose marriage is most like a crucifixion; whose wife receives most and gives least, is most unworthy of him, is—in her own mere nature—least lovable. For the Church has no beauty but what the Bride-groom gives her; he does not find, but makes her, lovely. The chrism of this terrible coronation is to be seen not in the joys of any man's marriage but in its sorrows, in the sickness and sufferings of a good wife or the faults of a bad one, in his unwearying (never paraded) care or his inexhaustible forgiveness: forgiveness, not acquiescence. As Christ sees in the flawed, proud, fanatical or lukewarm Church on earth that Bride who will one day be without spot or wrinkle, and labours to produce the latter, so the husband whose headship is Christ-like (and he is allowed no other sort) never despairs. He is a King Cophetua who after twenty years still hopes that the beggar-girl will one day learn to speak the truth and wash behind her ears.

To say this is not to say that there is any virtue or wisdom in making a marriage that involves such misery. There is no wisdom or virtue in seeking unnecessary martyrdom or deliberately courting persecution; yet it is, none the less, the persecuted or martyred Christian in whom the pattern of the Master is most unambiguously realised. So, in these terrible marriages, once they have come about, the "headship" of the husband, if only he can sustain it, is most Christ-like.

The sternest feminist need not grudge my sex the crown offered to it either in the Pagan or in the Christian mystery. For the one is of paper and the other of thorns. The real danger is not that husbands may grasp the latter too eagerly; but that they will allow or compel their wives to usurp it.

From Venus, the carnal ingredient within Eros, I now turn to Eros as a whole. Here we shall see the same pattern repeated. As Venus within Eros does not really aim at pleasure, so Eros does not aim at happiness. We may think he does, but when he is brought to the test it proves otherwise. Everyone knows that it is useless to try to separate lovers by proving to them that their marriage will be an unhappy one. This is not only because they will disbelieve you. They usually will, no doubt. But even if they believed, they would not be dissuaded. For it is the very mark of Eros that when he is in us we had rather share unhappiness with the Beloved than be happy on any other terms. Even if the two lovers are mature and experienced people who know that broken hearts heal in the end and can clearly foresee that, if they once steeled themselves to go through the present agony of parting, they would almost certainly be happier ten years hence than marriage is at all likely to make them — even then, they would not part. To Eros all these calculations are irrelevant — just as the coolly brutal judgment of Lucretius is irrelevant to Venus. Even when it becomes clear beyond all evasion that marriage with the Beloved cannot possibly lead to happiness — when it cannot even profess to offer any other life than that of tending an incurable invalid, of hopeless poverty, of exile, or of disgrace — Eros never hesitates to say, "Better this than parting. Better to be miserable with her than happy without her. Let our hearts break provided they break together." If the voice within us does not say this, it is not the voice of Eros.

This is the grandeur and terror of love. But notice, as before, side by side with this grandeur, the playfulness. Eros, as well as Venus, is the subject of countless jokes. And even when the circumstances of the two lovers are so tragic that no bystander could keep back his tears, they themselves—in want, in hospital wards, on visitors' days in jail—will sometimes be surprised by a merriment which strikes the onlooker (but not them) as unbearably pathetic. Nothing is falser than the idea that mockery is necessarily hostile. Until they have a baby to laugh at, lovers are always laughing at each other.

It is in the grandeur of Eros that the seeds of danger are concealed. He has spoken like a god. His total commitment, his reckless disregard of happiness, his transcendence of self-regard, sound like a message from the eternal world.

And yet it cannot, just as it stands, be the voice of God Himself. For Eros, speaking with that very grandeur and displaying that very transcendence of self, may urge to evil as well as to good. Nothing is shallower than the belief that a love which leads to sin is always qualitatively lower—more animal or more trivial—than one which leads to faithful, fruitful and Christian marriage. The love which leads to cruel and perjured unions, even to suicide-pacts and murder, is not likely to be wandering lust or idle sentiment. It may well be Eros in all his splendour; heart-breakingly sincere; ready for every sacrifice except renunciation.

There have been schools of thought which accepted the voice of Eros as something actually transcendent and tried to justify the absoluteness of his commands. Plato will have it that "falling in love" is the mutual recognition on earth of souls which have been singled out for one another in a previous and celestial existence. To meet the Beloved is to realise "We loved before we were born." As a myth to express what lovers feel this is admirable. But if one accepted it literally one would be faced by an embarrassing consequence. We should have to conclude that in that heavenly and forgotten life affairs were no better managed than here. For Eros may unite the most unsuitable yokefellows; many unhappy, and predictably unhappy, marriages were love-matches.

A theory more likely to be accepted in our own day is what we may call Shavian—Shaw himself might have said "metabiological"—Romanticism. According to Shavian Romanticism the voice of Eros is the voice of the *élan vital* or Life Force, the "evolutionary appetite." In overwhelming a particular couple it is seeking parents (or ancestors) for the superman. It is indifferent both to their personal happiness and to the rules of morality because it aims at something which Shaw thinks very much more important: the future perfection of our species. But if all this were true it hardly makes clear whether—and if so, why—we should obey it. All pictures yet offered us of the superman are so unattractive that one might well vow celibacy at once to avoid the risk of begetting him. And secondly, this theory surely leads to the conclusion that the Life Force does not very well understand its (or her? or his?) own business. So far as we can see the existence or intensity of Eros between two people is no warrant that their offspring will be especially satisfactory, or even that they will have offspring at all. Two good "strains" (in the stockbreeders' sense), not two good lovers, is the recipe for fine children. And what on earth was the Life Force doing through all those countless generations when the begetting of children depended very little on mutual Eros and very much on arranged marriages, slavery, and rape? Has it only just thought of this bright idea for improving the species?

Neither the Platonic nor the Shavian type of erotic transcendentalism can help a Christian. We are not worshippers of the Life Force and we know nothing of previous existences. We must not give unconditional obedience to the voice of Eros when he speaks most like a god. Neither must we ignore or attempt to deny the god-like quality. This love is really and truly like Love Himself. In it there is a real nearness to God (by Resemblance); but not, therefore and necessarily, a nearness of Approach. Eros, honoured so far as love of God and charity to our fellows will allow, may become for us a means of Approach. His total commitment is a paradigm or example, built into our natures, of the love we ought to exercise towards God and Man. As nature, for the nature-lover, gives a content to the word *glory*, so this gives a content to the word *Charity*. It is as if Christ said to us through Eros, "Thus—just like this—with this prodigality—not counting the cost—you are to love me and the least of my brethren." Our conditional honour to Eros will of course vary with our circumstances. Of some a total renunciation (but not a contempt) is required. Others, with Eros as their fuel and also as their model, can embark on the married life. Within which Eros, of himself, will never be enough—will indeed survive only in so far as he is continually chastened and corroborated by higher principles.

But Eros, honoured without reservation and obeyed unconditionally, becomes a demon. And this is just how he claims to be honoured and obeyed. Divinely indifferent to our selfishness, he is also demoniacally rebellious to every claim of God or Man that would oppose him. Hence as the poet says:

> *People in love cannot be moved by kindness,*
> *And opposition makes them feel like martyrs.*

Martyrs is exactly right. Years ago when I wrote about medieval love-poetry and described its strange, half make-believe, "religion of love," I was blind enough to treat this as an almost purely literary phenomenon. I know better now. Eros by his nature invites it. Of all loves he is, at his height, most god-like; therefore most prone to demand our worship. Of himself he always tends to turn "being in love" into a sort of religion.

Theologians have often feared, in this love, a danger of idolatry. I think they meant by this that the lovers might idolise one another. That does not seem to me to be the real danger; certainly not in marriage. The deliciously plain prose and businesslike intimacy of married life render it absurd. So does the Affection in which Eros is almost invariably clothed.

Even in courtship I question whether anyone who has felt the thirst for the Uncreated, or even dreamed of feeling it, ever supposed that the Beloved could satisfy it. As a fellow-pilgrim pierced with the very same desire, that is, as a Friend, the Beloved may be gloriously and helpfully relevant; but as an object for it—well (I would not be rude), ridiculous. The real danger seems to me not that the lovers will idolise each other but that they will idolise Eros himself.

I do not of course mean that they will build altars or say prayers to him. The idolatry I speak of can be seen in the popular misinterpretation of Our Lord's words "Her sins, which are many, are forgiven her, for she loved much" (*Luke* VII, 47). From the context, and especially from the preceding parable of the debtors, it is clear that this must mean: "The greatness of her love for Me is evidence of the greatness of the sins I have forgiven her." (The *for* here is like the *for* in "He can't have gone out, *for* his hat is still hanging in the hall"; the presence of the hat is not the cause of his being in the house but a probable proof that he is). But thousands of people take it quite differently. They first assume, with no evidence, that her sins were sins against chastity, though, for all we know, they may have been usury, dishonest shopkeeping, or cruelty to children. And they then take Our Lord to be saying, "I forgive her unchastity because she was so much in love." The implication is that a great Eros extenuates—almost sanctions—almost sanctifies—any actions it leads to.

When lovers say of some act that we might blame, "Love made us do it," notice the tone. A man saying, "I did it because I was frightened," or "I did it because I was angry," speaks quite differently. He is putting forward an excuse for what he feels to require excusing. But the lovers are seldom doing quite that. Notice how tremulously, almost how devoutly, they say the word *love*, not so much pleading an "extenuating circumstance" as appealing to an authority. The confession can be almost a boast. There can be a shade of defiance in it. They "feel like martyrs." In extreme cases what their words really express is a demure yet unshakable allegiance to the god of love.

"These reasons in love's law have passed for good," says Milton's Dalila. That is the point; *in love's law.* "In love," we have our own "law," a religion of our own, our own god. Where a true Eros is present resistance to his commands feels like apostasy, and what are really (by the Christian standard) temptations speak with the voice of duties—quasi-religious duties, acts of pious zeal to love. He builds his own religion round the lovers. Benjamin Constant has noticed how he creates for them, in a few weeks or months, a joint past which seems to them immemorial. They recur to it continually with wonder and reverence, as the Psalmists recur to the history of Israel. It is in fact the Old Testament of Love's religion; the record of love's judgments and mercies towards his chosen pair up to the moment when they first knew they were lovers. After that, its New Testament begins. They are now under a new law, under what corresponds (in this religion) to Grace. They are new creatures. The "spirit" of Eros supersedes all laws, and they must not "grieve" it.

It seems to sanction all sorts of actions they would not otherwise have dared. I do not mean solely, or chiefly, acts that violate chastity. They are just as likely to be acts of injustice or uncharity against the outer world. They will seem like proofs of piety and zeal towards Eros. The pair can say to one another in an almost sacrificial spirit, "It is for love's sake that I have neglected my parents—left my children—cheated my partner—failed my friend at his greatest need." These reasons in love's law have passed for good. The votaries may even come to feel a particular merit in such sacrifices; what costlier offering can be laid on love's altar than one's conscience?

And all the time the grim joke is that this Eros whose voice seems to speak from the eternal realm is not himself necessarily even permanent. He is notoriously the most mortal of our loves. The world rings with complaints of his fickleness. What is baffling is the combination of this fickleness with his protestations of permanency. To be in love is both to intend and to promise lifelong fidelity. Love makes vows unasked; can't be deterred from making them. "I will be ever true," are almost the first words he utters. Not hypocritically but sincerely. No experience will cure him of the delusion. We have all heard of people who are in love again every few years; each time sincerely convinced that "*this* time it's the real thing," that their wanderings are over, that they have found their true love and will themselves be true till death.

And yet Eros is in a sense right to make this promise. The event of falling in love is of such a nature that we are right to reject as intolerable the idea that it should be transitory. In one high bound it has overleaped the massive wall of our selfhood; it has made appetite itself altruistic, tossed personal happiness aside as a triviality and planted the interests of another in the centre of our being. Spontaneously and without effort we have fulfilled the law (towards one person) by loving our neighbour as ourselves. It is an image, a foretaste, of what we must become to all if Love Himself rules in us without a rival. It is even (well used) a preparation for that. Simply to relapse from it, merely to "fall out of" love again, is—if I may coin the ugly word—a sort of *disredemption*. Eros is driven to promise what Eros of himself cannot perform.

Can we be in this selfless liberation for a lifetime? Hardly for a week. Between the best possible lovers this high condition is intermittent. The old self soon turns out to be not so dead as he pretended—as after a religious conversion. In either he may be momentarily knocked flat; he will soon be up again; if not on his feet, at least on his elbow, if not roaring, at least back to his surly grumbling or his mendicant whine. And Venus will often slip back into mere sexuality.

But these lapses will not destroy a marriage between two "decent and sensible" people. The couple whose marriage will certainly be endangered by them, and possibly ruined, are those who have idolised Eros. They thought he had the power and truthfulness of a god. They expected that mere feeling would do for them, and permanently, all that was necessary. When this expectation is disappointed they throw the blame on Eros or, more usually, on their partners. In reality, however, Eros, having made his gigantic promise and shown you in glimpses what its performance would be like, has "done his stuff." He, like a godparent, makes the vows; it is we who must keep them. It is we who must labour to bring our daily life into even closer accordance with what the glimpses have revealed. We must do the works of Eros when Eros is not present. This all good lovers know, though those who are not reflective or articulate will be able to express it only in a few conventional phrases about "taking the rough along with the smooth," not "expecting too much," having "a little common sense," and the like. And all good Christian lovers know that this programme, modest as it sounds, will not be carried out except by humility, charity and divine grace; that it is indeed the whole Christian life seen from one particular angle.

Thus Eros, like the other loves, but more strikingly because of his strength, sweetness, terror and high port, reveals his true status. He cannot of himself be what, nevertheless, he must be if he is to remain Eros. He needs help; therefore needs to be ruled. The god dies or becomes a demon unless he obeys God. It would be well if, in such case, he always died. But he may live on, mercilessly chaining together two mutual tormentors, each raw all over with the poison of hate-in-love, each ravenous to receive and implacably refusing to give, jealous, suspicious, resentful, struggling for the upper hand, determined to be free and to allow no freedom, living on "scenes." Read *Anna Karenina*, and do not fancy that such things happen only in Russia. The lovers' old hyperbole of "eating" each other can come horribly near to the truth.

Charity

WILLIAM Morris wrote a poem called "Love Is Enough" and someone is said to have reviewed it briefly in the words "It isn't." Such has been the burden of this book. The natural loves are not self-sufficient. Something else, at first vaguely described as "decency and common sense," but later revealed as goodness, and finally as the whole Christian life in one particular relation, must come to the help of the mere feeling if the feeling is to be kept sweet.

To say this is not to belittle the natural loves but to indicate where their real glory lies. It is no disparagement to a garden to say that it will not fence and weed itself, nor prune its own fruit trees, nor roll and cut its own lawns. A garden is a good thing but that is not the sort of goodness it has. It will remain a garden, as distinct from a wilderness, only if someone does all these things to it. Its real glory is of quite a different kind. The very fact that it needs constant weeding and pruning bears witness to that glory. It teems with life. It glows with colour and smells like heaven and puts forward at every hour of a summer day beauties which man could never have created and could not even, on his own resources, have imagined. If you want to see the difference between its contribution and the gardener's, put the commonest weed it grows side by side with his hoes, rakes, shears, and packet of weed killer; you have put beauty, energy and fecundity beside dead, sterile things. Just so, our "decency and common sense" show grey and deathlike beside the geniality of love. And when the garden is in its full glory the gardener's contributions to that glory will still have been in a sense paltry compared with those of nature. Without life springing from the earth, without rain, light and heat descending from the sky, he could do nothing. When he has done all, he has merely encouraged here and discouraged there, powers and beauties that have a different source. But his share, though small, is indispensable and laborious. When God planted a garden He set a man over it and set the man under Himself. When He planted the garden of our nature and caused the flowering, fruiting loves to grow there, He set our will to "dress" them. Compared with them it is dry and cold. And unless His grace comes down, like the rain and the sunshine, we shall use this tool to little purpose. But its laborious—and largely negative—services are indispensable. If they were needed when the garden was still Paradisal, how much more now when the soil has gone sour and the worst weeds seem to thrive on it best? But heaven forbid we should work in the spirit of prigs and Stoics. While we hack and prune we know very well that what we are hacking and pruning is big with a splendour and vitality which our rational will could never of itself have supplied. To liberate that splendour, to let it become fully what it is trying to be, to have tall trees instead of scrubby tangles, and sweet apples instead of crabs, is part of our purpose.

But only part. For now we must face a topic that I have long postponed. Hitherto hardly anything has been said in this book about our natural loves as rivals to the love of God. Now the question can no longer be avoided. There were two reasons for my delay.

One—already hinted—is that this question is not the place at which most of us need begin. It is seldom, at the outset, "addressed to our condition." For most of us the true rivalry lies between the self and the human Other, not yet between the human Other and God. It is dangerous to press upon a man the duty of getting beyond earthly love when his real difficulty lies in getting so far. And it is no doubt easy enough to love the fellow-creature less and to imagine that this is happening because we are learning to love God more, when the real reason may be quite different. We may be only "mistaking the decays of nature for the increase of Grace." Many people do not find it really difficult to hate their wives or mothers. M. Mauriac, in a fine scene, pictures the other disciples stunned and bewildered by this strange command, but not Judas. He laps it up easily.

But to have stressed the rivalry earlier in this book would have been premature in another way also. The claim to divinity which our loves so easily make can be refuted without going so far as that. The loves prove that they are unworthy to take the place of God by the fact that they cannot even remain themselves and do what they promise to do without God's help. Why prove that some petty princeling is not the lawful Emperor when without the Emperor's support he cannot even keep his subordinate throne and make peace in his little province for half a year? Even for their own sakes the loves must submit to be second things if they are to remain the things they want to be. In this yoke lies their true freedom; they "are taller when they bow." For when God rules in a human heart, though He may sometimes have to remove certain of its native authorities altogether, He often continues others in their offices and, by subjecting their authority to His, gives it for the first time a firm basis. Emerson has said, "When half-gods go, the gods arrive." That is a very doubtful maxim. Better say, "When God arrives (and only then) the half-gods can remain." Left to themselves they either vanish or become demons. Only in His name can they with beauty and security "wield their little tridents." The rebellious slogan "All for love" is really love's death warrant (date of execution, for the moment, left blank).

But the question of the rivalry, for these reasons long postponed, must now be treated. In any earlier period, except the nineteenth century, it would have loomed large throughout a book on this subject. If the Victorians needed the reminder that love is not enough, older theologians were always saying very loudly that (natural) love is likely to be a great deal too much. The danger of loving our fellow-creatures too little was less present to their minds than that of loving them idolatrously. In every wife, mother, child and friend they saw a possible rival to God. So of course does Our Lord (*Luke* XIV, 26).

There is one method of dissuading us from inordinate love of the fellow-creature which I find myself forced to reject at the very outset. I do so with trembling, for it met me in the pages of a great saint and a great thinker to whom my own glad debts are incalculable.

In words which can still bring tears to the eyes, St. Augustine describes the desolation into which the death of his friend Nebridius plunged him (*Confessions* IV, 10). Then he draws a moral. This is what comes, he says, of giving one's heart to anything but God. All human beings pass away. Do not let your happiness depend on something you may lose. If love is to be a blessing, not a misery, it must be for the only Beloved who will never pass away.

Of course this is excellent sense. Don't put your goods in a leaky vessel. Don't spend too much on a house you may be turned out of. And there is no man alive who responds more naturally than I to such canny maxims. I am a safety-first creature. Of all arguments against love none makes so strong an appeal to my nature as "Careful! This might lead you to suffering."

To my nature, my temperament, yes. Not to my conscience. When I respond to that appeal I seem to myself to be a thousand miles away from Christ. If I am sure of anything I am sure that His teaching was never meant to confirm my congenital preference for safe investments and limited liabilities. I doubt whether there is anything in me that pleases Him less. And who could conceivably begin to love God on such a prudential ground—because the security (so to speak) is better? Who could even include it among the grounds for loving? Would you choose a wife or a Friend—if it comes to that, would you choose a dog—in this spirit? One must be outside the world of love, of all loves, before one thus calculates. Eros, lawless Eros, preferring the Beloved to happiness, is more like Love himself than this.

I think that this passage in the *Confessions* is less a part of St. Augustine's Christendom than a hangover from the high-minded Pagan philosophies in which he grew up. It is closer to Stoic "apathy" or neo-Platonic mysticism than to charity. We follow One who wept over Jerusalem and at the grave of Lazarus, and, loving all, yet had one disciple whom, in a special sense, he "loved." St. Paul has a higher authority with us than St. Augustine—St. Paul who shows no sign that he would not have suffered like a man, and no feeling that he ought not so to have suffered, if Epaphroditus had died (*Phil.* II, 27).

Even if it were granted that insurances against heartbreak were our highest wisdom, does God Himself offer them? Apparently not. Christ comes at last to say "Why hast thou forsaken me?"

There is no escape along the lines St. Augustine suggests. Nor along any other lines. There is no safe investment. To love at all is to be vulnerable. Love anything, and your heart will certainly be wrung and possibly be broken. If you want to make sure of keeping it intact, you must give your heart to no one, not even to an animal. Wrap it carefully round with hobbies and little luxuries; avoid all entanglements; lock it up safe in the casket or coffin of your selfishness. But in that casket—safe, dark, motionless, airless—it will change. It will not be broken; it will become unbreakable, impenetrable, irredeemable. The alternative to tragedy, or at least to the risk of tragedy, is damnation. The only place outside Heaven where you can be perfectly safe from all the dangers and perturbations of love is Hell.

I believe that the most lawless and inordinate loves are less

THE FOUR LOVES   317

contrary to God's will than a self-invited and self-protective
lovelessness. It is like hiding the talent in a napkin and for
much the same reason "I knew thee that thou wert a hard man."
Christ did not teach and suffer that we might become, even in
the natural loves, more careful of our own happiness. If a man
is not uncalculating towards the earthly beloveds whom he has
seen, he is none the more likely to be so towards God whom
he has not. We shall draw nearer to God, not by trying to avoid
the sufferings inherent in all loves, but by accepting them and
offering them to Him; throwing away all defensive armour. If
our hearts need to be broken, and if He chooses this as the way
in which they should break, so be it.

It remains certainly true that all natural loves can be inordinate. *Inordinate* does not mean "insufficiently cautious." Nor
does it mean "too big." It is not a quantitative term. It is probably impossible to love any human being simply "too much."
We may love him too much *in proportion* to our love for God;
but it is the smallness of our love for God, not the greatness of
our love for the man, that constitutes the inordinacy. But even
this must be refined upon. Otherwise we shall trouble some
who are very much on the right road but alarmed because they
cannot feel towards God so warm a sensible emotion as they
feel for the earthly Beloved. It is much to be wished — at least
I think so — that we all, at all times, could. We must pray that
this gift should be given us. But the question whether we are
loving God or the earthly Beloved "more" is not, so far as concerns our Christian duty, a question about the comparative intensity of two feelings. The real question is, which (when the
alternative comes) do you serve, or choose, or put first? To
which claim does your will, in the last resort, yield?

As so often, Our Lord's own words are both far fiercer and
far more tolerable than those of the theologians. He says nothing about guarding against earthly loves for fear we might be
hurt; He says something that cracks like a whip about tram-
pling them all under foot the moment they hold us back from

following Him. "If any man come to me and hate not his father and mother and wife . . . and his own life also, he cannot be my disciple" (*Luke* XIV, 26).

But how are we to understand the word *hate?* That Love Himself should be commanding what we ordinarily mean by hatred—commanding us to cherish resentment, to gloat over another's misery, to delight in injuring him—is almost a contradiction in terms. I think Our Lord, in the sense here intended, "hated" St. Peter when he said, "Get thee behind me." To hate is to reject, to set one's face against, to make no concession to, the Beloved when the Beloved utters, however sweetly and however pitiably, the suggestions of the Devil. A man, said Jesus, who tries to serve two masters, will "hate" the one and "love" the other. It is not, surely, mere feelings of aversion and liking that are here in question. He will adhere to, consent to, work for, the one and not for the other. Consider again, "I loved Jacob and I *hated* Esau" (*Malachi* I, 2–3). How is the thing called God's "hatred" of Esau displayed in the actual story? Not at all as we might expect. There is of course no ground for assuming that Esau made a bad end and was a lost soul; the Old Testament, here as elsewhere, has nothing to say about such matters. And, from all we are told, Esau's earthly life was, in every ordinary sense, a good deal more blessed than Jacob's. It is Jacob who has all the disappointments, humiliations, terrors, and bereavements. But he has something which Esau has not. He is a patriarch. He hands on the Hebraic tradition, transmits the vocation and the blessing, becomes an ancestor of Our Lord. The "loving" of Jacob seems to mean the acceptance of Jacob for a high (and painful) vocation; the "hating" of Esau, his rejection. He is "turned down," fails to "make the grade," is found useless for the purpose. So, in the last resort, we must turn down or disqualify our nearest and dearest when they come between us and our obedience to God. Heaven knows, it will seem to them sufficiently like hatred. We must not act on the pity we feel; we must be blind to tears and deaf to pleadings.

I will not say that this duty is hard; some find it too easy; some, hard almost beyond endurance. What is hard for all is to know when the occasion for such "hating" has arisen. Our temperaments deceive us. The meek and tender—uxorious husbands, submissive wives, doting parents, dutiful children—will not easily believe that it has ever arrived. Self-assertive people, with a dash of the bully in them, will believe it too soon. That is why it is of such extreme importance so to order our loves that it is unlikely to arrive at all.

How this could come about we may see on a far lower level when the Cavalier poet, going to the wars, says to his mistress:

> *I could not love thee, dear, so much*
> *Loved I not honour more.*

There are women to whom the plea would be meaningless. *Honour* would be just one of those silly things that Men talk about; a verbal excuse for, therefore an aggravation of, the offence against "love's law" which the poet is about to commit. Lovelace can use it with confidence because his lady is a Cavalier lady who already admits, as he does, the claims of Honour. He does not need to "hate" her, to set his face against her, for he and she acknowledge the same law. They have agreed and understood each other on this matter long before. The task of converting her to a belief in Honour is not now—now, when the decision is upon them—to be undertaken. It is this prior agreement which is so necessary when a far greater claim than that of Honour is at stake. It is too late, when the crisis comes, to begin telling a wife or husband or mother or friend, that your love all along had a secret reservation—"under God" or "so far as a higher Love permits." They ought to have been warned; not, to be sure, explicitly, but by the implication of a thousand talks, by the principle revealed in a hundred decisions upon small matters. Indeed, a real disagreement on this issue should make itself felt early enough to prevent a marriage or a Friendship from existing at all. The best love of either sort is not blind. Oliver Elton, speaking of Carlyle and Mill, said that they differed about justice, and that such a difference was naturally fatal "to any friendship worthy of the name." If "All"—quite seriously all—"for love" is implicit in the Beloved's attitude, his or her love is not worth having. It is not related in the right way to Love Himself.

And this brings me to the foot of the last steep ascent this book must try to make. We must try to relate the human activities called "loves" to that Love which is God a little more precisely than we have yet done. The precision can, of course, be only that of a model or a symbol, certain to fail us in the long run and, even while we use it, requiring correction from other models. The humblest of us, in a state of Grace, can have some "knowledge-by-acquaintance" (*connaître*), some "tasting," of Love Himself; but man even at his highest sanctity and intelligence has no direct "knowledge about" (*savoir*) the ultimate Being—only analogies. We cannot see light, though by light we can see things. Statements about God are extrapolations from the knowledge of other things which the divine illumination enables us to know. I labour these deprecations because, in what follows, my efforts to be clear (and not intolerably lengthy) may suggest a confidence which I by no means feel. I should be mad if I did. Take it as one man's reverie, almost one man's myth. If anything in it is useful to you, use it; if anything is not, never give it a second thought.

God is love. Again, "Herein is love, not that we loved God but that He loved us" (I *John* IV, 10). We must not begin with mysticism, with the creature's love for God, or with the wonderful foretastes of the fruition of God vouchsafed to some in their earthly life. We begin at the real beginning, with love as the Divine energy. This primal love is Gift-love. In God there is no hunger that needs to be filled, only plenteousness that desires to give. The doctrine that God was under no necessity to create is not a piece of dry scholastic speculation. It is essential. Without it we can hardly avoid the conception of what I can only call a "managerial" God; a Being whose function or nature is to "run" the universe, who stands to it as a head-master to a school or a hotelier to a hotel. But to be sovereign of the universe is no great matter to God. In Himself, at home in "the land of the Trinity," he is Sovereign of a far greater realm. We must keep always before our eyes that vision of Lady Julian's in which God carried in His hand a little object like a nut, and that nut was "all that is made." God, who needs nothing, loves into existence wholly superfluous creatures in order that He may love and perfect them. He creates the universe, already foreseeing—or should we say "seeing"? there are no tenses in God—the buzzing cloud of flies about the cross, the flayed back pressed against the uneven stake, the nails driven through the mesial nerves, the repeated incipient suffocation as the body droops, the repeated torture of back and arms as it is time after time, for breath's sake, hitched up. If I may dare the biological image, God is a "host" who deliberately creates His own parasites; causes us to be that we may exploit and "take advantage of" Him. Herein is love. This is the diagram of Love Himself, the inventor of all loves.

God, as Creator of nature, implants in us both Gift-loves and Need-loves. The Gift-loves are natural images of Himself; proximities to Him by resemblance which are not necessarily and in all men proximities of approach. A devoted mother, a beneficent ruler or teacher, may give and give, continually exhibiting the likeness, without making the approach. The Need-loves, so far as I have been able to see, have no resemblance to the Love which God is. They are rather correlatives, opposites; not as evil is the opposite of good, of course, but as the form of the blanc-mange is an opposite to the form of the mould.

But in addition to these natural loves God can bestow a far better gift; or rather, since our minds must divide and pigeon-hole, two gifts.

He communicates to men a share of His own Gift-love. This is different from the Gift-loves He has built into their nature.

These never quite seek simply the good of the loved object for the object's own sake. They are biased in favour of those goods they can themselves bestow, or those which they would like best themselves, or those which fit in with a pre-conceived picture of the life they want the object to lead. But Divine Gift-love—Love Himself working in a man—is wholly disinterested and desires what is simply best for the beloved. Again, natural Gift-love is always directed to objects which the lover finds in some way intrinsically lovable—objects to which Affection or Eros or a shared point of view attracts him, or, failing that, to the grateful and the deserving, or perhaps to those whose helplessness is of a winning and appealing kind. But Divine Gift-love in the man enables him to love what is not naturally lovable; lepers, criminals, enemies, morons, the sulky, the superior and the sneering. Finally, by a high paradox, God enables men to have a Gift-love towards Himself. There is of course a sense in which no one can give to God anything which is not already His; and if it is already His what have you given? But since it is only too obvious that we can withhold ourselves, our wills and hearts, from God, we can, in that sense, also give them. What is His by right and would not exist for a moment if it ceased to be His (as the song is the singer's), He has nevertheless made ours in such a way that we can freely offer it back to Him. "Our wills are ours to make them Thine." And as all Christians know there is another way of giving to God; every stranger whom we feed or clothe is Christ. And this apparently is Gift-love to God whether we know it or not. Love Himself can work in those who know nothing of Him. The "sheep" in the parable had no idea either of the God hidden in the prisoner whom they visited or of the God hidden in themselves when they made the visit. (I take the whole parable to be about the judgment of the heathen. For it begins by saying, in the Greek, that the Lord will summon all "the nations" before Him—presumably, the Gentiles, the *Goyim*.)

That such a Gift-love comes by Grace and should be called

Charity, everyone will agree. But I have to add something which will not perhaps be so easily admitted. God, as it seems to me, bestows two other gifts; a supernatural Need-love of Himself and a supernatural Need-love of one another. By the first I do not mean the Appreciative love of Himself, the gift of adoration. What little I have to say on that higher—that highest—subject will come later. I mean a love which does not dream of disinterestedness, a bottomless indigence. Like a river making its own channel, like a magic wine which in being poured out should simultaneously create the glass that was to hold it, God turns our need of Him into Need-love of Him. What is stranger still is that He creates in us a more than natural receptivity of Charity from our fellow-men. Need is so near greed and we are so greedy already that it seems a strange grace. But I cannot get it out of my head that this is what happens.

Let us consider first this supernatural Need-love of Himself, bestowed by Grace. Of course the Grace does not create the need. That is there already; "given" (as the mathematicians say) in the mere fact of our being creatures, and incalculably increased by our being fallen creatures. What the Grace gives is the full recognition, the sensible awareness, the complete acceptance—even, with certain reservations, the glad acceptance—of this Need. For, without Grace, our wishes and our necessities are in conflict.

All those expressions of unworthiness which Christian practice puts into the believer's mouth seem to the outer world like the degraded and insincere grovellings of a sycophant before a tyrant, or at best a *façon de parler* like the self-depreciation of a Chinese gentleman when he calls himself "this coarse and illiterate person." In reality, however, they express the continually renewed, because continually necessary, attempt to negate that misconception of ourselves and of our relation to God which nature, even while we pray, is always recommending to us. No sooner do we believe that God loves us than there is an impulse to believe that He does so, not because He is Love, but because we are intrinsically lovable. The Pagans obeyed this impulse unabashed; a good man was "dear to the gods" because he was good. We, being better taught, resort to subterfuge. Far be it from us to think that we have virtues for which God could love us. But then, how magnificently we have repented! As Bunyan says, describing his first and illusory conversion, "I thought there was no man in England that pleased God better than I." Beaten out of this, we next offer our own humility to God's admiration. Surely He'll like *that*? Or if not that, our clear-sighted and humble recognition that we still lack humility. Thus, depth beneath depth and subtlety within subtlety, there remains some lingering idea of our own, our very own, attractiveness. It is easy to acknowledge, but almost impossible to realise for long, that we are mirrors whose brightness, if we are bright, is wholly derived from the sun that shines upon us. Surely we must have a little — however little — native luminosity? Surely we can't be *quite* creatures?

For this tangled absurdity of a Need, even a Need-love, which never fully acknowledges its own neediness, Grace substitutes a full, childlike and delighted acceptance of our Need, a joy in total dependence. We become "jolly beggars." The good man is sorry for the sins which have increased his Need. He is not entirely sorry for the fresh Need they have produced. And he is not sorry at all for the innocent Need that is inherent in his creaturely condition. For all the time this illusion to which nature clings as her last treasure, this pretence that we have anything of our own or could for one hour retain by our own strength any goodness that God may pour into us, has kept us from being happy. We have been like bathers who want to keep their feet — or one foot — or one toe — on the bottom, when to lose that foothold would be to surrender themselves to a glorious tumble in the surf. The consequences of parting with our last claim to intrinsic freedom, power, or worth, are real freedom, power and worth, really ours just because God gives them and because we know them to be (in another sense) not "ours." Anodos has got rid of his shadow.

But God also transforms our Need-love for one another, and it requires equal transformation. In reality we all need at times, some of us at most times, that Charity from others which, being Love Himself in them, loves the unlovable. But this, though a sort of love we need, is not the sort we want. We want to be loved for our cleverness, beauty, generosity, fairness, usefulness. The first hint that anyone is offering us the highest love of all is a terrible shock. This is so well recognised that spiteful people will pretend to be loving us with Charity precisely because they know that it will wound us. To say to one who expects a renewal of Affection, Friendship, or Eros, "I forgive you as a Christian" is merely a way of continuing the quarrel. Those who say it are of course lying. But the thing would not be falsely said in order to wound unless, if it were true, it would be wounding.

How difficult it is to receive, and to go on receiving, from others a love that does not depend on our own attraction can be seen from an extreme case. Suppose yourself a man struck down shortly after marriage by an incurable disease which may not kill you for many years; useless, impotent, hideous, disgusting; dependent on your wife's earnings; impoverishing where you hoped to enrich; impaired even in intellect and shaken by gusts of uncontrollable temper, full of unavoidable demands. And suppose your wife's care and pity to be inexhaustible. The man who can take this sweetly, who can receive all and give nothing without resentment, who can abstain even from those tiresome self-depreciations which are really only a demand for petting and reassurance, is doing something which Need-love in its merely natural condition could not attain. (No doubt such a wife will also be doing something beyond the reach of a natural Gift-love, but that is not the point at present.) In such a case to receive is harder and perhaps more blessed than to give. But what the extreme example illustrates is universal. We are all receiving Charity. There is something in each of us that cannot be naturally loved. It is no one's fault if they do not so love it. Only the lovable can be naturally loved. You might as well ask people to like the taste of rotten bread or the sound of a mechanical drill. We can be forgiven, and pitied, and loved in spite of it, with Charity; no other way. All who have good parents, wives, husbands, or children, may be sure that at some times—and perhaps at all times in respect of some one particular trait or habit—they are receiving Charity, are loved not because they are lovable but because Love Himself is in those who love them.

Thus God, admitted to the human heart, transforms not only Gift-love but Need-love; not only our Need-love of Him, but our Need-love of one another. This is of course not the only thing that can happen. He may come on what seems to us a more dreadful mission and demand that a natural love be totally renounced. A high and terrible vocation, like Abraham's, may constrain a man to turn his back on his own people and his father's house. Eros, directed to a forbidden object, may have to be sacrificed. In such instances, the process, though hard to endure, is easy to understand. What we are more likely to overlook is the necessity for a transformation even when the natural love is allowed to continue.

In such a case the Divine Love does not *substitute* itself for the natural—as if we had to throw away our silver to make room for the gold. The natural loves are summoned to become modes of Charity while also remaining the natural loves they were.

One sees here at once a sort of echo or rhyme or corollary to the Incarnation itself. And this need not surprise us, for the Author of both is the same. As Christ is perfect God and perfect Man, the natural loves are called to become perfect Charity and also perfect natural loves. As God becomes Man "Not by conversion of the Godhead into flesh, but by taking of the

Manhood into God," so here; Charity does not dwindle into merely natural love but natural love is taken up into, made the tuned and obedient instrument of, Love Himself.

How this can happen, most Christians know. All the activities (sins only excepted) of the natural loves can in a favoured hour become works of the glad arid shameless and grateful Need-love or of the selfless, unofficious Gift-love, which are both Charity. Nothing is either too trivial or too animal to be thus transformed. A game, a joke, a drink together, idle chat, a walk, the act of Venus—all these can be modes in which we forgive or accept forgiveness, in which we console or are reconciled, in which we "seek not our own." Thus in our very instincts, appetites and recreations, Love has prepared for Himself "a body."

But I said "in a favoured hour." Hours soon pass. The total and secure transformation of a natural love into a mode of Charity is a work so difficult that perhaps no fallen man has ever come within sight of doing it perfectly. Yet the law that loves must be so transformed is, I suppose, inexorable.

One difficulty is that here, as usual, we can take a wrong turn. A Christian—a somewhat too vocally Christian—circle or family, having grasped this principle, can make a show, in their overt behaviour and especially in their words, of having achieved the thing itself—an elaborate, fussy, embarrassing and intolerable show. Such people make every trifle a matter of explicitly spiritual importance—out loud and to one another (to God, on their knees, behind a closed door, it would be another matter). They are always unnecessarily asking, or insufferably offering, forgiveness. Who would not rather live with those ordinary people who get over their tantrums (and ours) unemphatically, letting a meal, a night's sleep, or a joke mend all? The real work must be, of all our works, the most secret. Even as far as possible secret from ourselves. Our right hand must not know what our left is doing. We have not got far enough if we play a game of cards with the children "merely" to amuse them or to show that they are forgiven. If this is the best we can do we are right to do it. But it would be better if a deeper, less conscious, Charity threw us into a frame of mind in which a little fun with the children was the thing we should at that moment like best.

We are, however, much helped in this necessary work by that very feature of our experience at which we most repine. The invitation to turn our natural loves into Charity is never lacking. It is provided by those frictions and frustrations that meet us in all of them; unmistakable evidence that (natural) love is not going to be "enough"—unmistakable, unless we are blinded by egotism. When we are, we use them absurdly. "If only I had been more fortunate in my children (that boy gets more like his father every day) I could have loved them perfectly." But every child is sometimes infuriating; most children are not infrequently odious. "If only my husband were more considerate, less lazy, less extravagant" . . . "If only my wife had fewer moods and more sense, and were less extravagant" . . . "If my father wasn't so infernally prosy and close-fisted." But in everyone, and of course in ourselves, there is that which requires forbearance, tolerance, forgiveness. The necessity of practising these virtues first sets us, forces us, upon the attempt to turn—more strictly, to let God turn—our love into Charity. These frets and rubs are beneficial. It may even be that where there are fewest of them the conversion of natural love is most difficult. When they are plentiful the necessity of rising above it is obvious. To rise above it when it is as fully satisfied and as little impeded as earthly conditions allow—to see that we must rise when all seems so well already—this may require a subtler conversion and a more delicate insight. In this way also it may be hard for "the rich" to enter the Kingdom.

And yet, I believe, the necessity for the conversion is inexorable; at least, if our natural loves are to enter the heavenly life. That they can enter it most of us in fact believe. We may hope that the resurrection of the body means also the resurrection of what may be called our "greater body"; the general fabric of our earthly life with its affections and relationships. But only on a condition; not a condition arbitrarily laid down by God, but one necessarily inherent in the character of Heaven: nothing can enter there which cannot become heavenly. "Flesh and blood," mere nature, cannot inherit that Kingdom. Man can ascend to Heaven only because the Christ, who died and ascended to Heaven, is "formed in him." Must we not suppose that the same is true of a man's loves? Only those into which Love Himself has entered will ascend to Love Himself. And these can be raised with Him only if they have, in some degree and fashion, shared His death; if the natural element in them has submitted—year after year, or in some sudden agony—to transmutation. The fashion of this world passes away. The very name of nature implies the transitory. Natural loves can hope for eternity only in so far as they have allowed themselves to be taken into the eternity of Charity; have at least allowed the process to begin here on earth, before the night comes when no man can work. And the process will always involve a kind of death. There is no escape. In my love for wife or friend the only eternal element is the transforming presence of Love Himself. By that presence, if at all, the other elements may hope, as our physical bodies hope, to be raised from the dead. For this only is holy in them, this only is the Lord.

Theologians have sometimes asked whether we shall "know one another" in Heaven, and whether the particular love-relations worked out on earth would then continue to have any significance. It seems reasonable to reply: "It may depend what kind of love it had become, or was becoming, on earth." For, surely, to meet in the eternal world someone for whom your love in this, however strong, had been merely natural, would not be (on that ground) even interesting. Would it not be like meeting in adult life someone who had seemed to be a great friend at your preparatory school solely because of common interests and occupations? If there was nothing more, if he was not a kindred soul, he will now be a total stranger. Neither of you now plays conkers. You no longer want to swop your help with his French exercise for his help with your arithmetic. In Heaven I suspect, a love that had never embodied Love Himself would be equally irrelevant. For Nature has passed away. All that is not eternal is eternally out of date.

But I must not end on this note, I dare not—and all the less because longings and terrors of my own prompt me to do so—leave any bereaved and desolate reader confirmed in the widespread illusion that reunion with the loved dead is the goal of the Christian life. The denial of this may sound harsh and unreal in the ears of the broken hearted, but it must be denied.

"Thou hast made us for thyself," said St. Augustine, "and our heart has no rest till it comes to Thee." This, so easy to believe for a brief moment before the altar or, perhaps, half-praying, half-meditating in an April wood, sounds like mockery beside a deathbed. But we shall be far more truly mocked if, casting this way, we pin our comfort on the hope—perhaps even with the aid of *séance* and necromancy—of some day, this time forever, enjoying the earthly Beloved again, and no more. It is hard not to imagine that such an endless prolongation of earthly happiness would be completely satisfying.

But, if I may trust my own experience, we get at once a sharp warning that there is something wrong. The moment we attempt to use our faith in the other world for this purpose, that faith weakens. The moments in my life when it was really strong have all been moments when God Himself was central in my thoughts. Believing in Him, I could then believe in Heaven as a corollary. But the reverse process—believing first in reunion with the Beloved, and then, for the sake of that reunion, believing in Heaven, and finally, for the sake of Heaven, believing in God—this will not work. One can of course imagine things. But a self-critical person will soon be increasingly aware that the imagination at work is his own; he knows he is only weaving a fantasy. And simpler souls will find the phantoms they try to feed on void of all comfort and nourishment, only to be stimulated into some semblance of reality by pitiful efforts of self-hypnotism, and perhaps by the aid of ignoble pictures and hymns and (what is worse) witches.

We find thus by experience that there is no good applying to Heaven for earthly comfort. Heaven can give heavenly comfort; no other kind. And earth cannot give earthly comfort either. There is no earthly comfort in the long run.

For the dream of finding our end, the thing we were made for, in a Heaven of purely human love could not be true unless our whole Faith were wrong. We were made for God. Only by being in some respect like Him, only by being a manifestation of His beauty, loving-kindness, wisdom or goodness, has any earthly Beloved excited our love. It is not that we have loved them too much, but that we did not quite understand what we were loving. It is not that we shall be asked to turn from them, so dearly familiar, to a Stranger. When we see the face of God we shall know that we have always known it. He has been a party to, has made, sustained and moved moment by moment within, all our earthly experiences of innocent love. All that was true love in them was, even on earth, far more His than ours, and ours only because His. In Heaven there will be no anguish and no duty of turning away from our earthly Beloveds. First, because we shall have turned already; from the portraits to the Original, from the rivulets to the Fountain, from the creatures He made lovable to Love Himself. But secondly, because we shall find them all in Him. By loving Him more than them we shall love them more than we now do.

But all that is far away in "the land of the Trinity," not here in exile, in the weeping valley. Down here it is all loss and renunciation. The very purpose of the bereavement (so far as it affects ourselves) may have been to force this upon us. We are then compelled to try to believe, what we cannot yet feel, that God is our true Beloved. That is why bereavement is in some ways easier for the unbeliever than for us. He can storm and rage and shake his fist at the universe, and (if he is a genius) write poems like Housman's or Hardy's. But we, at our lowest ebb, when the least effort seems too much for us, must begin to attempt what seem impossibilities.

"Is it easy to love God?" asks an old author. "It is easy," he replies, "to those who do it." I have included two Graces under the word Charity. But God can give a third. He can awake in man, towards Himself, a supernatural Appreciative love. This is of all gifts the most to be desired. Here, not in our natural loves, nor even in ethics, lies the true centre of all human and angelic life. With this all things are possible.

And with this, where a better book would begin, mine must end. I dare not proceed. God knows, not I, whether I have ever tasted this love. Perhaps I have only imagined the tasting. Those like myself whose imagination far exceeds their obedience are subject to a just penalty; we easily imagine conditions far higher than any we have really reached. If we describe what we have imagined we may make others, and make ourselves, believe that we have really been there. And if I have only imagined it, is it a further delusion that even the imagining has at some moments made all other objects of desire—yes, even peace, to have no more fears—look like broken toys and faded flowers? Perhaps. Perhaps, for many of us, all experience merely defines, so to speak, the shape of that gap where our love of God ought to be. It is not enough. It is something. If we cannot "practise the presence of God," it is something to practise the absence of God, to become increasingly aware of our unawareness till we feel like men who should stand beside a great cataract and hear no noise, or like a man in a story who looks in a mirror and finds no face there, or a man in a dream who stretches out his hand to visible objects and gets no sensation of touch. To know that one is dreaming is to be no longer perfectly asleep. But for news of the fully waking world you must go to my betters.